Springer Series: SOCIETAL IMPACT ON AGING

K. Warner Schaie, PhD, Series Editor
Director, Gerontology Center
College of Health and Human Development
The Pennsylvania State University
University Park, PA

1993 Societal Impact on Aging: Historical Perspectives
K. Warner Schaie, PhD, and W. Andrew Achenbaum, PhD, Editors

1995 Adult Intergenerational Relations: Effects of Societal Change
Vern L. Bengtson, PhD, K. Warner Schaie, PhD, and Linda K. Burton, PhD, Editors

1996 Older Adults' Decision-Making and the Law
Michael Smyer, PhD, K. Warner Schaie, PhD, and Marshall Kapp, JD, MPH, Editors

1997 Societal Mechanisms for Maintaining Competence in Old Age
Sherry L. Willis, PhD, K. Warner Schaie, PhD, and Mark Hayward, PhD, Editors

Forthcoming volumes in the Series include . . .

1997 Impact of Work on Older Adults
K. Warner Schaie, PhD, and Carmi Schooler, PhD, Editors

Sherry L. Willis, PhD, is a professor of human development at the Pennsylvania State University. She received her BS degree from Memphis State University and her PhD degree from the University of Texas at Austin. She is best known for her research in developing and evaluating training programs to help older adults compensate for age-related declines in cognitive competence, and for her work on measuring practical intelligence. She is a past president of the Division of Adult Development and Aging of the American Psychological Association and a fellow of the Gerontological Society of America. She is a co-author, with K. Warner Schaie, of the textbook *Adult Development and Aging,* now in its fourth edition and co-editor with Samuel Dubin of *Contemporary Approaches to Professional Updating.*

K. Warner Schaie, PhD, is the Evan Pugh Professor of Human Development and Psychology and Director of the Gerontology Center at the Pennsylvania State University. He has previously held professional appointments at the University of Nebraska, West Virginia University, and the University of Southern California. Dr. Schaie received his BA from the University of California-Berkeley, and his MS and PhD degrees from the University of Washington, all in psychology. He is the author or editor of 22 books and over 150 journal articles and chapters related to the study of human aging. Dr. Schaie is the recipient of the Distinguished Scientific Contributions Award of the American Psychological Association and of the Robert W. Kleemeier Award for Distinguished Research Contributions from the Gerontological Society of America.

Mark D. Hayward, PhD, is Professor of Sociology at Penn State University. Dr. Hayward specializes in the area of the demography of aging, with an emphasis on the influence of the work career on the retirement and health experiences of the American older population. Recent publications have focused on topics including the role of health as a determinant of inequality in the retirement life cycle, how morbidity and mortality intersect to influence active life expenctancy, social inequality in active life expectancy, and the consequences of chronic morbidity for active life. Current research interests focus on how social circumstances over the life cycle combine to influence morbidity and mortality in late life.

Societal Mechanisms for Maintaining Competence in Old Age

Sherry L. Willis, PhD
K. Warner Schaie, PhD
Mark Hayward, PhD

Springer Publishing Company

Springer Publishing Company, Inc.
536 Broadway
New York, NY 10012-3955

Cover design by: Margaret Dunin
Acquisitions Editor: Helvi Gold
Production Editor: Kathleen Kelly

97 98 99 00 01 / 5 4 3 2 1

Library of Congress Cataloging-in-Publication Data

Societal mechanisms for maintaining competence in old age / Sherry L.
  Willis, K. Warner Schaie, Mark Hayward, editors.
    p. cm.
   Includes bibliographical references and indexes.
   ISBN 0-8261-9690-X
   1. Social work with the aged. 2. Aged—Services for. 3. Aging—
Psychological aspects. 4. Aged—Psychology. 5. Old age
assistance. I. Willis, Sherry L., 1947- . II. Schaie, K. Warner
(Klaus Warner), 1928- . III. Hayward, Mark D.
HV1451'S633 1997
362.6—dc21   97-16310
                                              CIP

Printed in the United States of America

Contents

Contributors   *vii*

Preface   *ix*

1. **What Can We Learn about Competence at the Older Ages from Active Life Expectancy?**   **1**
   Eileen M. Crimmins and Mark D. Hayward

   Commentary: Imprints of Disability   23
   Lois M. Verbrugge

   Commentary: Active Life Expectancy:
   Concept or Model for Research on Competency?   35
   Merrill F. Elias and Penelope K. Elias

2. **Psychological Issues Related to Competence**   **50**
   Timothy A. Salthouse

   Commentary: Psychological Issues Related
   to Competence: Cognitive Aging and Instrumental
   Activities of Daily Living   66
   Denise C. Park

   Commentary: The Social Context of Competence   83
   Neal Krause

3. **Does Being Placed in a Nursing Home
   Make You Sicker and More Likely to Die?**   **94**
   *Fredric D. Wolinsky, Timothy E. Stump and
   Christopher M. Callahan*

   Commentary: The Role of Physical Health
   in Understanding Societal Mechanisms
   for Maintaining Competence in Old Age   131
   Ilene C. Siegler

Commentary: Nursing Home Placement and
    Subsequent Morbidity and Mortality   136
Laurence G. Branch

**4. Long-Term Care Institutions and the
    Maintenance of Competence: A Dialectic Between
    Compensation and Overcompensation   142**
Margret M. Baltes and Ann L. Horgas

Commentary: Dependency Scripts and Competencies:
    New Direction or More of the Same?   165
Steven H. Zarit

Commentary: Quality Improvement and the Management
    of Dependency in Nursing Facilities   173
Diane Brannon and Theresa Barry

5. Social Support and the Maintenance of Competence   182
Toni C. Antonucci and Hiroko Akiyama

Commentary: Social Relationships in Context and
    as Context: Social Support and the Maintenance
    of Competence in Old Age   207
Laura L. Carstensen and Frieder R. Lang

Commentary: Emerging Theoretical and Empirical
    Issues in the Study of Social Support and
    Competence in Later Life   223
Merril Silverstein

**6. The Physical Environment and Maintenance
    of Competence   232**
Victor Regnier

Commentary: The FSU Approach to Design:
    Feedback from Senior Users   251
Neil Charness

Commentary: The Maintenance of ADL and
    IADL Functioning Through Design   266
Paul G. Windley

Author Index   275
Subject Index   285

Contributors

Toni C. Antonucci, PhD
Institute for Social Research
University of Michigan
Ann Arbor, MI

Hiroko Akiyama, PhD
The University of Michigan
Ann Arbor, MI

Margret M. Baltes, PhD
Research Unit, Psychological
  Gerontology
Freie Universitaet Berlin
Berlin, Germany

Laurence G. Branch, PhD
Duke University Medical Center
Center on Aging
Durham, NC

Theresa Berry, MHA
Brown University
Providence, RI

Diane Brannon, PhD
The Pennsylvania State
  University
Department of Health Policy and
  Administration
University Park, PA

Christopher M. Callahan, MD
Indiana University School of
  Medicine
Indianapolis, IN

Laura L. Carstensen, PhD
Stanford University
Department of Psychology
Stanford, CA

Neil Charness, PhD
Florida State University
Department of Psychology
Tallahassee, FL

Eileen M. Crimmins, PhD
Andrus Gerontology Center
University of Southern California
Los Angeles, CA

Merrill F. Elias, PhD, MPH
University of Maine
Department of Psychology
Orno, ME

Penelope K. Elias, PhD
Boston University
Boston, MA

Mark D. Hayward, PhD
The Pennsylvania State
  University
Department of Sociology
University Park, PA

Ann L. Horgas, RN, PhD
Institute of Gerontology
Wayne State University
Detroit, MI

Neal Krause, PhD
University of Michigan
School of Public Health and
  Research
Ann Arbor, MI

Frieder R. Lang, PhD
Free University
Berlin, Germany

Denise C. Park, PhD
University of Michigan
Institute of Gerontology
Ann Arbor, MI

Victor Regnier, PhD
University of Southern California
School of Architecture
Los Angeles, CA

Timothy A. Salthouse, PhD
Georgia Institute of Technology
School of Psychology
Atlanta, GA

Ilene C. Siegler, PhD, MPH
Duke University Medical Center
Durham, NC

Merrill Silverstein, PhD
University of Southern California
Andrus Gerontology Center
Los Angeles, CA

Timothy E. Stump, MA
Indiana University
Regenstrief Institute for Health
  Care
Indianapolis, IN

Lois M. Verbrugge, PhD, MPH
University of Michigan
Institute of Gerontology
Ann Arbor, MI

Paul G. Windley, PhD
University of Idaho
College of Arts and Architecture
Moscow, ID

Fredric Wolinsky, PhD
Saint Louis University
Health Sciences Center
School of Public Health
St. Louis, MO

Steven H. Zarit, PhD
The Pennsylvania State
  University
Department of Human Develop-
  ment and Family Studies
University Park, PA

Preface

This is the ninth volume in a series on the broad topic of "Societal Impact on Aging," and it is the fourth volume published in this series.* It is the edited proceedings of a conference held at the Pennsylvania State University, October 11–13, 1994.

The series of conferences originated from the deliberations of a subcommittee of the Committee on Life Course Perspectives of the Social Science Research Council chaired by Matilda White Riley in the early 1980s. That subcommittee was charged with developing an agenda and mechanisms that would serve to encourage communication between scientists who study societal structures that may affect the aging of individuals and those scientists who are concerned with the possible effects of contextual influences on individual aging. The committee proposed a series of conferences that would systematically explore the interfaces between social structures and behavior, and, in particular, would identify mechanisms through which society influences adult development. When the second editor, K. Warner Schaie, was named director of the Penn State Gerontology Center, he was able to implement this conference program as one of the center's major activities.

The previous eight volumes in this series have dealt with the societal impact on aging in psychological processes (Schaie & Schooler, 1989); age structuring in comparative perspective (Kertzer & Schaie, 1989); self-directedness and efficacy over the life span (Rodin, Schooler, & Schaie, 1990); aging, health behaviors, and health outcomes (Schaie, Blazer, & House, 1992); caregiving in families (Zarit, Pearlin, & Schaie, 1993);

---

*The first five volumes were published under the series title *Social Structure and Aging.*

aging in historical perspective (Schaie & Achenbaum, 1993); adult inter-generational relations (Bengtson, Schaie, & Burton, 1995); and older adults' decision making and the law (Smyer, Schaie, & Kapp, 1996). The present volume extends the theme of the previous volume by examining how societal mechanisms and social support systems serve to maintain adults' decision-making capacity into old age.

The strategy for each of these volumes has been to commission six reviews on three major topics by established subject-matter specialists who have credibility in aging research. We then invite two formal discussants for each chapter—usually one drawn from the writer's discipline and one from a neighboring discipline. This format seems to provide a suitable antidote to the perpetuation of parochial orthodoxies as well as to make certain that questions are raised with respect to the validity of iconoclastic departures in new directions.

To focus the conference, the editors chose three topics of broad interest to gerontologists. Social and behavioral scientists with a demonstrated track record were then selected and asked to interact with those interested in theory building within a multidisciplinary context.

The purpose of the conference reported in this latest volume was to summarize knowledge and to stimulate research regarding the societal mechanisms by which older individuals are supported in their efforts to maintain themselves as competent individuals leading independent lives within their communities. More than poverty or even death, older adults report fearing a loss of independence and resulting institutionalization. Maintenance of competence in older people is a major societal concern given the changing demographic structure.

In addition to the maintenance of the individual's cognitive skills into advanced old age, a variety of environmental support mechanisms (social and physical) are required. We therefore explored the changing nature of competence as the individual progresses from young-old to advanced old age. Competence in old age is both a personal and societal phenomenon. Issues of diversity and person by environment ''fit'' were therefore included to help us understand whether an individual can maintain his or her independence in the community or whether that person requires institutionalization. Even though societal institutions that maintain physical health are obviously important to the maintenance of competence, this volume does not focus on them since they were dealt with extensively in previous conference volumes. Given our concern with examining competence over the entire period of old age, we considered those changes in social and environmental support mechanisms that come into place with advancing age.

The volume begins with an examination of the alternative approaches taken by different disciplines in defining the concept of competence. For the purposes of this conference, competence is defined as the older person's ability to maintain personal independence within the context of societal supporting institutions and mechanisms. This definition is closely related to what is often referred to as active life expectancy; that is, competence to live independently in the community is differentiated from mere physical survival. The first chapter therefore deals explicitly with this issue, followed by a more technical discussion of the psychological issues related to competence.

The third topic in this volume deals with the maintenance of residual competence within institutional settings that may be required when independent living is no longer possible; in particular, after nursing home placement. This chapter examines the question whether institutionalization actually leads to a further decline in function and whether it escalates the time line toward death. The fourth chapter considers the conflict between attempts to maintain maximum residual independence for residents of nursing homes and the desire of nursing home staff to provide adequate and efficient care.

Chapter 5 addresses major support mechanisms for the maintenance of competence that are external to the aging individual. The chapter analyzes the effect of social support on the maintenance of competence. The last chapter reflects the views of architect and human factor psychologists on how principles of design might be used to provide environments that are conducive to the maintenance of competence.

Because our definition of competence in old age involves both societal and personal aspects, the conference brought together scientists interested in individual development, social structures, person-environment fit, and social policy. We hope that the resultant interplay of views from various disciplines contributes to our theoretical understanding of basic issues in maintaining competence in old age and provides an in-depth review of the literature that will inform policy development and practice.

We are grateful for the financial support of the conference that led to this volume, which was provided by conference grant AG (09787-04) from the National Institute on Aging, and by additional support from the Vice-President for Research and Dean of the Graduate School of the Pennsylvania State University. We are also grateful to Judy Hall and

Alvin Hall for handling the conference logistics, to Anna Shuey for coordinating the manuscript preparation, and to Joan Houtz for preparing the indexes.

K. Warner Schaie

April 1996

REFERENCES

Bengtson, V. L., Schaie, K. W., & Burton, L. (1995). *Adult intergenerational relations: Effects of societal changes.* New York: Springer.

Kertzer, D., & Schaie, K. W. (1989). *Age structuring in comparative perspective.* Hillsdale, NJ: Erlbaum.

Rodin, J., Schooler, C., & Schaie, K. W. (1990). *Self-directedness and efficacy: Causes and effects throughout the life course.* Hillsdale, NJ: Erlbaum.

Schaie, K. W., & Achenbaum, W. A. (1993). *Societal impact on aging: Historical perspectives.* New York: Springer.

Schaie, K. W., Blazer, D., & House, J. (1992). *Aging, health behaviors, and health outcomes.* Hillsdale, NJ: Erlbaum.

Schaie, K. W., & Schooler, C. (1989). *Social structure and aging: Psychological processes.* Hillsdale, NJ: Erlbaum.

Smyer, M., Schaie, K. W., & Kapp, M. B. (1996). *Older adults' decision-making and the law.* New York: Springer.

Zarit, S. H., Pearlin, L., & Schaie, K. W. (1993). *Social structure and caregiving: Family and cross-national perspectives.* Hillsdale, NJ: Erlbaum.

CHAPTER 1

What Can We Learn about Competence at the Older Ages from Active Life Expectancy?

Eileen M. Crimmins and Mark D. Hayward

Measures of active life expectancy offer easily comprehensible summary indicators of the length of competent life for a population and for subgroups of that population. Competency can be defined as the ability to carry out the requisite activities associated with the major social domains of life. According to a given set of criteria, a person can be defined as competent or not competent. Like competency, active life also is defined in terms of ability to perform these major social activities. However, it frames the concept of competency in terms of the life cycle. That is, active life expectancy is a measure of the average length of competent life. A population's mortality and its functioning or competency experiences determine the length of active life. This property is useful because it provides the means of decomposing historical changes or group differences in the effects of change or differences in mortality, competency, or both. For instance, competent life can be lengthened through lower mortality, lower rates of becoming incompetent, or because people learn new ways to compensate for losses in competence. Life tables provide an accounting framework to identify effects of each of these sources of increasing competent life.

Researchers in the field of active life expectancy and disability have increasingly documented that change in functioning and competence is a complicated life cycle process at the individual level, often involving multiple and recurrent changes in ability status. For instance, some individuals experience increasing functioning problems that result in death, others experience little loss of functioning, while still others experience intermittent spells of disability (Verbrugge, Reoma, & Gruber-Baldini, 1994; Branch & Ku, 1989; A. Rogers, Rogers, & Branch, 1989; Crimmins, Hayward, & Saito, 1994a). Active life expectancy summarizes these experiences over the life cycle for the average individual.

The aims of this chapter are to demonstrate how the models and methods underlying research in active life expectancy are appropriate for addressing issues of competency, to assess the relevance to competency of existing studies of active life expectancy, and to discuss how we can better use the active life expectancy model to understand more fully and to clarify the process of changes in competence that often occurs with advancing age. As part of this discussion, we also examine the sources of historical change in active life expectancy as well as differences in active life expectancy across population subgroups. This discussion is relevant to understanding competency change and differences within the population.

THE CONCEPT OF ACTIVE LIFE EXPECTANCY

Life Tables

Understanding the life table model is essential to understanding the concept of active life expectancy. The calculation of a conventional life table is based on the simple input of a series of age-specific death rates. One of the appealing features of life table summary measures is that they are comparable across time, place, and subgroups of the population. This results from the fact that they are based solely on mortality conditions and are not affected by the age composition of the population. The most familiar measure derived from the life table is life expectancy at a given age, or the average years of life to be lived after that birthday, assuming that persons experience current mortality rates from that age through the rest of life. While life tables used to determine active life expectancy are more complicated than conventional life tables, they retain the feature of comparability across time, place, and subgroups of the population.

Active Life Expectancy

As demographers' interest grew in the issues of health and functioning, researchers suggested the possibility of a more complex life table model that would decompose life expectancy into the years of active and inactive life, where active life is an indicator of the average number of "healthy" years a person can expect to live (Sanders, 1964; Sullivan, 1971). Active life expectancy is computed using both mortality rates and age-specific rates of health and functioning. Mortality rates define the limits to life, while the rates indicating health and functioning ability determine the limits to active life. When combined in a life table, these rates produce estimates of expected years of both active and inactive life over the life cycle. The life table model also can identify the number of people who become inactive or die at any age. Further, the distribution of health in the population can be determined by the number of survivors who are active or inactive at a given age or at any combination of ages. Thus the life table model on which active life expectancy is based provides useful characteristics of both expected individual life cycles and the populations comprised of those individuals.

After years of dramatic mortality decline at the older ages, interest in the concept of active life expectancy increased as both researchers and policy makers began to ask whether we were adding healthy or unhealthy years to life with continued mortality decline (Verbrugge, 1984). They could have asked whether the years were competent or incompetent, or disabled or nondisabled. Active life expectancy provides a powerful measure for answering these questions.

What Is the Meaning of "Active" in Active Life Expectancy?

No standard definition of "active life expectancy" is used in the literature. Various researchers have defined "active life" as years one is "able to perform expected social roles," years one is "able to perform certain functions," or years one is "without specific diseases or disabilities." In some research projects with particular emphasis on the quality of life, years of life have been adjusted for quality to produce "quality adjusted expected years of life." This array of definitions is not surprising given the wide interests of both the research and policy communities in the idea of active life expectancy as well as the various streams of research within which investigations of active life expectancy developed.

While there have been attempts to standardize the definition of active life expectancy, particularly within the International Network on Active Life Expectancy (REVES), these have been largely unsuccessful. In part, this results from a continuing international debate on how to define "disabilities," "handicaps," and "impairments," but primarily, it results from the limited availability of data for use in computing estimates of active life expectancy.

Active Life as Nondisabled Life

Most surveys of the "health" of national populations have collected some indicator of whether individuals have "long-term disability." For instance, this has been true for ongoing surveys in the United States, Canada, and Great Britain (Bebbington, 1988; Wilkins & Adams, 1983; Crimmins, Saito, & Ingegneri, 1989). In all of these surveys, long-term disability has been defined as an inability to carry out one's usual activity or the activity that is "normal" for a specified age. This may include going to school, working, or keeping house.

For older persons, what constitutes "normal activity" has been less clear. For this reason almost all surveys of the older population in the last 15 years have adopted "functioning ability" as the general health outcome of interest. Around the world, this has increasingly been measured as ability to perform Activities of Daily Living (ADLs) and Instrumental Activities of Daily Living (IADL), which are indicative of one's ability to provide "self-care" and "independent living," respectively. Competence in providing self-care and maintaining an independent household are of interest to those thinking of the needs of the older population.

Because of the availability of data on disability, disabled life has been the operational definition of inactive life and, conversely, active life has been nondisabled life. "Disability" is difficulty or incompetence in performing socially expected activities. Active life expectancy definitions based on disability provide good summary measures of the competence of the population or population subgroups in various domains of life such as work, home management, self-care, and social and community life.

Active Life as Life Without Impairments or Diseases

Estimating life without impairments or specific diseases is another approach to defining active life expectancy. A number of researchers, for example, have attempted to estimate the length of life without cognitive impairment (Ritchie, Jagger, Brayne, & Letenneur, 1993). This provides an indicator of the expected years of cognitive competence and incompetence. We also could assess how active life expectancy might be affected by changing the rate of the onset of disease or the rate of death among those persons with the disease for any specific disease. Such an analysis of trends in the age at onset and death rates from heart disease would provide a better understanding of the implications of the remarkable success we have had in controlling death rates from heart disease. More specifically, the life table model could be used to show the increase in life expectancy with and without heart disease; how much life expectancy among those who had heart disease had increased; and how the number of people in the population with heart disease as well as the years of heart disease requiring treatment increased.

The "Disablement Process"

Verbrugge (1994) and Verbrugge and Jette (1994) have improved the conceptual clarity of the various approaches to defining population "health" and "disability" by developing a conceptual framework of the relationships among the stages of what they call "the disablement process." The process described by them is relevant to understanding the different approaches to estimating active life expectancy and thinking about the process of changes and differences in competency. Their scheme clarifies conceptually how the different dimensions of health—diseases, impairments, functional limitations, and disability—are ordered in the process of disablement or loss of competence. As outlined by Verbrugge and Jette, disease and impairment are generally the beginning of the process that may then result in functioning loss and disability. While these components can be thought of as hierarchical and sequential over the course of the process, this is not necessarily so in each individual life. Active life expectancy is pertinent to each component of the process: life without specific diseases, impairments, and functional limitations, and life without disability. Understanding the process of health change or competence change in a population requires an understanding of each phase of this process.

External Factors Affecting Disability

Verbrugge and Jette also clarify how factors external to the individual may influence the process of disablement. While this has been largely ignored in work on active life expectancy, it is a very important consideration in thinking about time trends or social differences in any estimates of either disability, active life, or competent life.

Disability and competence are general concepts that reflect a variety of medical and nonmedical conditions. Disability or loss of competency is not exclusively a biomedical process, but rather the outcome of dysfunction (organ system or bodily function) as well as the demands of the functions and activities used to define disability or competence. Very often, disability has been interpreted as a reflection of the level of organic or bodily dysfunction. Much of differential disability may reflect these dysfunctions, but, depending upon the operational definition, group differences also could reflect different levels of physical and social supports and challenges, either real or perceived.

Changes (or group differences) in active life expectancy may reflect changes (or differences) in the level of social and environmental support as well as changes in physical or mental functioning. For example, changes in marital status or living arrangements can result in persons reporting they "get" or "need" more or less help with tasks, meaning that their level of ability or competence has changed. Technological change resulting in the development of assistive devices or the adoption of existing assistive devices can lead persons to report that they are "able" rather than "unable" to perform tasks. Changing housing environments can result in changes in a person's ability to perform tasks in the home.

Disability or competence thus is the intersection at a given point in time of the individual's level of dysfunction and the physical and social support and challenges in the environment. Disability transitions potentially reflect changes in dysfunction, the physical and social environment, or both. Casting disability as a dynamic concept thus complicates the interpretation of disability changes in individuals' lives. Because active life expectancy is usually measured by individuals' reports of their abilities or needs, perceptions of environmental challenges can change over time. An accommodation can be reached such that problems are no longer perceived. Even when the level of dysfunction remains constant, the level of reported disability may decline because of changes in the environment or perception. Conversely, some persons may be unable to make adaptive changes, perhaps due to the lack of personal and social resources. In this instance, disability minimally remains constant and probably increases over time.

Researchers have paid scant attention to the possible differences and changes that occur in persons' surroundings (both adaptive and nonadaptive), some of which are endogenous to the process of health and functioning. While differentiating dysfunctional changes from environmental changes may not be an impediment to obtaining reasonable estimates of active life expectancy under current conditions for the population (i.e., the period with and without disability or competence), it is important in interpreting age-related changes in disability, and population heterogeneity in the onset and recovery from disability.

METHODS OF COMPUTING ACTIVE LIFE EXPECTANCY

Methodologically as well as conceptually, there have been a variety of approaches to estimating active life expectancy. Again, the variety of approaches is due to differences in the eventual use of estimates and to the availability of data. Some approaches are only possible with longitudinal data for large samples of individuals, a scarce commodity for many age groups and time periods.

The Prevalence Approach to Active Life Expectancy

Most studies of active life expectancy have used a prevalence-based method to estimate active or nondisabled life. All studies of change over time in active life and differences across countries have been based on such methods. Researchers have been limited to this method because only prevalence data are available for national populations of all ages and for different time periods. For this method the age-specific percentages of the population in the active state are used along with mortality rates to produce estimates of active life expectancy. Estimates of active and inactive life are produced by applying these percentages to the years lived by the life table population in each age range to divide years lived into active and inactive years. When summed over the age range, years of active and inactive life expectancy are produced. (For more details on methodology, see Robine et al., 1986, or Crimmins et al., 1989.)

Dynamic Methods of Estimating Active Life Expectancy

Dynamic methodology for estimating active life expectancy has been employed in some studies of the older population of the United States, for whom panel data are available. As noted previously, demographers now readily acknowledge the dynamic quality of individuals' disability experiences over time and the appropriateness of active life expectancy as a summary measure of these experiences. The estimation of active life expectancy using dynamic models is different and significantly more complicated than prevalence-based life table models. The results, although more complicated, also are potentially more informative.

Most dynamic estimates of active life expectancy for the older population use Markov-based multistate (increment-decrement) life table methods to estimate total, active, and inactive life. Multistate estimates are based on age-specific transition rates reflecting movements both into and out of active life, and from each health state to death (Figure 1.1). Unlike a prevalence-based life table model, this approach allows both the death rates to vary by health state and bidirectional movements between the active and inactive states. It also uses incidence-based measures of health change rather than prevalence-based measures. This produces a more realistic and dynamic model of the process of health and functioning than is allowed by the traditional prevalence-based life table model, since actual changes in health are captured. The drawback of this approach is that it places heavy demands on the data because of the difficulty in producing reliable incidence rates. (For more details on methodology, see Crimmins et al., 1994a or Land, Guralnik, & Blazer, 1994.)

SUMMARY OF DISCUSSION OF ACTIVE LIFE EXPECTANCY

What the previous discussion should make clear is that there is no single number that is "the" active life expectancy of a population at a given moment. Like other models employed in social science research, the number computed for active life expectancy depends on the definition of active life and the method used to estimate it. It is the input to the construction of active life expectancy and the potential comparability of the life table results that are the important outcomes of the active life

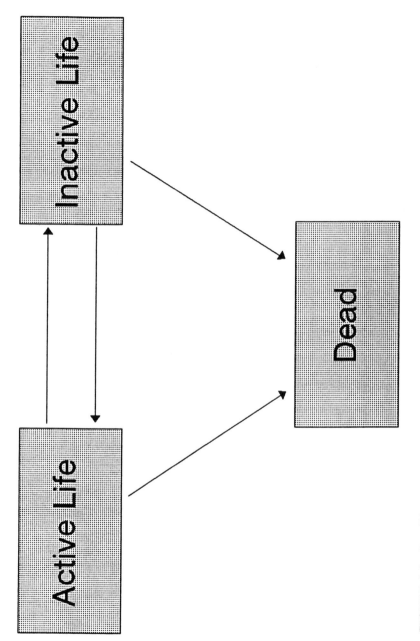

FIGURE 1.1   Possible transitions across states in a multistate life table model.

9

expectancy model. It should also be clear that active life, as it has been estimated, is very relevant to understanding the expected length of competent life for individuals and the expected level of competence in populations under different circumstances.

WHAT HAVE WE LEARNED FROM EXISTING STUDIES OF ACTIVE LIFE EXPECTANCY?

Our discussion of existing studies will divide them into those based on the prevalence method and those based on multistate methods. This methodological separation also results in a division into studies aimed at producing point estimates of active life expectancy across the life span for individual countries, including studies examining historical change, and studies concentrating on the older population of the United States.

Prevalence Estimates of Active Life Expectancy

Jean-Marie Robine and colleagues have provided a number of assessments of knowledge stemming from prevalence studies, so our examination of these will be brief (Robine, Mathers, & Brouard, 1993; Robine, Bucquet, & Ritchie, 1991; Robine & Ritchie, 1993).

1.   National estimates of active life expectancy: As discussed previously, national estimates have all used the prevalence method and have defined active life as life without disability. Estimates of disability-free life at birth as well as total life and the percentage of disability-free life expectancy for a number of countries are shown in Table 1.1. The estimates for countries show a wide range in the length of disability-free life, from a low in the United States to a high in Switzerland. The differences across countries are a good indicator of the effect of societal differences in either attitudes or policies toward disability. There is a clear influence of social programs relevant to disability on the length of disabled life. Countries in which it is easier to survive out of the workforce with a disability are likely to have more disabled years. These societal differences in disability-relevant attitudes and policies make difficult the interpretation of the meaning of the differences in active life expectancy observed across countries. For instance, few people believe that the almost 5-year differ-

TABLE 1.1 Disability-Free Life Expectancy at Birth in Developed Countries

Country	Year	Male			Female		
		Total Life Expectancy	Disability-free Life Expectancy	% of Disability-free Life Expectancy	Total Life Expectancy	Disability-free Life Expectancy	% of Disability-free Life Expectancy
United States	1980	70.1	55.5	79.2	77.6	60.4	77.8
France	1982	70.7	61.9	87.6	78.9	67.1	85.0
Italy	1983	71.6	64.3	89.8	78.2	68.3	87.3
Netherlands	81–85	72.8	58.8	80.8	79.5	57.3	72.1
Federal Republic of Germany	1986	71.8	63.4	88.3	78.4	68.4	87.2
Canada	1986	73.0	61.3	84.0	79.8	64.9	81.3
Spain	1986	73.2	60.8	83.1	79.6	62.6	78.6
United Kingdom	1988	72.4	58.5	80.8	78.1	61.2	78.4
Australia	1988	73.1	58.4	79.9	79.5	63.4	79.7
Switzerland	88–89	74.0	67.1	90.7	80.9	72.9	90.1

Source: Robine & Ritchie, 1993. Measuring changes in population health through changes in disability-free life expectancy calculation. *Internation Population Conference, Montreal, Canada, 1, 523–535.*

ence in disability-free life between the United States and Canada is due to a difference in physical ability. It is probably due in part to definitional differences in disability but also to societal attitudes toward disability.

2.   Sex differences in active life expectancy: Meta-analysis of disability-free life expectancy for large numbers of countries, however, has provided important information about differences by sex in active life. In virtually all countries, despite the variety of disability definitions, the estimates show that women have longer disabled lives as well as disability-free lives than men (Table 1.1). The active life expectancy model thus helps us understand how the generally lower level of female mortality and the higher prevalence of female disability combine to produce different life cycle health and functioning experiences for men and women. We will return to the discussion of the male-female difference in active life expectancy in the next section to demonstrate the relative richness of understanding produced with a multistate analysis.

3.   Active life expectancy change over time: For a few countries where disability data were collected in a relatively consistent manner over time (Great Britain, Australia, and the United States), estimates of changes over the 1970 and 1980 decades in life expectancy and disability-free life expectancy are available. The pattern of results consistently indicates that as total life expectancy increased over the last 2 decades, disability-free life expectancy has not increased. The increased years of life expectancy were years with some disability. However, when disability is categorized according to severity, the increase in the years spent with disability during the 1970s and 1980s occurs in the mild to moderate range, while decreases in the years of severe disability are observed (Robine et al., 1993). The two explanations that have been put forth for this increase in moderate disability are either that disability really did increase or that only ''reported'' disability increased. Attitudinal change is thought to be the source of the increase in ''reported'' disability. We will also return to this topic in the next section.

Multistate Estimates of Active Life Expectancy

Multistate estimates of active life expectancy and total life expectancy are currently available for the United States and some subareas of the United States (Table 1.2). Because these studies use slightly different definitions of active life expectancy and a variety of methods, the resulting

TABLE 1.2   Multistate Estimates of Active Life Expectancy for the Older U.S. Population

Source	Population	Age		Life Expectancy		
				Total	Active	% Active
Rogers et al.[1] (1990)	U.S. 1984–86	70	Active Population	13.36	10.13	76
			Inactive Population	12.40	6.20	50
Branch et al.[2] (1991)	East Boston Whites	65	Male	11.9	10.6	89
			Female	18.9	14.4	76
	Iowa Whites	65	Male	15.3	12.3	80
			Female	20.5	16.7	81
	New Haven Whites	65	Male	12.6	10.4	83
			Female	19.1	15.8	83
Land et al.[3] (1994)	Piedmont, N.C.	65	Females— Low Education			
			Black	18.2	15.6	86
			White	17.8	15.2	85
			Females— High Education			
			Black	22.8	19.5	86
			White	21.1	18.0	85
Crimmins et al.[4] (1994, 1996)	U.S. 1984–90	70		12.16	9.27	76
			Male	10.3	8.9	86
			Female	13.9	11.1	80

Definitions
1. Rogers et al.—Need assistance with at least one task: eating, bathing, dressing, transferring, using toilet, getting outside, walking.
2. Branch et al.—Need help to perform one of the following: bathing, dressing, transferring, eating.
3. Land et al.—Need help or unable to perform one or more of the following: walking across room, bathing, dressing, eating.
4. Crimmins et al.—Unable to perform by oneself at least one of the following functions: bathing, dressing, eating, transferring, using toilet, preparing own meal, shopping for personal items, manage money, use telephone, do light housework (institutionalized).

numbers are not directly comparable across studies but for subgroups within studies. For this reason, we will summarize the important results of each study to indicate what can be learned about life cycle competence and population ability using multistate methods.

A. Rogers, Rogers, and Belanger (1990) were the first to use the multistate model to estimate active life expectancy. They produced "status-based" multistate life tables for the active and inactive populations. Status-based tables can be used to demonstrate the different life cycle outcomes for groups who differ at the initial age of the life table. For instance, Rogers et al. (1990) divided the older population into those needing assistance with ADL activities and those who could accomplish these activities on their own. Their analysis showed that these groups differ in total life expectancy with those who are active having a year longer of expected life at age 70 (Table 1.2). However, the differential in expected active life is even longer. People who need ADL assistance have an expected active life of about 6 years, while those not in need of assistance have an active life of 10 years on average. Their analysis was also important in demonstrating the effect of returning to active functioning from the inactive state on the length of active life.

Branch et al. (1991) provided estimates of active life expectancy for whites in three very different communities in the United States: East Boston, Iowa, and New Haven. The range of these estimates indicates that populations of different socioeconomic circumstances living in different areas of the country differ substantially in both their life expectancy and their active life expectancy. Their estimates also are important in producing insights into sex and age differences in active life expectancy in these three areas. They found, for example, that the added years of life experienced by women were neither "solely added years of vigor nor solely added years of disability, but added years with the same mix of independence/dependence that shorter-lived males experience" (p. M145). They also noted a relative constancy of the length of inactive life as age increased after 65. This is important in indicating that longer life does not necessarily mean longer dependent life and has implications for how we evaluate the benefits of longer life.

Land et al. (1994) incorporated indicators of race and education into their analysis of active life expectancy in the Piedmont region of North Carolina. While they do not find large race differences in active life expectancy, they do find substantial educational effects on both total and active life. They conclude that education acts as a powerful protector in delaying the onset of health problems and in prolonging an active life. Their results are an important demonstration of the effect of socioeconomic status on the length of competent and incompetent lives.

Crimmins, Hayward, and Saito (1994, 1996) have collaborated on two studies of active life expectancy in which multistate active life table models are used to explain two paradoxes observed by disability and mortality researchers: lengthening life seems to be accompanied by deteriorating health, and women have longer lives but worse health than men. These studies differ from others in that much of the focus is on the inputs to the active life expectancy model and the clarity they provide in understanding the processes leading to differences and changes in active life and the health of the population. Both of these studies refer to the population 70 years of age and over in the United States.

The effect of the differing mortality and disability rates for men's and women's active life expectancies is shown in Table 1.2. Life expectancy for men at age 70 is 10.3 years, and for women it is 13.9 years. As in other studies, women have both a longer total expected life and a longer active and inactive life than men at age 70. The expected length of inactive life for women is twice that for men: 2.8 years versus 1.4 years, respectively.

Sex differences in active life expectancy could arise either because of differences in mortality, differences in the onset of and recovery from disability, or both. Men have a higher mortality rate than women from both the active and the inactive states. In the active state, a woman is half as likely to die as a man; in the inactive state, women are 33% less likely to die.

Sex, however, is not consistently related to functioning change or the movement into and out of disability. Where there is a difference in the likelihood of making a functioning change, women are more likely to experience deteriorated functioning, while men are more likely to experience improved functioning. Thus sex affects mortality and disability in the opposite direction. Men experience higher mortality, while women are more subject to deteriorating functioning.

Most of the sex difference in active life expectancy arises from the differences in mortality rather than differences in the rates of disability onset. Women gain inactive years through their longer survival in the inactive states. If men and women differed only in the functioning transitions and not in mortality, there would be very little sex difference in either life expectancy or active life expectancy. The mortality differences between men and women also result in a greater proportion of disabled women at every age (Crimmins et al., 1996).

Because actual data are unavailable to study the effect of changing mortality and morbidity on the length of active and inactive life, Crimmins et al. (1994) used a simulation approach to determine the likely effects of the mortality reduction at the older ages between 1968 and 1987 on the length of active life and the health of the population. To do this, the higher mortality rates of 1968 are substituted into the multistate life table instead of the mortality rates for the late 1980s. The consequence of worse mortality is clear. There is a decrease in the overall length of life in each state and a decrease in the proportion of life that is inactive (Table 1.3). This suggests that longer life does not necessarily signify better health. The simulation shows that the way to reduce the proportion of inactive life in the future would be to increase mortality (an unlikely occurrence) or to increase the age of onset to the inactive or disabled state—keeping everything else constant. These are also the ways to reduce the prevalence of disability in the population (Crimmins et al., 1994).

The results of this analysis have implications for understanding the supposed paradox of lengthening life but deteriorating health observed in a number of countries during the 1970s. If the first attack on chronic disease reduced death rates for those with disease but there was no change in the rate of onset of disease, the result should have been an increase in the level of disability in the population; this is the trend generally reported in disability data for the United States and other industrialized countries. This analysis supports the idea that the observed increase in disability was real and not just an increase in "reported" disability. There has been

TABLE 1.3   Life Expectancy at Age 70 Under Various Assumptions

	Total	Active	Inactive	% Inactive
Baseline (1984–90)	12.16	9.27	2.88	0.24
Mortality Conditions of 1968	10.32	8.36	1.95	0.19
Age at Onset to Worse Functioning Increased	13.32	11.95	2.37	0.18

Source: Crimmins, Hayward, & Saito, 1994.

a suggestion that in the 1980s the trend toward worsening disability had stopped and there even was some hint of improvement in the percent disabled in the late 1980s (Manton, Corder, & Stallard, 1993). Such a change can only come about if the rate of onset of disability has started to decline. Lower rates of the onset of disability can occur because of a change in cohort characteristics or through prevention.

The use of active life expectancy models to understand the expectancy of mentally competent life is demonstrated in Hayward, Crimmins, and Friedman (1994). In this analysis, dementia-free life expectancy is estimated for the chronically impaired population of the United States 65 years of age and over. Using the 1982–1984 longitudinal data from the National Long-Term Care Survey, the community-dwelling population is categorized as cognitively intact, mildly impaired, or moderately to severely impaired, using the "Short Portable Mental Status Questionnaire." Information is also available to identify people who are institutionalized.

Transition rates are calculated showing the age-specific risks of experiencing a change in cognitive impairment, where change can denote both onset and recovery. These rates are then input into a multistate life table to estimate cognitive impairment-free life expectancy. For chronically impaired persons aged 65, total life expectancy is estimated to be 8.3 years (Table 1.4). Of this, over 6 years are spent dementia-free living in the community, about 1 year is spent living in the community with dementia, and slightly over 1 year living in an institution. Note that the years expected to be lived in the community with dementia do not increase as age increases. At age 85, the expected length of community life with dementia is less than that at age 65, although institutional life is longer. This is an insight gained from a life table approach that incorporates mortality as well as the rates of the onset of impairment and recovery.

Multistate tables for the population divided according to cognitive states at age 65 show that expected length of cognitively impaired life varies considerably among individuals in the population (Table 1.5). Persons who are cognitively intact at age 65 can expect to live longer, with fewer years of impairment, compared to those who have already experienced functioning problems. For example, as shown in Table 1.5, persons aged 65 with moderate to severe impairment can expect to live almost 3 fewer years than those who are intact. The expectation is that they will live more impaired years both absolutely and relatively.

TABLE 1.4   Cognitive Impairment-Free Life Expectancy for Chronically Impaired, Community-Dwelling Persons Aged 65 and Older

Age	Total	Intact	Mild	Mod./Sev.	Instit.
65	8.33	6.30	0.43	0.49	1.12
75	5.97	3.75	0.32	0.48	1.41
85	4.05	1.83	0.22	0.42	1.58
95	2.74	0.84	0.13	0.26	1.51

Notes: Cognitive impairment status is measured using the Short Portable Mental Status Questionnaire. The categories are intact (0–2 errors), mild (3–4 errors), and moderate/severe (5 or more errors).

DATA SOURCE: National Long-Term Care Survey, 1982–1984; Multistate Life Table Estimates.

Source: Hayward, Crimmins, & Friedman, 1994.

TABLE 1.5   Cognitive Impairment-Free Life Expectancy by Impairment Status at Age 65: Chronically Impaired Persons Aged 65 Years and Older

Status at Age 65	Life Expectancy in:				
	Intact	Mild	Mod./Sev.	Instit.	Total
Intact	7.16	0.39	0.40	0.84	8.79
Mild	4.75	1.72	0.51	0.86	7.83
Mod./Sev.	3.07	0.30	1.76	0.86	6.00
Instit.	1.89	0.18	0.20	4.35	6.63

Notes: Cognitive impairment status is measured using the Short Portable Mental Status Questionnaire. The categories are intact (0–2 errors), mild (3–4 errors), and moderate/severe (5 or more errors).

DATA SOURCE: National Long-Term Care Survey, 1982–1984; Multistate Life Table Estimates.

Source: Hayward, Crimmins, & Friedman, 1994.

We think that the models of active life expectancy have added considerably to our understanding of the relationships between mortality and health change for expected lives of individuals and the dynamics giving rise to the prevalence of disability in the population. The models also have improved our understanding of how differences in mortality and disability interact to determine different disability or competency experiences over the life cycle for important social and demographic groups, as well as the demographic determinants of group differences in the prevalence of disability.

SUMMARY

The previous discussion provides a brief description of the value of active life expectancy in describing competency experiences over the life cycle. Several important lessons for understanding competence can be drawn from the work on active life expectancy. Perhaps foremost, this work shows the importance of viewing competence as a dynamic, life cycle process. Individuals can lose or gain the ability to manage their social environment, and this is an age-dependent process. Prior work also illustrates the possible ways in which competence, and the years individuals can anticipate spending as competent, may change over time. Years added to life are not necessarily years added to competence without an accompanying delay in the loss of competency. Finally, what determines the length of competence may vary significantly across population subgroups. Population heterogeneity in competence may be sensitive to underlying group differences in the length of life, and population characteristics, both ascribed and achieved, may differentially define the risks of competency loss and gain.

The variety of definitions employed in estimating active life expectancy has limited demographers' ability to gauge the gradient of active life expectancy across time as well as social and demographic groups. The sex difference in active life expectancy is a case in point. Estimates of active life expectancy for men and women are based on a common definition of ''disability'' without regard for sex differences in expected social roles. Similarly, the estimates of historical changes in active life expectancy are based on the assumption of no change in the socially expected or acceptable levels of impairment with which to continue performing social roles or attitudes concerning disabilities. These assumptions, while necessary to produce estimates within the constraints of available data, nonetheless need to be kept in mind.

The challenge for future research, therefore, is to develop measurement strategies that align more closely with the notion of disability or competence as a life cycle process involving both changes in dysfunction and changes in the environment's challenges. Increasingly, longitudinal data are available that provide sample paths of individuals' disability or competency status over time. Dynamic modeling techniques also are being applied to these longitudinal data in an attempt to resolve analytic problems imposed by the traditional cross-sectional and static approaches to disability analysis. Both the collection of new longitudinal data and the application of dynamic models have occurred apart from the development of more conceptual models of disability as a life cycle process. Implicitly, it appears that a static conceptualization of disability has been adopted in these instances with little attention given to assessing how the definition of "disability" might affect its manifestation of a dynamic process. Thus it is important to understand the ways in which the physical and social environments may change surrounding changes in dysfunction and vice versa. As part of this conceptualization, it becomes important to acknowledge explicitly how the social and physical environments are defined in relation to dysfunction, that is, functional difficulty compared to disability or competency, since these definitions may vary in their sensitivity to environmental changes. Ultimately, it is not clear how far new longitudinal data or the application of dynamic models to these data can improve our understanding of disability or competence. The challenge for future research lies in the definition of "competence" or "disability" as a dynamic concept.

REFERENCES

Bebbington, A. C. (1988). The expectation of life without disability in England and Wales. *Social Science and Medicine, 27,* 321–327.

Branch, L., Guralnik, J. M., Foley, D. J., Kohout, F. J., Wetle, T. T., Ostfeld, A., & Katz, S. (1991). Active life expectancy for 10,000 Caucasian men and women in three communities. *Journal of Gerontology, 46,* M145–150.

Branch, L., & Ku, L. (1989). Transition probabilities to dependency, institutionalization, and death among the elderly over a decade. *Journal of Aging and Health, 1*(3), 370–408.

Crimmins, E. M., Hayward, M., & Saito, Y. (1994). Changing mortality and morbidity rates and the health status and life expectancy of the older population. *Demography, 31,* 159–175.

Crimmins, E. M., Hayward, M., & Saito, Y. (1996). Differentials in active life expectancy among older Americans. *Journal of Gerontology: Social Sciences, 51B,* S109–S120.

Crimmins, E. M., Saito, Y., & Ingegneri, D. (1989). Changes in life expectancy and disability-free life expectancy in the United States. *Population and Development Review, 15,* 235–267.

Hayward, M., Crimmins, E., & Friedman, S. (1994). *Dementia-free life expectancy among the chronically impaired American elderly.* Paper presented at the annual meetings of the Population Association of America, Miami, FL.

Land, K., Guralnik, J., & Blazer, D. (1994). Estimating increment-decrement life tables with multiple covariates from panel data: The case of active life expectancy. *Demography, 31,* 297–319.

Manton, K. G., Corder, L., & Stallard, E. (1993). Estimates of change in chronic disability and institutional incidence and prevalence rates in the U.S. elderly population from the 1982, 1984, and 1989 National Long-Term Care Survey. *Journal of Gerontology: Social Sciences, 48,* S153–S166.

Ritchie, K. C., Brayne, C., & Letenneur, L. (1993). Dementia-free life expectancy: Preliminary calculations for France and the United Kingdom. In J. M. Robine, C. Mathers, M. Bone, & I. Remieu (Eds.), *Calculation of health expectancies: Harmonization, consensus achieved and future perspectives* (pp. 233–244). Montrouge, France: John Libby Eurotext.

Robine, J. M., Bucquet, D., & Ritchie, K. (1991). L'espérance de vie sons incapacité, un indicateur de l'évolution des conditions de santé au cours du temps: vingt ans de calcul [Life expectancy without incapacity, an indicator of the evolution of health conditions through the course of time: Twenty years of calculation]. *Cahiers Québécois de Démographie, 20,* 205–236.

Robine, J. M., Colvez, A., Bucquet, D., Hatton, F., Morel, B., & Lelaidier, S. (1986). L'espérance de vie sans incapacité en France en 1982 [Life expectancy without incapacity in France in 1982]. *Population, 41*(6), 1025–1042.

Robine, J. M., Mathers, C., & Brouard, N. (1993). *Health and mortality trends among elderly populations: Determinants and implications.* Paper presented at IUSSP meetings in Sendai, Japan, 1993.

Robine, J. M., & Ritchie, K. (1993). Measuring changes in population health through changes in disability-free life expectancy calculation. *International Population Conference, Montreal, Canada, 1,* 523–535.

Rogers, A., Rogers, R., & Belanger, A. (1990). Longer life but worse health? Measurement and dynamics. *The Gerontologist, 30,* 640–649.

Rogers, A., Rogers, R., & Branch, L. G. (1989). A multistate analysis of active life expectancy. *Public Health Reports, 104,* 222–226.

Sanders, B. (1964). Measuring community health level. *American Journal of Public Health, 54,* 1063–1070.

Sullivan, D. F. (1971). A single index of mortality and morbidity. *HSMHA Health Reports, 86,* 347–354.

Verbrugge, L. (1984). Longer life but worsening health? Trends in the health and mortality of older persons. *Milbank Memorial Fund Quarterly/Health and Society, 62,* 475–519.

Verbrugge, L. (1994). Disability in late life. In R. Abeles, H. Gift, & M. Ory (Eds.), *Aging and quality of life* (pp. 79–98). New York: Springer.

Verbrugge, L., & Jette, A. (1994). The disablement process. *Social Science and Medicine, 38,* 1–14.

Verbrugge, L., Reoma, J., & Gruber-Baldini, A. (1994). Short-term dynamics of disability and well-being. *Journal of Health and Social Behavior, 35,* 97–117.

Wilkins, R., & Adams, O. (1983). Health expectancy in Canada, late 1970s: Demographic, regional, and social dimensions. *American Journal of Public Health, 73,* 1073–1080.

Commentary: Imprints of Disability

Lois M. Verbrugge

Active life expectancy (ALE) is a compact statistic that describes a population's disability status. As a small imprint of disability, ALE is attractive to statistics users in government, journalism, and public health, who usually want information that is telling but brief. Demographers are generating ALE estimates and developing estimation procedures to meet user demands and to address scientific questions about past and future population health.

This commentary concerns the content and utility of ALE estimates and then the intertwined roles of demography and sociology in disability research. It is prepared as a separate chapter, rather than as a focused response to Crimmins and Hayward (this volume).

CONTENT AND UTILITY OF ALE

What is the general notion of "active life expectancy" about?[1] It estimates time spent in various disability states during life. Values are computed for nondisabled years ("active") and disabled years ("inactive"; often

---

[1]In this commentary, ALE will often appear as a global term, covering statistics that divide life into disabled and nondisabled portions. When precision is required, ALE is the specific statistic for the nondisabled portion.

split by severity levels). A given value represents cumulative years in a nondisabled or disabled state on average for a population. This is parallel to life expectancy, which also represents cumulative years in a state (alive) on average.

ALE values are derived from age-specific rates of disability and mortality. The disability data may be cross-sectional (prevalence rates) or longitudinal for several years (prevalence rates and transition rates into and out of disability). In both instances, the ALE values are effectively period estimates; they do not reflect the actual history of a birth cohort.

Real Life and Its Reflection in ALE

Disability is changeable in people's lives, varying as illnesses progress and retreat, as therapies and rehabilitation fail or succeed. The presence and severity of disability influence a person's risk of dying in a time interval. How well are these real-life dynamics and variety reflected in ALE estimates?

Prevalence-based ALE estimates have three embedded assumptions that do not match real-life experience. They assume that "once disabled, always disabled," that risks of dying are the same for all disabled persons, and that people must be disabled before they die. Formally, these assumptions are called absorption, homogeneity, and hierarchy. ALE values based on prevalence rates overestimate time spent disabled (because no functional restoration is allowed). Techniques that relieve absorption and homogeneity have been developed. They require longitudinal data with transitions (incidence into and out of disability) and gradations of disability (severity). Called multistate life table procedures, they have helped produce ALE estimates that are more veridical.

But the problem of hierarchy has not been solved. It occurs whenever researchers use several indicators of dysfunction in an analysis; for example, problems in basic physical or mental functioning, in household management (IADLs), and in personal care (ADLs). Institutional residence may also be included as an indicator of dysfunction. These are different dimensions of disability, and there are many possible profiles of scores people can have. But multistate life table procedures require mutually exclusive states, that is, a person can be in just one state at a given time. In response to this constraint, researchers impose a hierarchy on multiple indicators, grading them by presumed severity. In the previous example, this could be operationalized as: no functional problems, some functional problems but not IADLs or ADLs, IADLs but not ADLs, ADLs, and institutionalized. Once a hierarchy is established, individuals are scored by their most severe status.

The hierarchy assumption is seldom openly considered and studied by researchers. One way to relieve it is to compute ALEs for a variety of disability indicators, each by itself. In this way, disability's multidimensionality is maintained. But having multiple ALE values can confuse statistics users. Alternatively, an approach developed by Manton and colleagues relieves the assumption (Manton, Stallard, & Liu, 1993). Whether the multistate life table techniques now publicly available can be made flexible enough to handle multiple concurrent states is uncertain.

Quality Adjustments

Active life expectancy computes quantities of life in various disability states. Researchers have argued that quality of life differs for persons in the states, that is, a year of severe disability is subjectively worse than a year of mild disability. This assertion has prompted the development and use of quality adjustments (Patrick & Erickson, 1993; Robine, Mathers, & Bucquet, 1993).

Quality-adjusted years use weights that reflect how terrible or wonderful life is in various disability states. In the simplest format, death is set at 0.00 (zero quality), various disability states are scored > 0.00 but < 1.00 (with severe ones close to zero and mild ones close to 1.00), and the nondisabled stated is 1.00 (best quality). A weight of .35 means someone has about one-third the life quality as a nondisabled person, in a given time period such as a year. Once the weights are applied to individual or aggregate data, a new kind of life expectancy is calculated that expresses the number of years people can expect to live with top-quality function. It goes by various labels, for example, quality-adjusted life expectancy (QALE) or health-adjusted life expectancy (HALE). The obverse (years with less than top quality) can also be calculated; an example is the World Bank's indicator of disability-adjusted life years (DALY). Quality-adjusted life expectancy values tend to be higher than active life expectancy for the simple reason that disabled persons contribute some fraction of good-quality time, however small, to QALE, whereas ALE effectively assumes zero quality in the same time period.

Two problems with quality adjustments are the effort needed to derive them and their uncertain generalizability. The weights are derived from detailed and laborious studies of preferences or health utilities in which subjects are asked to compare and rate numerous states of morbidity and disability. The studies have genuine psychometric interest, but researchers often hope to produce a practical result, namely, weights that can be applied to other data sets for quality-adjusted values. To date, most studies have used selective samples such as patients with specific diseases, and this has spurred concerns about whether the weights can indeed be exported. Community-based preferences are now being gathered to remedy this. Taking another approach to the matter, some researchers have relied on expert judgments of quality for morbidity and disability states to be used on large-scale data sets. These are derived by careful query of a group of specialists or by discussion among the research team. Accuracy and generalizability are also issues here.

In sum, quality adjustments can be a worthy addition to ALE calculations, but they should be skipped if there are doubts about the weights. There is one more caution: Quality adjustments put expectancy values one step farther from the initial data, and this increases the likelihood of confusing statistics.

Variety in Terminology and Indicators

Disability is extensively multidimensional: People can have health-related problems walking, opening doors, reading road signs, getting into a bathtub, performing their job, doing their favorite hobby, taking a public bus, etc. It is no wonder that disability terminology and indicators are so diverse. But unnecessary confusion now exists. Names of variables are overblown or scarcely related to the content; underlying theoretical concepts are muddled or absent; and ill-defined words connote different things to various disciplines.

In the past decade, there have been strong efforts to develop conceptual schemes for use in disability research across many fields. One such effort is represented in the Nagi/Institute of Medicine scheme (Pope & Tarlov, 1991; Verbrugge & Jette, 1994), and another in the *International Classification of Impairments, Disabilities, and Handicaps* (World Health Organization, 1993). The existence of two simultaneous efforts prompted conflict between advocates of each scheme, but this is lessening over time as they recognize the distinctive contributions of each. The first serves especially well as a theoretical architecture for research design, and the second as a data classification scheme. Gradually, language is becoming clearer and more standard, but there is still a great deal of novelty and vagueness in the disability literature. Realism tells us that even if conceptual consensus continues to grow, there will always be other terms used in research reports, public laws and policies, and public health plans. Such diversity is acceptable if it is well defined; otherwise, it promotes and sustains bedlam.

I shall note one particularly bothersome terminology issue. Active life expectancy refers to *disability*; the two basic measurements are years without disability and years with disability; the computations are based on disability and mortality data. But the word ''active'' is sometimes used to distinguish years without chronic *morbidity* from those with chronic morbidity. That is something else and, when properly labeled, is called ''healthy life expectancy'' (HLE). To compute HLE, morbidity and mortality data are needed. Despite its interest, healthy life expectancy is seldom calculated because researchers are reluctant to define a cutoff for significant chronic morbidity versus insignificant or no chronic morbidity, and because of an odd tendency (even among mainstream researchers) to confound morbidity and disability. If researchers were as attentive to divisions of healthy versus ill states, as they are to nondisabled and disabled states, we would have sets of statistics about years in four basic states: well nondisabled, well disabled (potentially small but must be estimated), ill nondisabled, and ill disabled. These calculations can be based on cross-sectional (prevalence) or longitudinal (prevalence and incidence) data.

Other complaints, such as (1) how disability indicators are limited to ADLs, IADLs, and paid jobs, thus ignoring the many other valued activities of life and (2) how dependency indicators do not really measure disability, but instead a buffer introduced to alleviate disability, are discussed in Verbrugge (1990) and in Verbrugge and Jette (1994).

Utility of ALE Estimates

Journalists, politicians, and health officers see two virtues in ALE. It describes a population's functional status in a compact way, and it can be readily introduced into public discourse because of its similarity to life expectancy, already well established in lay and political settings. Strong outside demand is a major reason for scientists' enthusiasm to develop and interpret ALE estimates. Scientists are legitimately concerned about underlying problems of data quality, assumptions embedded in statistical techniques and possibilities for misinterpretation. These considerations are largely absent from the public literature; that is appropriate. Wide use of ALE in public settings is having a fine consequence, bringing the notions of functioning, disability at all ages, and well-being into broad view and parlance.

Actual values of ALE depend largely on the indicators and techniques used. Cross-national comparisons of ALE are especially hazardous because the underlying data and procedures are so varied. But as research accumulates, we discover that distilled aspects of ALE, such as percentage of lifetime spent disabled or the direction of gender differences, have great consistency across populations. This is a very important and felicitous point. Systematic aspects of disability in modern populations manage to percolate through many different ALE formats. Noisiness of data and techniques cannot snuff them out.

DEMOGRAPHY AND SOCIOLOGY OF DISABILITY

Demography and sociology are associated disciplines, but they differ in some fundamental ways. Demography's distinctive feature is production of high-quality statistics about population structure and dynamics. Health and disability are relatively new topics to demography. The expertise and perspectives devoted to long-standing topics (fertility, mortality, migration, age structure) are being applied to health and disability, and the results are widely used and well respected. Sociology concentrates on explaining social structure and dynamics by formulating and testing hypotheses about causes and consequences. There is now strong theoretical and empirical activity on topics such as reasons for population trends in disability, causes of the onset of disability and recovery, and efficacious interventions to reduce disability. Researchers often contribute solely to demography or solely to sociology, but there are others, such as Crimmins and Hayward (this volume), who bridge both disciplines to offer integrated descriptive and explanatory work.

Demography of Disability

Three issues have especially inspired demographers: population trends in disability prevalence and incidence, relative changes in population disability and mortality, and sociodemographic differentials in active life expectancy. Key questions prompting the work are: Is population morbidity and disability increasing despite marked declines in mortality in recent decades? Are the fractions of life spent ill or disabled decreasing ("compression of morbidity and disability")? Which population subgroups (gender, race, education) spend more years disabled or larger portions of life disabled?

1.   Trends in Prevalence and Incidence. Disability prevalence in the U.S. population has been traced over several decades, using the National Health Interview Survey (a repeated cross-sectional survey). Disability incidence (transitions into and out of disability) and trends in incidence require longitudinal panel data. Such data were not collected until the 1980s in the United States, specifically in the Longitudinal Study of Aging (LSOA) and the National Long-Term Care Survey (NLTCS). Analyses of incidence are data-greedy; estimating one incidence rate requires two time points, and trends in incidence require at least three and preferably more. Results to date are confined to the span of about a decade, and they show inconsistent changes in disability prevalence and incidence in the 1980s. This is not really a surprise given the short time span being studied; more time is needed to be certain.

Using the LSOA, Crimmins and Hayward (this volume) provide fine data and discussion on this issue. By contrast, the widely reported findings for NLTCS (Manton, Corder, & Stallard, 1993) are overstated and incomplete. First, the reported percentage decline in disability is true, but actual rates of disability are low and the absolute decline is small; relative changes have a tendency to look large when based on low rates. Second, the reported decline in disability incidence is true, but it a small part of the whole empirical story; more generally, stasis of disability states has increased over time (people are more likely to remain disabled or nondisabled than before).

2.   Compression of Morbidity and Disability. This intriguing question is far easier to discuss than to address empirically. The data requirements are excellent; one needs consistently measured values of healthy life expectancy, active life expectancy, and life expectancy for many decades. With such data, changes in proportions of life spent ill and disabled can then be determined: Are the proportions decreasing (compression) or increasing (expansion)? Whatever the answer is, the specific morbidity, disability, and mortality components that figure into the changes must be spelled out at the same time. Data to answer the compression versus expansion question do not exist, and their chances of being generated are

not very high given funding constraints and researchers' proclivity to alter survey items over time. In this situation, demographers have used innovative approaches to study relevant aspects of the compression hypothesis (e.g., changes in old-age mortality, distribution of ages at death, relationships of risk factors to disability and mortality in data sets from different decades), or they have set aside the issue to work on more tractable ones.

If I could design data to be collected for coming decades that are relevant to compression and expansion, they would include indicators about presence of specific chronic conditions and presence of difficulties performing physical, mental (cognitive and emotional), and role activities. Repeated in cross-sectional and longitudinal studies (combined designs are possible and efficient), they would provide the basis for estimating healthy life expectancy and active life expectancy in various formats over time. Scholars engaged in ALE research would agree with the previously mentioned list of data and indicators. But other aspects of population health need to be tracked in the future as well. Elsewhere, I have discussed the importance of severity, comorbidity, and the relative distribution of fatal and nonfatal conditions (Verbrugge, 1989, 1991). I now add "codisability," an unbecoming term for multiple disabilities. These aspects need to be viewed as imperative for monitoring and analyzing population health, rather than "nice to know when possible."

3. Gender Differences in ALE. There is now repeated confirmation that women spend more years disabled, and larger percentages of life disabled, than do men. The differences are sometimes small, but they are highly consistent across data sets and nations.

Why do women have more disability? An explanation emerges from these distinctive aspects of women's health: Women have higher age-specific prevalence rates for most nonfatal chronic conditions. Assuming no selective mortality due to having them, a higher *incidence of nonfatal conditions* for women is implied. There are far more nonfatal than fatal conditions in the human repertoire, so it is logical to posit that women accumulate *more chronic problems* than men by a given age. The average number of conditions is indeed higher for women (Guralnik, LaCroix, Everett, & Kovar, 1989). The combination of higher risks of acquiring and also accumulating nonfatal problems is likely to generate higher age-specific incidence and duration of disability. To date, analyses of ALE confirm the second aspect (longer duration in disabled states for women) but are inconsistent on the first (higher disability incidence for women).

(See Crimmins, Saito, & Reynolds, 1997; Manton, 1988; Manton et al., 1993.)

Women's current health and disability statuses give us vision toward the future. Consider first that women predominate in the older population, and this will continue for many decades even if sex mortality differences stabilize or begin to narrow. Second, biomedical and clinical research emphasis on fatal conditions is likely to continue, with applications in preventive and therapeutic care. The conjunction of these two features means that, gradually, late-life health for individuals and the population will become dominated by nonfatal conditions such as arthritis, hearing impairment, visual impairment, bunions, frequent constipation, and hemorrhoids. These will bother and disable women for many years until a fatal condition (with lower incidence and slower progression than today) finally prompts death.

In sum, demographers have provided fine statistics about morbidity, disability, and mortality states of the population and developed apt techniques to produce those statistics. By detailing the components of active life expectancy (rates that constitute the building blocks), components of changes in prevalence, and sociodemographic differentials, they launch the process of explanation. This is where sociology comes in.

Sociology of Disability

Determining reasons for differential levels of health and disability, and for changes in those levels, is the task of sociology. Why have population morbidity and disability increased (or shown initial increase then decrease) in recent decades? What epidemiologic, social, and medical factors account for increases in years spent disabled and in the proportion of life disabled? Can one prove that women's higher nonfatal morbidity is the main reason for their higher rates of disability both at a given time point and over their lifetime?

For these particular questions, sociologists are acting in a responsive manner to demographic results. But far more of their work on disability is proactive, generated and executed in the context of medical sociology and health psychology. Here, notions of disability dynamics and multidimensionality are commonplace rather than considered theoretically or technically troublesome. In sociology, some current research issues are to determine the effectiveness of medical and personal interventions in reducing disability, to operationalize the idea that disability is a gap between individual capability and environmental demand, to measure the experience of "handicap" or "social disadvantage," and to study long-term trajectories of disability in individuals' lives. These are very challenging for empirical research, but the challenge is being taken rather than ignored. Demographers are less likely to find such issues appealing or tractable. Still, thinking about them gives demographers a better perspective of what ALE statistics measure about the disability experience, and what they miss. Crimmins and Hayward (this volume) voice this perspective in their chapter's final section.

One topic causes a repeated rift in thinking between demographers and sociologists, and it should be noted. Increasingly, data are being produced that allow researchers to study trends in ALE. Disability trends reflect underlying changes in morbidity incidence, duration, and severity, and also societal changes that affect role demands and perceptions of being disabled. Demographers think of the societal changes as artifacts that are bothersome and should ideally be absent from data series. By contrast, sociologists acknowledge that causes of disability trends are indeed diverse (both epidemiological and sociocultural), and consider it silly to think or wish otherwise. Demographers could relax if they accepted this view rather than wishing for sociocultural-free data. With the broader perspective, disability prevalence and incidence rates and trends are accepted as true rather than suspect, even if their social and morbidity constituents vary across time and cannot be measured fully.

Summing up, demography and sociology are separate but related disciplines, and they have separate but intertwined roles in disability research. When working together, they produce descriptive and explanatory results that have value in both lay and professional circles—an outcome that is rare for scientific research products.

CONCLUSION

ALE estimates are tight little statistics about a population's diverse and changeable experiences of disability. From a sociological perspective, their brevity borders on the ridiculous. From a demographic one, brevity is fine so long as its quality is high. These points are virtuous and need to be maintained by scientists, but they scarcely bother disseminators and lay users of ALE. For them, the statistics give clear, simple messages about the potential for good functioning as people age. They are telling, useful, and welcome. ALE statistics are promoting notions of successful aging and quality of life in medical professions, public health offices, and the broad population. The small statistical imprints have big public power.

REFERENCES

Crimmins, E. M., Saito, Y., & Reynolds, S. L. (1997). Further evidence on recent trends in the prevalence and incidence of disability among older Americans from two sources: The Longitudinal Study on Aging and the National Health Interview Survey. *Journal of Gerontology: Social Sciences, 52*(2).

Guralnik, J. M., LaCroix, A. X., Everett, D. F., & Kovar, M. G. (1989). Aging in the eighties: The prevalence of comorbidity and its association with disability. *Advance Data,* No. 170. Hyattsville, MD: National Center for Health Statistics.

Manton, K. G. (1988). A longitudinal study of functional change and mortality in the United States. *Journals of Gerontology: Social Sciences, 43,* S153–161.

Manton, K. G., Corder, L. S., & Stallard, E. (1993). Estimates of change in chronic disability and institutional incidence and prevalence rates in the U.S. elderly population from the 1982, 1984, and 1989 National Long Term Care Survey. *Journals of Gerontology: Social Sciences, 48,* S153–166.

Manton, K. G., Stallard, E., & Liu, K. (1993). Forecasts of active life expectancy: Policy and fiscal implications. *Journals of Gerontology: Social Sciences, 48* (special issue), 11–26.

Patrick, D. L., & Erickson, P. (1993). *Health status and health policy: Allocating resources to health care.* New York: Oxford University Press.

Pope, A. M., & Tarlov, A. R. (Eds.). (1991). *Disability in America: Toward a National Agenda for Prevention.* Institute of Medicine, Division of Health Promotion and Disease Prevention. Washington, DC: National Academy Press.

Robine, J. M., Mathers, C. D., & Bucquet, D. (1993). Distinguishing health expectancies and health-adjusted life expectancies from quality-adjusted life years. *American Journal of Public Health, 83,* 797–798.

Verbrugge, L. M. (1989). Recent, present, and future health of American adults. In L. Breslow, J. E. Fielding, & L. B. Lave (Eds.), *Annual Review of Public Health* (Vol. 10, pp. 333–361). Palo Alto, CA: Annual Reviews.

Verbrugge, L. M. (1990). The iceberg of disability. In S. M. Stahl (Ed.), *The legacy of longevity.* Newbury Park, CA: Sage.

Verbrugge, L. M. (1991). Survival curves, prevalence rates, and dark matters therein. *Journal of Aging and Health, 3,* 217–236.

Verbrugge, L. M., & Jette, A. M. (1994). The disablement process. *Social Science and Medicine, 38,* 1–14.

World Health Organization. (1993). *International classification of impairments, disabilities, and handicaps.* (Reprint of 1980 edition, with a new foreword.) Geneva, Switzerland.

Commentary: Active Life Expectancy: Concept or Model for Research on Competency?

Merrill F. Elias and Penelope K. Elias

stimation of active life expectancy is an important objective from a demographic perspective. It has profound implications for public health programs and for informed policy decisions. At last, at a population level, we have a potentially systematic way of assessing progress toward national and international goals of achieving better life, not just longer life.

We direct our discussion of Crimmins' and Hayward's (this volume) chapter to the central question posed by these investigators: "What can we learn about competence at the older ages from active life expectancy?" There are two meanings we can attach to this question. Does active life expectancy research give us some conceptually creative ideas and directions for research on competency? Does active life expectancy, as a model, provide a useful theoretical framework for understanding age-related competency?

The answer to the first question is obvious. Yes, methodologically, one can decompose activity into competence and incompetence, or into relative degrees of competence, and then apply the statistical tools necessary to understand expectancy of competent life at any segment of the adult life span.

The answer to the second question requires that we consider a number of issues raised by Crimmins' and Hayward's (this volume) comprehensive review of research on active life expectancy. First we take up these issues. Then we discuss specific applications of active life expectancy methodology to population research on cognitive competence.

THE MODEL

Crimmins and Hayward (this volume) point out that "differing conceptual and operational definitions of disability give rise to the majority of cross-sectional variability in estimates of disability-free life." Does the active life expectancy model promise less variability if employed consistently in studies with U.S. populations or in cross-national studies?

It represents a beginning in this direction, but seems more a concept than a model, at least in the formal sense of providing consistent operational definitions that can be utilized successfully across various populations. Definitions of its key elements, activity, health, and competence, are either circular or have come full circle as research driven by the model has progressed.

Active life expectancy is defined as life without specific diseases, life without impairment, life without disability, life without functional limitations. Crimmins and Hayward (this volume) tell us that "[w]hile these processes can be thought of as hierarchical and sequential over the course of the process [of disablement], this is not necessarily so." (See chapter 1, p. 5.) We are left with the expectation that we will understand what *is so* at the end of the chapter. This expectation is frustrated. The investigators, cited by Crimmins and Hayward, make use of these processes or constructs (disease, impairment, disability, functional limitations), but operationalize them in different ways or construct their own hierarchies. The result, as Crimmins and Hayward point out, has been chaos. A dynamic view of active life expectancy is necessary to bring order from chaos, but with the addition of the dynamic component, we are left only with a more complex concept of active life expectancy, not an immediately useful model.

DEFINING ACTIVE LIFE

Crimmins and Hayward (this volume) begin with a definition of active life that defines its relationship to competency.

Active life also is defined in terms of ability to perform these major social activities. . . . That is a measure of the average length of competent life. (p. 1)

This definition emphasizes the important point that competency is not an absolute intrapersonal attribute, but must be understood within a social context. However, it does not make clear whether competency is being viewed as a unipolar correlate of competent life or as a bipolar correlate. If we assume a bipolar correlate, the definition needs to be more exact; if we assume a unipolar correlate, some comment on an underlying premise is necessary. By a unipolar definition, the more active one is, the more competent one is and vice versa; each is a proxy for the other. By a bipolar definition, activity can be competent or incompetent, and vary along a positive or negative continuum. A unipolar definition can only have merit if, in fact, society (broadly or narrowly defined as the family, co-workers, and friends) never expects, and thus never reinforces, incompetency. Appeal to personal experience suggests that this view is untrue.

One may behave in an actively incompetent manner and do so to meet internal (self) or external (others) expectations. Many personal examples come to mind. Incompetency allows one to escape distasteful chores and is all the easier when there is an expectation of inadequate performance. The senior author of this paper has never learned to clean the house competently; the second author cannot pump diesel fuel into her car. If our argument requires empirical support to be convincing, we refer the reader to the social psychology literature on learned helplessness (Maier, 1989). One can come to expect incompetency in oneself and, thus, behave incompetently. It seems clear that activity is not a proxy for competence.

The only way one can defend the argument that active life is an index of "average length of competent life in a population" (p. 1) is to define competence and activity in a circular manner, and, by definition, nothing is to be gained by including both terms under the umbrella of a single "model."

HEALTH AND ACTIVITY

If not circular by intent, the definitions of "health" and "activity" evolved in a circular fashion as research progressed.

As demographers' interests grew in the issue of health and functioning, researchers suggested the possibility of a more complex life table model that would decompose life expectancy into the years of active and inactive life, where active life is an indicator of the average number of healthy years a person can expect to live. (p. 3)

It would appear that as research progressed, the definition came full circle. Health became an index of activity. In fact, neither is a good index of the other. Life-threatening health events, occurring more often in old age, for example, stroke, malignant tumor, may result in disability and reduce activity. On the other hand, diagnoses of acute diseases in an early stage, chronic diseases, or symptoms of these diseases can stimulate increased social activity in relation to going to the physician, arranging transportation, and discussing the health problems with friends, family, and support groups. In response to such possibilities, Crimmins and Hayward recognize social-psychological dynamics as they influence relations among health, activity, and competence.

DYNAMIC MODELS

The Crimmins-Hayward argument for a dynamic model reflects wisdom born or their respective backgrounds in demography and life-span sociology. They provide good examples of the interactive dynamics of activity, health, and competency in social contexts, and devote some time to the discussion of statistical solutions. Abundant examples of the inadequacy of the static models and the importance of dynamic modeling come from the health psychology and aging literature (M. F. Elias, Elias, & Elias, 1990; Siegler & Costa, 1985).

With increasing age, symptoms diagnosed as health-related in the young are often dismissed as age-related in the elderly (Grimley-Evans, 1988). Men and women are often diagnosed, and treated differently, although displaying similar symptoms, for example, symptoms predictive of heart attack and stroke (Wisoki & Keuthen, 1988).

Ill health with respect to one disease category may lead to improved health habits over time or lead to the discovery of life-threatening disease, and thus may actually reduce the risk of catastrophic events such as stroke, or multiinfarct disease, a process that ultimately will lower the risk of cognitive incompetence in later life.

Because self-report of health and the experience of illness take place in a dynamic social context, self-report of health is an imperfect index of disease. In a dynamic model, self-report must be viewed as a product of dynamic social forces that shape what we report and how we feel about what we experience. Thus we are concerned to find that much of the information on health status in population research studies is based on global health report. This raises issues with respect to estimates of the prevalence of diseases in men and women over 65 years of age, and the precision and validity of these estimates are critical to active life expectancy tables. It is the awareness of this problem that leads Crimmins and Hayward to their emphasis on dynamic models of active life expectancy and competency.

> Estimates of active life expectancy for men and women are based on a common definition of disability without regard for sex differences in expected social roles. Similarly, the estimates of historical change in active life expectancy are based on the assumption of no change in the socially expected or acceptable levels of impairment with which to continue performing social roles or attitudes concerning disabilities. (p. 19)

Strickland (1988) takes this same argument to the level of how health and disability are measured. She points out that gender differences in perception of health may confound estimates of illness in men and women over 65 years of age. Strickland makes a convincing argument that identical instruments do not necessarily yield comparable information on men and women. She cites a literature indicating that women and men differ in their perceptions of illness, even of the same illness, because they have existed in different social environments since childhood.

In this context, it is important to recognize that much of the data on health in population research studies of active life expectancy is based on self-report, often with global health ratings. Are gender differences in symptom reporting the only problem with respect to this dependence on self-reported health ratings as indices of health or disease?

SELF-REPORT OF HEALTH STATUS

It is obvious that one can have disease, but either not report it or be unaware of it. Conversely, one may report symptoms of a disease that

one does not have (Costa & McCrae, 1985, 1987). In two excellent reviews
of the relevant literature, Costa and McCrae point out that correlations
between self-report of health and physicians' ratings are often used to
justify self-report of health as a proxy for health, but that these correlations
are modest. Global health ratings are related to health attitudes, psychological adjustment, and morale. While those who survive to old age do so
only to be exposed to increasing illness (the demographers' life expec-
tancy-health paradox), global ratings often fail to show marked associations with age. Considering the possibility that it is the undifferentiated
nature of global health ratings that lead to their deficits as proxies of the
state of disease, Costa and McCrae (1985) point out that symptom checklists such as the Cornell Medical Index (CMI) offer advantages relative
to global health ratings because they employ items dealing with specific
symptoms of disease categories. Unfortunately, they too reflect both objective health and social-psychological factors. This point is dramatically
illustrated by studies of symptom reporting in relation to coronary artery disease.

For example, we (M. F. Elias & Robbins, 1987; M. F. Elias, Robbins,
Blow, Rice, & Edgecomb, 1982) examined correlations between the number of symptoms reported for the various physical symptom categories
on the Cornell Medical Index and indices of coronary artery stenosis in
19 segments of the coronary arteries. Participants ($n = 85$) were undergoing
heart catheterization at Maine Medical Center because physicians judged
their chest pain symptoms to be indicative of coronary artery disease.

Presence of clinically significant disease in the coronary artery segments
was determined by cinearteriography, a procedure requiring heart catheterization. Table 1.6 shows correlations between the number of symptoms
reported for each symptom category and maximum stenosis (the maximum
amount of stenosis in the most occluded coronary artery); number of
diseased arterial segments (> 50% stenosis); and the Gensini Index, a
comprehensive index of arterial stenosis based on a classification scheme
proposed by Gensini (1975) and adapted by the American Heart
Association.

As may be seen in Table 1.6, with age and education controlled statistically, symptom reporting for various subcategories was *negatively* correlated with these indices of coronary artery disease. In a separate set of
analyses, it was found that those who reported angina-like chest pain in the
absence of clinically significant stenosis of the coronary arteries showed
significantly higher levels of anxiety and depression. Costa and McCrae
(1987) review a number of studies with similar findings.

TABLE 1.6   Correlations between Number of Symptoms (in Specific Categories) Reported on the Cornell Medical Index and Different Criteria for Number of Arteries Stenosed and Degree of Stenosis (n = 85)

Symptom Category	[a]Maximum Stenosis	[b]Number Stenosed	[c]Gensini Index
Sensory	−.14	−.16	−.01
Respiratory	−.27**	−.25**	−.17
Cardiovascular	−.27**	−.28**	−.23*
Digestive	−.04	−.17	−.01
Musculoskeletal	−.17	−.17	−.03
Skin	−.05	−.18*	−.16
Nervous System	−.38***	−.39***	−.20*
Genitourinary	−.14	−.15	−.10
Fatigue	−.30**	−.36***	−.19*
Illness Frequency	−.00	−.01	−.01
Miscellaneous	−.04	−.04	−.04
(Good) Habits	−.15	−.19*	−.06

*p < .05; **p < .01; ***p < .001.

a. Maximum stenosis in the most stenosed artery as measured by the percentage reduction in the diameter of the arterial lumen, ranging from 0% to 100% (total occlusion).

b. Stenosis exceeding 50% defines an arterial segment as stenosed. Nineteen segments were evaluated.

c. A comprehensive index proposed by Gensini (1975) and adapted by The American Heart Association. It takes into account stenosis, the configuration of the lesion, the presence of collaterals, and the size and location of the arterial segment or branch involved.

From: Use of cinearteriography in behavioral studies of patients with chest pain in the absence of clinically significant coronary artery disease. In J. W. Elias & P. H. Marshall (Eds.), *Cardiovascular disease and hypertension.* New York: Hemisphere. Copyright 1987 by Hemisphere Publishing Company. Reprinted with permission.

Our skepticism about self-reported health has been viewed as a heretical argument against use of self-health report instruments. Such is not the case. Clearly, it is impracticable to obtain objective data on health in population research studies where large study populations are used. Moreover, global self-report of health and symptoms' checklists provides important information about perceived health.

This argument applies to the relation between self-reported health and functional disability. Wolinsky, Coe, Miller, and Prendergast (1984) found low correlations between self-report of health and functional disability, and recommended that both measures be used.

THE MANY FACES OF COMPETENCE

While the active life expectancy model is still in its embryonic stage, Hayward, Crimmins, and Friedman (1994) have used it in a very creative way. To estimate the expectancy of life that is free from dementia, Hayward et al. (1994) used the Short, Portable Mental Status Questionnaire to arrange community dwelling individuals, over the age of 65, into categories of normal functioning and mild to more severe dementia. Once the categorization was achieved, age-specific risks of experiencing a change in levels of impairment in bipolar directions (onset or impairment or recovery) were calculated. These rates were then entered into a multistage life table to estimate cognitive impairment-free life expectancy. Here, a unipolar definition of ''competency'' was used, that is, it was defined in terms of disease, and the analyses were designed to be sensitive to varying degrees of incompetency that reflect the progression of the disease.

While the Mini-Mental Questionnaire and other screening devices are useful with regard to gross classifications of cognitive competence, impairment versus no impairment, or degrees of impairment within the general category of dementia, they are of limited usefulness for assessing competency across the full range of human cognitive abilities. Further, they do not allow the demographer to apply the multistage life table approach to multiple domains of cognitive functioning. The Halstead-Reitan neuropsychological battery (Lezak, 1983) is ideal for this purpose (M. F. Elias, Robbins, Schultz, & Pierce, 1990), but obviously impracticable for population research studies. But there are much shorter neuropsychological batteries that measure multiple domains of cognitive functioning and that are sensitive to age-cohort differences and disease. We can illustrate this point with data obtained from the Framingham Heart Study archive in collaboration with Professors Cupples, D'Agostino, White, and Wolf, all of Boston University. The Kaplan-Albert (Farmer et al., 1987) battery was designed as a short 20- to 25-minute battery that would measure performance in multiple cognitive domains but would be suitable for research with large study populations.

Beginning in 1950 a subset of 55- to 88-year-old participants in the Framingham study were examined for hypertension, stroke, and other vascular risk factors and events. Between 1976 and 1978 they were administered the Kaplan-Albert Neuropsychological Test battery (n = 2,123). The Kaplan-Albert (KA) battery (Farmer et al., 1987) includes eight short tests taken from the Weschler Adult Intelligence Scale, the Weschler Memory Scale, and the Multilingual Aphasia Examination (Lezak, 1983): Digit Span Forward; Digit Span Backward; Logical Memory; Logical Memory Delayed Recall; Fluency; Similarities; Paired Associates Learning; and Visual Reproductions. With our Boston colleagues, we have examined relations among age, averaged blood pressure level, chronic hypertension and stroke, and neuropsychological test performance for subsets of these individuals (M. F. Elias, Wolf, D'Agostino, Cobb, & White, 1993; M. F. Elias et al., 1995).

Blood pressure level was the focus of the first study (M. F. Elias et al., 1993). The average of blood pressure values measured at 5 biennial examinations (1956 to 1964) was employed as the predictor variable and related to neuropsychological test scores obtained between 1976 and 1978. We predicted that multiple measures of blood pressure would be inversely associated with cognitive functioning even though 12 to 14 years intervened between blood pressure measurement and neuropsychological testing. Age, occupation, education, gender, alcohol consumption, and cigarette use were controlled statistically. None of the participants had a history of stroke. Age × Blood Pressure interactions were not significant, and neither were Gender × Blood Pressure interactions. The left-hand (facing) column in Table 1.7 summarizes results for the full sample of 1,702 individuals. Of these participants, 29% were hypertensive and 13% had received antihypertensive medications during the blood pressure measurement window (1956 to 1964). We (M. F. Elias et al., 1993) presented data for the test scores that were significantly ($p < .05$) related to blood pressure. These data have been abstracted from the *American Journal of Epidemiology* and are summarized in Table 1.7. Regression coefficients express change in performance level (z scores) in relation to 10 mmHg increments in blood pressure. Averaged blood pressure (5 biennial examinations) was inversely associated with the composite of 8 scores, and 3 of 8 subtests, Logical Memory, Visual Reproductions, and Logical Memory Delayed.

In a second-pass analysis, participants who had received antihypertensive medications anytime prior to, or during, neuropsychological testing were excluded from the sample, and the analyses were repeated. Diastolic blood pressure values ranged from 56 to 99 mmHg, and systolic blood

TABLE 1.7 **Regression Coefficients* (β) from Multiple Regression Analyses Expressing the Association between 10 mmHg Increments in Averaged Diastolic Blood Pressure and 4 Test Scores on the Kaplan-Albert Battery that Were Related to Blood Pressure for One or More Analyses**

Test Score	Full Sample (*n* = 1,702)	Untreated Subsample (*n* = 1,038)
Logical Memory		
β	−.0819***	−.1329***
SE	.0231	.0407
Visual Reproductions		
β	−.0581*	−.0773*
SE	.0226	.0401
Digit Span Backward		
β	−.0374	−.1077**
SE	.0232	.0422
Logical Memory Delayed		
β	−.0588**	−.0994**
SE	.0229	.0398
Kaplan-Albert Composite	−.0428**	−.0678**
Score (8 tests)	.0135	.0236

*p < .05; **p < .01; ***p < .001.
*Regression coefficients are adjusted for age, education, occupation, gender, alcohol consumption, and cigarette smoking.

Notes: Data abstracted from a paper published in 1993 in the *American Journal of Epidemiology*, *138*(6), 361. Copyright 1993 by The Johns Hopkins University. Reprinted with permission.

pressure from 95 mmHg to 182 mmHg. As may be seen in the right-hand (facing) panel of Table 1.7 (*n* = 1,038), significant inverse associations between blood pressure and cognitive functioning were now observed for Digit Span Backwards, as well as the Logical Memory tests and Visual Reproductions. For the full sample and the subsample, blood pressure level was inversely related to cognitive functioning. The same pattern of results was obtained when systolic blood pressure and chronicity of hypertension (proportion of examinations in which hypertensive blood pressures were detected), rather than diastolic blood pressure were employed as the predictor variable.

Recently, data for this study population was reanalyzed (M. F. Elias, 1994), with age as the predictor variable of central interest. For a linear regression analysis with no statistical controls, age was significantly associated with every test score in the KA battery. The question raised in the study was whether statistically significant associations between age and each test measure would be obtained with statistical control for gender, education, occupation, marital status, alcohol and cigarette consumption, blood pressure level, diabetes mellitus, myocardial infarction, and stroke. For this analysis, blood pressure was averaged over *all* biennial examinations prior to neuropsychological testing (1950 to 1975). Data used to classify participants with regard to diabetes, myocardial infarction, and stroke were obtained for this same time period. Table 1.8 summarizes the tests employed in the KA battery and statistical associations between age (range 56 to 88) and the test scores for participants of the Framingham study who completed every test in the Kaplan-Albert battery ($n = 1,853$) and for whom data were available for all the covariables. The regression coefficients (Table 1.8) express the magnitude of change in the test scores (expressed as standard scores, z scores) in relation to *10-year* increments in age at the time of the neuropsychological testing (1976 to 1978). Despite controls for demographic variables and the other risk factors, age was inversely related to performance level for every test measure and the composite of all tests. The same results were obtained when persons with stroke history were removed from the sample.

A multiple regression analysis was used in this study. Thus each covariable in the model was controlled for all other covariables. Data with respect to blood pressure and diabetes were submitted for publication (1996) and thus cannot be presented here. The M. F. Elias et al. (1993) findings for blood pressure (Table 1.7) were replicated.

With control for all covariates, including age and blood pressure, history of stroke (yes/no) was related to the composite of all 8 scores ($\beta = -.2478$, $p < .0002$), Digit Span Backward ($\beta = -.3859$, $p < .0023$); Digit Span Symbol Forward ($\beta = -.2684$; $p < .0001$); Word Fluency ($\beta = -.4535$; $SE = .1159$, $p < .0001$), and marginally to Visual Reproductions ($\beta = -.2199$, $p < .07$). The same pattern of results was obtained when diastolic blood pressure was substituted for systolic blood pressure in the regression model. Even though only 3% of the sample experienced stroke, it had a dramatic impact on performance, as indicated by the regression coefficients. For example, for word fluency persons with stroke history performed almost one-half standard deviation below those free from stroke.

TABLE 1.8   Regression Coefficients (β) from Multiple Regression Analyses Expressing Change in Performance (in *z* Score Units) as a Function of 10-Year Increments in Age for 56- to 88-Year-Old Participants of the Framingham Heart Study Who Completed the Kaplan-Albert Neuropsychological Examination (*N* = 1,853)

Test Score	β	SE
Digit Span Backward	−.1524****	.0034
Logical Memory Delayed	−.2834****	.0326
Fluency	−.1768****	.0313
Digit Span Forward	−.1586****	.0346
Logical Memory	−.2440****	.0328
Similarities	−.2778** **	.0289
Paired Associates	−.3121****	.0337
Visual Reproductions	−.4099****	.0322
Composite *z* Score [All 8 Tests]	−.2451****	.0186

****$p < .0001$.

Note: Regression coefficients controlled for age, gender, education, occupation, marital status, blood pressure, alcohol consumption, smoking, myocardial infarction, and stroke. The analysis was done in collaboration with Dr. Adrienne Cupples, Department of Biostatistics and Epidemiology, School of Public Health, Boston University.

It is clear from these data that the KA battery is sensitive to age-cohort differences, blood pressure level, and stroke, but the pattern of tests affected by these predictor variables is different for each of these predictors. Gross screening measures, while useful with regard to some research questions, for example, the Hayward et al. (1994) study of dementia-free life expectancy, do not capture relationships between age, or disease, and the pattern of cognitive deficit.

We need short batteries of tests, including tests that measure a wide range of ability within specific domains of cognitive functioning. The KA battery takes 30 minutes on average to give in our laboratory. Test batteries of this length could be used with representative subsets of studies drawn from national study populations. We are not advocating the KA battery, but if pressed to suggest a battery for population research, we would consider it, at least as a prototype. The Digit-Symbol Substitution test (Lezak, 1983) should be added to the battery, where limitations on vision or motor dexterity are not affected adversely by disability. The stimulus materials may be enlarged for use with older individuals (e.g., Croog et al., 1994). Obviously, any battery used in population research for persons over age 65 would need to be modified, or would employ modified tests, to accommodate visual, hearing, motor, and other age-related disabilities.

SUMMARY

The concept of active life expectancy gives us a fresh approach to the study of maintenance and loss of competency in relation to chronological age, health, and functional disability. It will need to be revised and formalized if it is to bring order to the chaos that now exists in active life expectancy research. It is not unusual for definitions of constructs, and relations among them, to change as research progresses. Thus we anticipate evolution toward a formal model that addresses the following questions: How, specifically (in terms of a causal model), should fundamental constructs (health, functional disability, functional limitations, and cognitive impairment) relate to each other within defined social contexts? How should these constructs be indexed (i.e., what measurement instruments should be used for each) so that they are independently defined? A more disciplined definition of key components of the active life expectancy "concept" and identification of clear causal pathways between these components, as affected by social context, are necessary steps in the direction of a formal model.

Crimmins and Hayward are describing the state of the art in active life expectancy research and are themselves critical of the chaos that has evolved from multiple definitions and failure to place the model in a dynamic context. They make effective use of their provocative chapter to advocate dynamic expectancy models and provide us with a specific illustration of how multistage life tables can be used to estimate life expectancy free from dementia.

ACKNOWLEDGMENTS

We acknowledge the following colleagues who have been so important in our work with the Framingham Heart Study data archive and have served as collaborators on these studies: Drs. Adrienne Cupples, Ralph

B. D'Agostino, Lon R. White, and Philip A. Wolf. We also acknowledge computer programmers Janet Cobb and Halit Silbershatz (Statistics and Consulting Unit, Boston University).

Preparation of this chapter was supported by a grant from the National Institute on Aging (R37-AG03055) to Merrill F. Elias and a Special Career Emphasis Award from the National Institute on Aging to Penelope K. Elias (KO1-AG00646-01).

REFERENCES

Costa, P. T., & McCrae, R. R. (1987). Role of neuroticism in perception of chest pain symptoms and coronary artery disease. In J. W. Elias & P. H. Marshall (Eds.), *Cardiovascular disease and hypertension* (pp 39–66). New York: Hemisphere.

Costa, P. T., & McCrae, R. R. (1985). Hypochondriasis, neuroticism, and aging: When are somatic complaints unfounded? *American Psychologist, 40,* 19–28.

Croog, S. H., Elias, M. F., Colton, T., Baume, R. M., Leibum, S. R., Jenkins, C. D., Perry, H. M., & Hall, W. D. (1994). Effects of antihypertensive medications on quality of life in elderly hypertensive women. *American Journal of Hypertension, 7,* 323–339.

Elias, M. F. (1994). Longitudinal studies of hypertension and cognitive functioning: Epidemiological perspectives. *Symposium on the Inevitability of Age and Health: Natural Partners for Research Excellence.* Washington, DC: American Psychological Association.

Elias, M. F., Elias, P. K., & Elias, J. W. (1990). Biological and health influences on aging. In J. E. Birren & K. W. Schaie (Eds.), *Handbook on the psychology of aging* 3rd Ed., (pp. 80–102). New York: Academic Press.

Elias, M. F., Elias, P. K., Cobb, J., D'Agostino, R. B., White, L. R., & Wolf, P. A. (1995). Blood pressure affects cognitive functioning: The Framingham studies revisited. In J. E. Dimsdale & A. Baum, *Quality of life in behavioral medicine research* (pp. 121–143). New York: Lawrence Erlbaum.

Elias, M. F., & Robbins, M. A. (1987). Use of cinearteriography in behavioral studies of patients with chest pain in the absence of clinically significant coronary artery disease. In J. W. Elias & P. H. Marshall (Eds.), *Cardiovascular disease and hypertension* (pp. 67–106). New York: Hemisphere.

Elias, M. F., Robbins, M. A., Blow, F. C., Rice, A. P., & Edgecomb, J. L. (1982). Symptom reporting, anxiety, and depression in arteriographically classified middle-aged chest pain patients. *Experimental Aging Research, 8,* 45–51

Elias, M. F., Robbins, M. A., Schultz, N. R., Jr., & Pierce, T. W. (1990). Is blood pressure and important variable in research on aging and neuropsychological test performance? *Journals of Gerontology: Psychological Sciences*, *45*, 138–135.

Elias, M. F., Wolf, P. A., D'Agostino, R. B., Cobb, J., & White, L. R. (1993). Untreated blood pressure level is inversely related to cognitive functioning: The Framingham Study. *American Journal of Epidemiology*, *138*, 353–364.

Gensini, G. G. (1975). *Coronary arteriography*. New York: Future.

Grimley-Evans, J. (1988). Ageing and disease. In D. Evered & J. Whelan (Eds.), *Research and the ageing population* (pp. 38–57). Chichester, England: John Wiley.

Hayward, M. E., Crimmins, E. M., & Friedman, S. (1994). *Dementia-free life expectancy among the chronically impaired American elderly*. Paper presented at the annual meetings of the Population Association of America, Miami, FL.

Farmer, M. E., White, L. R., Kittner, S. J., Kaplan, E., Mars, E., Wolz, M., McManara, P., Wolf, P. A., & Feinleib, M. (1987). Neuropsychological test performance in Framingham: A descriptive study. *Psychometric Reports*, *60*, 1023–1040.

Lezak, M. D. (l983). *Neuropsychological assessment* (pp. 266–270). New York: Oxford Press.

Maier, S. F. (1989). Learned helplessness. Event covariation and cognitive changes. In S. B. Klein & R. R. Mower (Eds.), *Contemporary learning theories* (pp. 73–110). Hillsdale, NJ: Erlbaum.

Siegler, I. C., & Costa, P. T., Jr. (1985). Health behavioral relationships. In J. E. Birren & K. W. Schaie (Eds.), *Handbook of the psychology of aging*, 2nd Ed., (pp. 144–166). New York: Van Nostrand Reinhold.

Strickland, B. R. (1988). Menopause. In E. A. Blechman & K. D. Brownell (Eds.), *Handbook of behavioral medicine in women* (pp. 41–47). New York: Pergamon.

Wisoki, P. A., & Keuthen, N. K. (1988). Later life. In E. A. Blechman & K. D. Brownell (Eds.), *Handbook of behavioral medicine in women* (pp. 48–58). New York: Pergamon.

Wolinsky, F. D., Coe, R. M., Miller, D. K., & Prendergast, J. M. (1984). Measurement of the global and functional dimensions of health status in the elderly. *Journal of Gerontology*, *39*, 88–92.

CHAPTER 2

Psychological Issues Related to Competence

Timothy A. Salthouse

The title of this chapter implies a conjunction of the field of psychology and the concept of competence; therefore, it is appropriate to begin with a brief discussion of these two terms. We will start with psychology by considering what it is that psychologists do. It is probably fair to say that much of the activity of psychologists is concerned with the measurement and modification of behavior. Job descriptions for psychologists seldom contain only a phrase such as "measure and modify behavior"; nonetheless, those are key aspects of the profession because a large proportion of psychologists devote a substantial amount of their professional time to activities of assessment and intervention. The target behavior can range from cognitive to emotional in nature, and can be embedded in situations ranging from academic to interpersonal. Psychologists do more than just measure and modify behavior, but at least when interpreted broadly, these appear to be two of the primary responsibilities of many psychologists.

Now what is meant by the term "competence"? This term is not as easy to describe because while psychology is a well-established discipline, the concept of competence has numerous meanings and connotations.

One reasonable place to start is with definitions of ''competence'' obtained from dictionaries. For example, the *American Heritage Dictionary of the English Language* (1992) lists the following meanings for competence: ''properly or sufficiently qualified; adequate for the purpose; and capable.'' *Webster's Seventh New Collegiate Dictionary* (1972) defines ''competence'' as ''having requisite ability or qualities.'' It is apparent from these definitions that competence often refers to minimum levels of proficiency, as opposed to high levels of excellence. Indeed, it would be considered very faint praise to characterize an artist or a professional as merely competent, rather than with a more laudatory adjective.

A somewhat different usage of the term ''competence'' has been employed in certain professional literatures. For example, in some discussions in the literature concerned with aging, competence is used as though it referred *only* to an individual's capability of living independently in the period of later life. A recent example of this usage is apparent in the following quotation from Willis (1991): ''Competence represents the ability to carry out, when necessary, a broad array of activities considered essential for independent living, even though in daily life the adult may not perform those activities or only perform a subset of those activities'' (p. 81).

Although this statement is useful for emphasizing the distinction between potential and actual performance that is inherent in the concept of competence, it may be an overly narrow and limited interpretation of what is generally meant by the term ''competence.'' It is clearly desirable to refine the meaning of terms when they are used in scientific or technical discourse, but confusion can result if the word already has a broader meaning in general society.

NEW DEFINITION OF COMPETENCE

An alternative definition of ''competence'' can therefore be proposed that may be more consistent with the common meaning of the term and yet incorporate several important aspects. According to this definition, competence is a judgment about an individual's capability in a particular activity based on an assessment, which can be formal or informal and objective or subjective, of two or more aspects presumed relevant to the successful performance of that activity.

Let us now unpack this definition by considering its key characteristics. First, competence is specific to a particular activity and is not universal or general. It is therefore a property or quality of functioning in certain contexts or situations and is not a global characteristic of an individual.

The limited scope of competence is important because very few people are totally incompetent in the sense that they lack a minimum level of adequacy in all possible dimensions or domains of activity. Although someone could be devoid of competence within a single domain, it is unlikely that he or she is not competent in at least some other domains. It thus seems essential in discussions of competence to be explicit about the activity or domain to which one is referring.

Second, competence is usually multidimensional in that it is based on several aspects or dimensions rather than a single critical dimension. Proficiency in a single aspect or dimension is probably more appropriately characterized as a skill, or possibly an ability, because the term ''competence'' typically refers to activities requiring several different components or dimensions.

Third, competence implies some type of assessment or evaluation. Informal characterizations of competence are frequently based on personal opinions, but to be scientifically acceptable, the assessment should be objective and yield measures with high reliability and validity. Only if the assessments meet conventional standards of evaluation would the judgments based on them be truly meaningful and appropriate for use in scientific discourse.

Finally, competence involves a judgment. Some criterion or threshold is imposed on the measurement scale to classify the individual's level of functioning. The resulting classification may be a dichotomy, such as competent or incompetent, or it may reflect a continuum corresponding to degrees of competence. In either case, however, some type of mapping is required to convert the values of the relevant measurements to a decision regarding competence.

An advantage of the proposed definition is that it reflects the fact that the concept of competence can be, and is, applied in many different situations. For example, lawyers and physicians are accused of being incompetent when they are charged with negligence or malpractice. Furthermore, political partisans frequently claim that politicians of the opposite party are incompetent even when no one would deny that the politicians are capable of independent living.

The breadth of the competence concept can also be illustrated in a variety of personal situations. For example, senior faculty members are sometimes asked to make judgments of competence in the context of membership on university tenure and promotion committees. In that role the decision is whether a junior faculty member has met the criteria for competence as a faculty member at a major research institution. The individual under consideration therefore has to be evaluated in terms of dimensions of teaching, quality and quantity of research, and service. Considerable subjectivity is involved in evaluating the individual on these dimensions, and in deciding how to weight and combine the dimensions to arrive at an overall recommendation. The assessment and decision-making processes in this situation are thus unlikely to meet scientific standards of measurement even though those involved in the process almost certainly attempt to be as thorough and conscientious as possible.

Another situation is more closely related to the current focus on issues of aging and competence, and concerns a decision whether an elderly parent whose spouse has recently died should be moved to a residential care facility. The factors entering into this decision are likely to be perceptions of the parent's capability for self-care, and especially meal preparation, housekeeping, and shopping. Again, the evaluation of these dimensions is probably highly subjective, as is the process of combining the impressions into a decision—thus the assessment and decision procedures are inadequate from a scientific perspective.

These are obviously different types of situations, and the target individuals varied dramatically in their overall levels of functioning. However, a similar issue of competence assessment can be required in both cases. Specifically, a decision has to be reached with respect to whether the individual was capable of functioning at an acceptable level in the relevant situation. The point of these examples, then, is that even though scientific standards of evaluation are not always employed, judgments of competence are frequently made in a wide range of situations.

MEASUREMENT AND MODIFICATION
OF COMPETENCE

Now that some background has been provided concerning the role of psychologists and the meaning of the term "competence," it is appropriate to return to the title of this chapter, namely, "Psychological Issues Related to Competence.'' A useful way of discussing this linkage is by describing how the measurement and modification tools of a psychologist may be applied to the concept of competence. As noted previously, competence is best understood with respect to functioning within a particular activity or domain, and thus the term is meaningful only when referring to a particular context. The specific domain of competence to be considered in the initial example is that of an automobile mechanic because the word ''incompetent'' seems to be frequently mentioned in references to car mechanics. Certain adjectives have become closely linked with particular professions and occupations in our society, such as rich and doctor, greedy and lawyer, ambitious and politician, and the words ''incompetent'' and ''auto mechanic'' are probably also strongly associated for many people who have had to deal with auto repairs.

The first step is to define the domain of interest and to identify the relevant activity for which competence is to be assessed. We have already specified auto mechanic competence as the target domain, and because the primary role of an automobile mechanic is the repair of cars, the relevant activity in this example will be effectiveness in car repair.

Before any evaluation can be carried out, it is important to identify essential components of the target activity. Although a formal job analysis has not been conducted, the following aspects seem necessary in the repair of automobiles: diagnosis of the problem, in the sense of determining what is wrong; intervention to repair the problem, which frequently involves replacing a defective component; and evaluation of the effectiveness of the intervention, or determining if the problem has been solved.

These dimensions may not encompass all of the requirements of the job of an auto mechanic. To the extent that they do not, they may not be sufficient to provide a comprehensive evaluation of the functioning or competence of an auto mechanic. Nevertheless, they are still useful to illustrate the importance of analyzing an activity in terms of its components to facilitate assessment.

Several possible methods could be employed to assess proficiency of the relevant dimensions. Because a trade-off often exists between the efficiency of paper-and-pencil tests and the validity of direct behavioral observations, a reasonable compromise may involve some type of work simulation in which representative aspects of the job are assessed in a controlled and standardized setting.

Regardless of the assessment method used, it is important to document that the measurement is scientifically acceptable concerning properties of reliability and validity. As is well known, reliability refers to the consistency and stability of measurement across time, and across different evaluators. It is the minimum requirement for adequate measurement because the assessment is of dubious scientific or practical value if it is not reliable. Validity refers to whether the measures actually reflect what is intended, which in this case is the individual's proficiency as an automobile mechanic. Evaluations of validity frequently consist of examining relations with other criteria measures, which in the case of an auto mechanic might consist of supervisor ratings, the frequency of customer complaints, or some other indications of the quality of the repairs.

Assuming that suitable measurement instruments have been identified and appropriately administered, it should be possible to combine the relevant information to reach a decision about the individual's competence as a mechanic. The question of interest to many psychologists then becomes, What should an employer do if the mechanic's performance level is judged to be incompetent? (Different alternatives are available from the perspective of the customer because he or she could simply avoid that mechanic in the future, or could engage a greedy lawyer to sue the mechanic for incompetence.)

One option for the employer is to remove the individual from the relevant situation, which in this case may consist of firing the employee. Because there may be legal challenges regarding the appropriateness of the evaluation criteria and the assessment procedures, it is important for legal as well as scientific reasons to follow accepted guidelines in the assessment and decision-making process.

However, options other than dismissal could also be considered in this situation. Specifically, because lack of competence implies a mismatch of demands and skills, either the demands could be lowered or the level of skills could be raised.

Reduction of the demands requires some type of alteration of the environment. In the case of the auto mechanic, the demands could be decreased by assigning the employee to simpler jobs, or by switching his or her responsibilities to less demanding activities such as tire repair, or washing and waxing. Alternatively, certain types of instructional aids or reminders could be introduced in the worksite to provide guidance in the diagnosis and evaluation of problems, or in the procedures to be used in the replacement of parts.

Improving the skill level of the individual usually involves some type of intervention or behavioral modification, which depending on the field of psychology may be classified as therapy, training, or education. A wide variety of modification techniques could be employed, but in all cases the goal is to increase relevant skills of the individual so that he or she will be able to cope with the demands of the target activity.

Competence for Independent Living

With this example of a psychological approach to assessment and intervention involving competence as background, we can turn to a consideration of how similar procedures may be employed when competence for independent living is the target activity. That is, in this section the focus is on the concept of competence as the term is used by care providers and professionals concerned with providing services to older adults.

MEASUREMENT

First, in a manner analogous to the identification of critical elements in a job analysis, the requirements for independent living need to be determined. One area in which the requirements for independent living have been discussed is legal writings concerned with issues of guardianship. Legal criteria for independent living often refer to the ability of the individual to make rational decisions concerning oneself and one's property. However, this guideline is rather abstract because it is seldom accompanied by any details on how rational decision making can be assessed. Moreover, the legal approach to competence assessment is typically limited to a single aspect of functioning, namely, decision making, and thus would probably not be useful for evaluating other factors that contribute to an individual's ability to live alone without assistance.

Fortunately, several prerequisites or criteria for independent living have been widely discussed and accepted in the fields of gerontology and geriatrics. One set of criteria is known as the Activities of Daily Living (ADL), because they are intended to represent "common activities whose performance is required for self-maintenance and independent community residence" (Fillenbaum, 1987). Activities within the ADL categories are primarily concerned with self-care, and include tasks such as feeding, bathing, toileting, and basic mobility.

More complex activities associated with independent living are included within a second set of criteria known as the Instrumental Activities of

Daily Living (IADL). The seven primary IADL domains are: managing medications, shopping for necessities, managing one's finances, using transportation, using the telephone, maintaining one's household, and meal preparation and nutrition (Lawton & Brody, 1969).

Functioning in each of these domains is frequently assessed on a 3-point scale with categories corresponding to "can do without help," "can do with help," or "cannot do." As one may expect, the percentage of individuals who have difficulty with various activities of daily living has been found to be greater with increased age. One illustration of this relationship is portrayed in Figure 2.1, which contains percentages of adults in three age groups with no difficulties, difficulties in either ADL or IADL domains, or difficulties in both domains.

The primary limitation of the ADL and IADL scales is that the ratings are subjective, and hence may be biased. Bias is particularly likely when the ratings are provided by the target individual, as opposed to spouses or other care providers, because people frequently overestimate their own capabilities. Primarily for this reason, there has been growing interest in the identification and development of more objective methods for the assessment of competence for independent living.

One method of assessment involves the use of scales that were originally developed to provide gross information about the individual's level of cognitive functioning. These brief tests typically involve questions concerning orientation in time and space, ability to attend and concentrate, short-term memory, visual-spatial function, and comprehension and production of language. The scores are often combined to yield a global index of overall mental status that has been found useful in the diagnosis of dementia and other disorders affecting mental functioning. Two of the most frequently used instruments are the Mini-Mental Status Exam (MMSE) (M. F. Folstein, Folstein, & McHugh, 1975; Tombaugh & McIntyre, 1992), and the Dementia Rating Scale (DRS) (Mattis, 1973), although several other similar instruments are available. The reliability of global measures from these types of scales is generally in the moderate to high range.

The primary limitation of mental functioning scales is that they yield a single index designed to reflect overall mental status rather than measures of the individual's ability to live independently. Of course, this is not a defect of the instruments per se, but it is a weakness when they are used to assess competence for independent living.

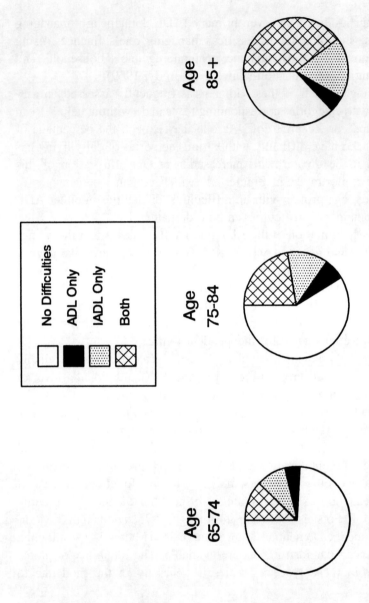

FIGURE 2.1 Proportion of adults at different ages experiencing difficulties with Activities of Daily Living. Data from Table C2-12, F. L. Schick & R. Schick, *Statistical handbook on aging Americans: 1994 edition.* Phoenix, AZ: Oryz Press. Copyright 1994 by Oryz Press. Reprinted with permission.

A second approach to the assessment of competence for independent living has relied on paper-and-pencil procedures, with written materials and written responses. One test of this type is the ETS Basic Skills Test (Educational Testing Service, 1977). This test was designed to assess real-life competencies of high-school seniors, but it has been administered to several samples of older adults by Willis and colleagues (e.g., Willis & Schaie, 1986; Willis, Jay, Diehl, & Marsiske, 1992).

The items in the test have been grouped into eight content domains concerned with: understanding labels on household articles, reading a street map, understanding charts and schedules, understanding paragraphs, filling out forms, reading newspaper and phone directory ads, understanding technical documents, and comprehending newspaper text. Reliability of the total score is high, as Willis and Schaie (1986) have reported that the split-half reliability is .94, and Willis et al. (1992) have reported a test-retest stability coefficient of .82.

A similar paper-and-pencil test is the Everyday Problems Test (EPT), which was recently described by Marsiske and Willis (1995). There are 84 items on this test, with 12 for each of 7 scales concerned with different domains of daily living. The domains are: food preparation, medication use, telephone use, shopping and consumerism, financial management, housekeeping, and transportation.

Reliability of the EPT is in the moderate to high range, particularly for the total score. To illustrate, Marsiske and Willis (1995) have reported that internal consistency reliabilities of the scales ranged from .62 to .74, with 1-year test-retest stabilities ranging from .74 to .82. Corresponding values for the total score were .94 for internal consistency and .91 for stability.

Although paper-and-pencil tests are efficient and the resulting measures frequently have high reliability, there are important limitations of relying on paper-and-pencil procedures for assessing competence for independent living. Of course, one obvious limitation is that the tests can only be administered in the standard format if the respondent can read and write. Adaptations could be made to the testing procedure by allowing spoken questions and answers, but it would then have to be determined whether the norms and measurement properties obtained under standard testing conditions were applicable for scores obtained in these special conditions.

Another potential weakness of paper-and-pencil testing procedures is that even though the content of the items may appear relevant to activities of daily living, the mode of response is different from that of real-life activities. This is a concern because the responses an individual provides in a written test may have little correspondence to actual behavior of the individual in a real situation.

It is primarily in response to this criticism of paper-and-pencil testing that a third approach to the assessment of competency for independent living has been based on behavioral observations of a subset of tasks postulated to be representative of real-life activities. The assumption has been that observation of an individual's performance in simulated activities, such as counting change, telling time, and using a phone book, is more informative about his or her actual capabilities in everyday situations than subjective ratings, global assessments of mental status, or performance in paper-and-pencil tests.

One test based on behavioral observation is the Direct Assessment of Functional Status (DAFS) (Loewenstein et al., 1989). This test was originally designed for use with patient populations such as those with Alzheimer's Disease, but it is relevant in the present context because it explicitly incorporates functional assessment based on behavioral observations. Items on the test assess time orientation, communication, finances, shopping, eating, and dressing. Each of the subscales on the test has been reported to have good reliability, with test-retest correlations ranging from .55 to .82.

Another test based on behavioral observations is the recently developed Observational Tasks of Daily Living (OTDL) (Diehl, Willis, & Schaie, 1995). This test consists of 31 tasks designed to be performed in the individual's own home. All items require the examinee to read material and then perform appropriate actions with actual materials. Domains represented in the OTDL consist of food preparation, medication intake, and telephone use. Only preliminary information is available about the OTDL, but the average item-total correlations for the 3 subscales have been reported to range from .63 to .84 (Diehl et al., 1995).

The preceding review indicates that a variety of different assessment procedures are available for evaluating competence for independent living. Each type of procedure has advantages and disadvantages, but most of the instruments have respectable reliability. An important unresolved question, however, concerns the validity of these instruments for the purpose of evaluating competence for independent living. Unfortunately, as noted by Willis (1996), a critical problem in this area is the lack of an agreed-upon criterion for validating potential measures of competence for independent living. Professional opinions are sometimes used for this purpose, but they are not ideal because the opinions are also often of unknown validity. A similar objection applies to the method of assessing validity by relying on correlations with scores on other instruments (i.e., construct validity), because the validity of scores on those other instruments for assessing competence for independent living is still an open question.

The ultimate criterion outcome for competence for independent living may be death, because failure to survive can be interpreted as the complete inability to live independently. However, there are a great many causes of death, and not all of them can be attributed to failures on the part of the individual. Furthermore, death is a very extreme outcome, and it may be more informative, and is certainly more humane, to rely on physical or emotional health status as an indication of the individual's ability to care for himself or herself. Another criterion for independent living may be changes in the individual's level of cognitive functioning if one assumes that at least some cognitive declines are consequences of deficiencies in one's nutritional, physical, or emotional lifestyle. Unfortunately, none of these measures is completely satisfactory at the current time. It is thus essential that the search continue for a meaningful criterion that can be used in validating assessments of competence for independent living.

MODIFICATION

Let us now turn from the issue of measurement to that of modification or intervention. The question of primary interest in this context is, How can we modify an individual's level of competency for independent living? That is, if an individual is judged to be incapable of living independently, what are the alternatives to placing him or her in an institution, or some other type of residential care facility? As with other behavioral interventions, the focus can be on reducing the demands placed on the individual from the environment, or in increasing relevant capabilities of the individual. Each of these will be considered in turn.

There are many environmental interventions that may increase an individual's capability for independent living. For example, physical modifications of the environment could be implemented to make it easier to bathe (e.g., by providing grab bars in the bath), to cook (e.g., by increasing reliance on labor-saving devices such as a microwave oven), and to shop (e.g., by using a grocery delivery service). Modifications in the social environment could also occur in the form of home visits by medical care professionals, a meals-on-wheels program, or providing accessible transportation for shopping.

Interventions at the level of the individual could have either a narrow or a broad focus. Narrow interventions typically concentrate on one or two dimensions or symptoms, such as food preparation and medication adherence. The primary rationale for a specific emphasis is the assumption that it may be easier to modify a limited aspect of an individual's behavior than to alter all relevant aspects simultaneously.

However, a convincing argument for a focus on broader abilities in intervention has been provided by Willis (1987):

> The number of specific tasks of daily living on which training might be useful is very large. Training on cognitive abilities that underlie performance on these tasks may therefore be more efficient and result in broader transfer of training than training that is restricted to a specific practical task. (pp. 179–180)

Additional research is needed to determine which type of intervention— physical or social at the level of the environment, or narrow or broad at the level of the individual—is most effective in improving competence for independent living. Because it is likely that the effectiveness of the intervention will vary according to the number or type of limitations of the individual, it is important that research investigating the efficacy of different interventions be sensitive to individual differences in the nature of competency limitations.

DECLINES IN COMPETENCE

The possibility that competence for independent living can decline from earlier levels leads to questions of why there is a loss of competence and what can be done to prevent similar losses in the future. Note that these questions did not arise in the example of an auto mechanic because it was assumed that the competence of the target individual in that situation had never been at a higher level. However, if competence does in fact decline over time, and if the limitations in functioning are not simply made more salient by the loss of some type of support system, then issues of causation and prevention become relevant. Prevention can be considered a proactive form of intervention, but like other types of intervention, the reasons for the low levels of functioning need to be identified for it to be effective.

Longitudinal research, with detailed information about each individual's level of functioning before and after any detectable loss of competence for independent living, is needed to reach strong conclusions about the causes of decline in this type of competence. However, results from concurrent correlational studies can be informative in identifying correlates of measures of competence for independent living. Of particular interest is the relative importance of factors related to physical health compared to those related to cognitive functioning.

Preliminary evidence relevant to this issue has been provided by Willis and her colleagues, who have found that fluid cognitive abilities are among the most important correlates of measures of competence for independent living. For example, Willis and Schaie (1986) found moderate to high correlations between measures of cognitive ability and performance on the ETS Basic Skills Test, and Willis et al. (1992) found moderate correlations between cognitive ability measures and ETS Basic Skills performance in both current and subsequent (i.e., 7 years later) assessments. Moreover, the relations are not restricted to paper-and-pencil tests because moderate correlations, in the range from .3 to .7, have been reported by Diehl et al. (1994) between cognitive ability measures and performance on the OTDL.

Much of the literature concerned with correlates of measures of competence has been reviewed by Willis (1991), who suggested that cognitive factors are more important than factors related to physical health as determinants of competence for independent living. This claim should be considered tentative until additional evidence is available, with a wider range of health measures and a broader variety of competence measures. It is nevertheless intriguing because of the implication that basic research concerned with age-related declines in cognitive functioning may play an important role in understanding, and possibly preventing, some of the losses in competence for independent living that sometimes occur in later adulthood.

SUMMARY

This chapter has emphasized the following major points.

1.   It started by claiming that the measurement and modification of behavior are primary activities of psychologists, and a definition of "com-

petence'' was provided that was designed to reflect both everyday and scientific meanings of the concept.

2. Measurement and modification activities concerned with one type of competence, that of an automobile mechanic, were then discussed to illustrate how measurement and modification could be applied to the concept of competence.

3. Competence for independent living was considered next, beginning with a review of various types of assessment procedures that have been proposed. It was suggested that no strong conclusion can yet be reached about the best methods of assessment because of the current lack of meaningful criteria against which measures of competence for independent living can be validated.

4. Different types of intervention approaches were discussed next, including those based on environmental modifications and either narrow or broad training of the individual.

5. Finally, the topic of prevention, and the importance of understanding the causes of any losses of functioning relevant to independent living that might occur, was discussed.

It should be obvious from the preceding material that psychologists can make important contributions to the measurement and modification of all types of competence, including that concerned with independent living. It remains to be seen whether these potential contributions can be realized.

REFERENCES

American heritage dictionary of the English language. (1992). Boston, MA: Houghton-Mifflin.

Diehl, M., Willis, S. L., & Schaie, K. W. (1995). Practical problem solving in older adults: Observational assessment and cognitive correlates. *Psychology and Aging, 10,* 478–491.

Educational Testing Service. (1977). *Basic skills assessment test: Reading.* Princeton, NJ: Educational Testing Service.

Fillenbaum, G. G. (1987). Activities of daily living. In G. L. Maddox (Ed.), *Encyclopedia of aging* (pp. 3–4). New York: Springer.

Folstein, M. F., Folstein, S. E., & McHugh, P. R. (1975). Mini-Mental State: A practical method for grading the cognitive state of patients for the clinician. *Journal of Psychiatric Research, 12,* 189–198.

Lawton, M. P., & Brody, E. M. (1969). Assessment of older people: Self-maintaining and instrumental activities of daily living. *Gerontologist, 9,* 179–185.

Loewenstein, D. A., Amigo, E., Duara, R., Guterman, A., Hurwitz, D., Berkowitz, N., Wilkie, F., Weinberg, G., Black, B., Gittelman, B., & Eisdorfer, C. (1989). A new scale for the assessment of functional status in Alzheimer's Disease and related disorders. *Journal of Gerontology: Psychological Sciences, 44,* 114–121.

Marsiske, M., & Willis, S. L. (1995). Dimensionality of everyday problem solving in older adults. *Psychology and Aging, 10,* 269–283.

Mattis, S. (1973). *Dementia Rating Scale professional manual.* Odessa, FL: Psychological Assessment Resources, Inc.

Schick, F. L., & Schick, R. (1994). *Statistical handbook on aging Americans: 1994 edition.* Phoenix, AZ: Oryx Press.

Tombaugh, T. N., & McIntyre, N. J. (1992). The Mini-Mental State Examination: A comprehensive review. *Journal of the American Geriatrics Society, 40,* 922–935.

Webster's seventh new collegiate dictionary. (1972). Springfield, MA: G. C. Merriam.

Willis, S. L. (1987). Cognitive training and everyday competence. In K. W. Schaie (Ed.), *Annual Review of Gerontology and Geriatrics, Vol. 7* (pp. 159–188). New York: Springer.

Willis, S. L. (1991). Cognition and everyday competence. In K. W. Schaie & M. P. Lawton (Eds.), *Annual Review of Gerontology and Geriatrics, Vol. 11* (pp. 80–109). New York: Springer.

Willis, S. L. (1996). Assessing everyday competence in the cognitively challenged elderly. In M. A. Smyer, M. B. Kapp, & K. W. Schaie (Eds.), *Impact of the law on older adults' decision making capacity* (pp. 87–127). New York: Springer.

Willis, S. L., Jay, G. M., Diehl, M., & Marsiske, M. (1992). Longitudinal change and prediction of everyday task competence in the elderly. *Research on Aging, 14,* 68–91.

Willis, S. L., & Schaie, K. W. (1986). Practical intelligence in later adulthood. In R. J. Sternberg & R. K. Wagner (Eds.), *Origins of competence in the everyday world* (pp. 236–268). New York: Cambridge University Press.

Commentary: Psychological Issues Related to Competence: Cognitive Aging and Instrumental Activities of Daily Living

Denise C. Park

althouse has provided us with a definition of "competence" and has addressed important aspects of measurement of competent behaviors. One important point that Salthouse made was that competence is not a general quality, but rather it is specific to an activity or a set of related activities. This chapter will be based on Salthouse's view that competence is domain-specific and will focus on specific domains of behavior of importance to older adults—namely, the instrumental activities of daily living (IADLs), described initially by Lawton and Brody (1969). As Salthouse has noted, the ability to perform these seven activities is considered to be of great importance by gerontologists and geriatricians for maintaining independence in late adulthood. These seven activities include the ability to use the telephone, to prepare meals, to maintain a household, to shop, to use public or private transportation, to manage finances, and to take medication correctly.

In this chapter, these seven behaviors will be discussed within a cognitive aging framework. I will address not only the cognitive aspects of each IADL, but also the sensory and physical requirements associated with each behavior. I will also examine how these requirements may change when an appropriate environmental support is available to relieve some of the cognitive, sensory, or physical demands of the task. The component behaviors that comprise the different IADLs span a range of complexity, and the physical, cognitive, and sensory demands vary substantially across these tasks. Thus these behaviors are ideal for such an analysis because there are such large age differences in the task demands, as well as how easily such support can be made available. In general, it is easier to provide physical environmental supports than cognitive and sensory supports, as will be seen in the subsequent discussion.

In reflecting on the way I manage the IADLs in my own life, I realized how many things one can do to minimize the cognitive, physical, and sensory demands of the IADLs. I recognized that I actually allocate relatively little time to such IADLs as preparing meals, shopping, maintaining my household, and managing my finances. This is partially because I use environmental supports to manage the demands of these activities. The supports can be obvious, like eating microwave dinners, which minimize the cognitive, sensory, and physical demands of cooking, to more sophisticated strategies like having as many bills as possible automatically deducted from my checking account to limit the effort involved in paying bills. I also use mail-order shopping and a maid service to preserve my time and limited cognitive resources for other tasks.

To understand the role of cognition in IADLs, I will initially provide a brief overview of several important constructs from the cognitive aging literature that have implications for the function or competence of older adults in their everyday environment. Following this, I will present a systematic analysis of the sensory/perceptual, cognitive, and physical requirements instrumental to daily living, examining the requirements of each test under ''free-ranging'' conditions and under those where some type of support is introduced that would typically be available to many Americans. This type of analysis will help focus on particularly problematic IADLs where appropriate environmental supports are not easily available. We will isolate domains within the IADLs where it is not so easy to find support or to maintain competence in the face of declining cognitive, physical, and sensory resources and where more research and innovative solutions are needed to permit older adults to maintain independence. Because decline does not occur in parallel in the cognitive, physical, and sensory domains with age, it will be particularly useful to isolate what components of an IADL need support, so that it will be clearer as to what IADLs will be problematic for individuals with varying problems. I will close the chapter with a brief discussion of technology and aging, because technology has reached a stage of development where it can play an increasingly larger role in helping to manage IADLs for frail older people.

IMPORTANT CONCEPTS
FROM THE COGNITIVE AGING LITERATURE

There are three major constructs from the cognitive aging literature that can be applied in a straightforward manner to analysis of the instrumental activities of daily living.

Processing Resources

There is a large body of evidence that has accrued from the cognitive aging literature that suggests that older adults have limited processing resources (Craik & Byrd, 1982; Craik & Jennings, 1992, Salthouse, 1992). Cognitive aging researchers view measures of working memory and speed of processing as estimates of cognitive resource. There are a growing number of studies that demonstrate that nearly all age-related variance in most cognitive activities is mediated by deficiencies in working memory and speed of processing.

Working memory is measured by determining how many pieces of information an individual can simultaneously hold in memory and manipulate at the same time (Baddeley, 1986). Perhaps the simplest example of a task that some consider a working memory task is the Backward Digit Span from the Wechsler Adult Intelligence Scale (WAIS) (Wechsler, 1981), where the subject must maintain the forward digits in memory and then transpose them mentally into the reverse order. Similarly, the Digit-Symbol task from the WAIS is also viewed as a simple but accurate estimate of the speed of processing (Salthouse, 1992). This is a task where the subject must match a set of 10 abstract symbols to random digits. The subject's task is to copy the relevant symbols under each digit in a long series as rapidly as possible.

There is little question that as we age, these cognitive resources decline, and it has been an exciting and recent development to learn that they are the basis for most age-related decline observed on a broad range of cognitive tasks, including memory, reasoning, verbal fluency, and spatial cognition (Lindenberger, Mayr, & Kliegl, 1993; Park et al., in press; Salthouse, 1993). To relate the resource construct to the performance of

IADLs, we need to recognize that older adults do have less processing resources available to perform tasks like managing finances or developing a medication plan that may be fairly intensive in their cognitive requirements. Similarly, older adults will be disadvantaged on tasks that demand a higher speed of processing, such as some decisions that might occur when driving a car. Thus, when an IADL is described in this chapter as being relatively high in its cognitive demands, it will mean that it is a task that is relatively intensive in its processing resource requirements as defined by speed and working memory.

Deliberate Recollection and Familiarity

The next construct relates to the very important role that familiarity plays in offsetting cognitive resource demands on IADLs. Psychologists who have studied expert behaviors like chess playing, typing, and bridge playing have noted that older adults are capable of performing at very high levels of competence on these tasks (Charness, 1987, 1989; Salthouse, 1984; Salthouse, Babcock, Mitchell, Skovronek, & Palmon, 1990) despite their demanding cognitive requirements. Moreover, there is little evidence that older adults' competence in the workplace declines—the correlations between age and work performance are near zero in nearly all work settings (Rhodes, 1983; Park, 1994a). Although a detailed discussion of age and its relationship to expertise and work performance is beyond the scope of this chapter, the important point to extract from these findings is that there are innumerable examples of older adults performing at a very high level of competence on cognitively demanding tasks.

Typically, if you examine the conditions under which this competence occurs, the task is a highly practiced, highly familiar one. Thus the second construct that is important to emphasize is the increasingly important role that familiarity is beginning to play in our thinking about cognitive aging. We are beginning to recognize that tasks that are highly complex but familiar do not place the same demands on our cognitive resources as equally complex but unfamiliar tasks do. An obvious example is finding one's way around a city. If you have, for example, lived in Philadelphia your whole life, driving to the art museum from the airport would not represent a cognitively challenging task. If, however, you had never been to Philadelphia and were renting a car and were going to follow a map to the art museum, this would be a very intensive cognitive task, indeed. One would expect an older adult to be at no disadvantage to a younger one in the familiar situation, but the younger adult would likely have an advantage in the unfamiliar situation, because it would be a highly resource demanding task that had almost no element of familiarity to it.

Basic memory research conducted by Jacoby and associates on familiarity has important implications for age-related changes in cognitive function and the performance of IADLs. Jacoby, Yonelinas, and Jennings (in press) postulated that in a verbal learning task, memory for items is due to two processes: an automatically activated familiarity component and a more effortful, deliberate recollection component. Jacoby provided subjects with lists of words to study and then presented the subjects with word fragments—incomplete words with missing letters, much like a partially solved puzzle in the Wheel of Fortune game. The subject's task was to determine a word that correctly completed the fragment. Jacoby (1992) told subjects in an inclusion condition that they should try to complete the fragments *only* with words that they had just studied. In what he calls the ''exclusion condition,'' he asked subjects to complete the fragments only with words that they had *never* studied. Despite these instructions, subjects frequently completed the fragments with previously studied words in the exclusion condition. By performing some simple mathematical operations on the 2 values obtained from the inclusion and exclusion condition, Jacoby was able to compute values for what he calls ''deliberate recollection,'' a resource-intensive process, and the familiarity component of memory, an automatic, low-resource process that some even describe as unconscious.

What is interesting and of relevance here is that the elderly showed marked impairment in the deliberate recollection condition relative to young adults but no impairment in a number of different experiments in the familiarity component of recall (Jacoby, 1992; Jacoby, Jennings, & Hay, 1996). Jacoby et. al (1996) speculate from this that because the deliberate recollection component is impaired with age, older people are much more likely to respond in many situations on the basis of familiarity or habit via the procedural or unconscious components of memory. This interpretation is a profoundly important empirical point for understanding the everyday behavior of older adults. It supports an observation made by many gerontologists—that older adults are not impaired when they are responding to situations where they can use highly familiar, automatized aspects of behavior. Impairment or deficits only become noticeable when the individual must engage in deliberate recollection or processing-intensive tasks.

This type of finding can explain why adults may become much more dysfunctional when they move to a nursing home or some other unfamiliar environment. Suddenly, they are in a situation where they must engage in an enormous amount of deliberate recollection to function in their daily environment. Even the simple act of getting a drink of water, finding the television, or finding their bedroom can require a substantial amount of deliberate recollection and processing because the familiar, automatized responses they have to their environment no longer work. Thus it appears to be critically important to distinguish between IADLs that occur in a familiar context and that rely on the familiarity component of the cognitive system in the older adult, and those IADLs that might occur in a more novel situation where greater reliance on deliberate recollection is required—a process that becomes impaired with age. It is entirely possible that an individual who is highly competent in a familiar setting might not be functional in a new setting, particularly an institutional one, or in an entirely new community, where much new processing would be required to meet the criteria for competence in the IADLs.

Environmental Support

The third concept from the cognitive aging literature that is particularly germane to the issue of competence and IADLs is that of environmental support. Craik and Byrd (1982) have suggested that deficits in deliberate recollection can be repaired or mitigated in older adults by structuring information in such a manner that less self-initiated processing is required, that is, less processing resources are required. Thus, to the extent that we can understand the cognitive resource requirements of IADLs like medication-taking and financial management, we may be in a position to relieve some of the cognitive demands through restructuring the information or organizing the task in a way that will reduce demands associated with it.

The next section consists of a review of the seven IADLs within the cognitive aging framework previously described, as well as a discussion of how particular environmental supports can make a difference in reducing the demands of these tasks. There have been numerous demonstrations of introducing successful cognitive supports for old and young adults in the form of structured cues (Park, Cherry, Smith, & Lafranza, 1990; Park, Smith, Morrell, Puglisi, & Dudley, 1990) as well as in the form of visual elaboration (Park, Puglisi, & Smith, 1986; Park, Puglisi, & Sovacool,

1984), but little is known about how to support cognition in real-world environments. The environmental support principle expressed by Craik (Craik & Jennings, 1992), however, should be entirely applicable to every-day life.

AN ANALYSIS OF THE SENSORY, COGNITIVE, AND PHYSICAL DEMANDS OF THE INSTRUMENTAL ACTIVITIES OF DAILY LIVING

The demands of each IADL will be discussed within the context of three domains: sensory/perceptual requirements, cognitive activities, and physical strength. A summary of these requirements appears in Table 2.1. One problem with this approach is that, at present, there are no independent measures available of the actual demands of these domains. Thus the present discussion should be viewed as preliminary, with the recognition that more attention needs to be directed toward defining an objective continuum of task demands. For the purposes of this commentary, a taxonomy of the physical, cognitive, and sensory task demands of the IADLs is presented. Low task demands would be those that could be performed by an individual who was moderately impaired on the behavioral dimension in question (e.g., physical, cognitive, or sensory). Moderate task demands would be those an individual who was mildly impaired could still perform, and high task demands would be a task that required low normal function on the dimension in question to perform correctly.

Using the Telephone

Using the telephone, if one has an old-fashioned rotary phone, would be a task that is relatively high in its sensory/perceptual requirements, medium in its cognitive demands, and low in its strength requirements. The introduction of a preprogrammed push-button phone as an environmental support, however, reduces the cognitive and sensory/perceptual demands of the task. Even a severely impaired individual could learn to press the relevant buttons if the buttons had large labels that were already programmed to reach family, friends, or emergency and health services. Thus it would appear that use of the telephone should not be an IADL of great concern with respect to maintenance of competence. It would be easy to

TABLE 2.1 The Physical, Sensory, and Cognitive Demands of the Instrumental Activities of Daily Living With and Without Cognitive Supports

IADL	Requirements without Support			Requirements with Support		
	Sensory	Cognition	Physical	Sensory	Cognition	Physical
Using Telephone	High	Medium	Low	Medium	Low	Low
Meal Preparation	Medium	High	Medium	Medium	Low	Low
Maintaining Household	Medium	Low	High	Low	Low	Low
Shopping	Medium	Medium	High	Low	Medium	Low
Using Transportation* (private auto)	High	Medium	Low	—	—	—
Managing Medications	Medium	Medium	Low	Low	Medium	Low
Financial Management**	Medium	High	Low	—	—	—

Notes:
*Training intervention rather than environmental support is recommended.
**Specific supports not recommended pending further research.

introduce the relatively inexpensive environmental support of a prepro-grammed telephone into an older adult's environment and no longer be concerned that an inability to use a phone directory or to understand complex, long-distance dialing requirements could impact on an individu-al's ability to live independently.

Meal Preparation

If one prepares homemade traditional meals, the demands of this task can be relatively high at the cognitive level given the multitasking nature and the complex instructions that often accompany meal preparation. An individual must frequently keep track of multiple events while foods cook, and at the same time, continue food preparation on another item for the meal. Time estimation is also required if the individual is to successfully finish all of the meal components to be served at the same time. Of course, individuals who prepared complex dishes that they had been making all their lives might not find this type of preparation cognitively challenging, because of the high familiarity component. The reliance on old schemes and existing knowledge despite declining cognition may result in a high level of competence within this domain. Difficulties would likely manifest themselves if an individual attempted to prepare an unfamiliar meal that was from a complex recipe.

The sensory/perceptual as well as strength requirements of preparing a meal would appear to be medium. However, if one considers the use of fully prepared microwave meals as an environmental support, these could reduce cognitive and strength demands to the low level. Sensory/perceptual requirements would be maintained at the medium level, because some sensory ability would be required to read the instructions on the packages as well as to read and to manipulate the microwave dials. Please note that there is the assumption that the individual already understands and is able to use the microwave oven. The cognitive demands of learning how to use a new microwave, as we all know, can be high. Overall, with the use of appropriate environmental supports in the form of prepared meals, meal preparation need not be a task that has a particularly high cognitive, sensory, or physical demand.

Maintaining a Household

To maintain a household, one has to be able to keep a house clean, do laundry, take out garbage, and call repairmen to fix things. The cognitive demands of these tasks are relatively low, the perceptual demands are medium, and the strength requirements are high for at least some of these tasks. Because of the low cognitive and moderate sensory demands, there will not be much discussion of this IADL. The services of a relative or of a weekly maid service of some sort, if affordable, could reduce the physical demands to the medium range, bringing household maintenance within the reach of many elderly adults. The primary limiting factor to maintain this IADL with support is cost, and for this reason, support could be well out of reach for many older adults.

Shopping

Shopping, mainly for groceries and other essentials, has higher cognitive demands than housekeeping, and is also physically demanding, when one considers that the individual must get the bags of groceries into the house. With respect to cognitive demands, the individual must make numerous choice decisions from an array of items, keeping track of what one has at home as well as in the grocery cart. Moreover, for many people, particularly the elderly, the choices must be related to the total amount of money available to be spent on groceries. The task also has high sensory/perceptual demands because food must be selected from very complex arrays, which anyone who has ever tried to find a specific brand of cereal can testify. Writing things down and making lists is an obvious environmental support to relieve some of the demands of this task (Park, Smith, & Cavanaugh, 1990). Nevertheless, a frail elderly adult may need an environmental support to mitigate the task requirements on all three dimensions, perhaps in the form of a helper who reviews needs with the older adults, and then purchases and delivers groceries.

Another mechanism for relieving the physical burdens of shopping would be to develop user-friendly, icon-based software for home computers, where the individual could log on and point to groceries and then send an order over a computer-fax or a network. This would reduce the physical requirements to a very low level, but the perceptual/sensory component would continue to be high as would the cognitive component, because the individual would still have to make complex decisions about costs and choices of items. Overall, shopping appears to be a problematic behavior for frail older people that can only be supported by either a relatively expensive computer system (which could mitigate the physical demands assuming grocery delivery was available) or by help from another individual—friend, family, or paid assistant. At the same time, an individual who couldn't shop could still manage to maintain daily competence because assistance might be only needed for an hour a week, and a person doing his or her own shopping could also help another individual shop at the same time. Thus cost to the helper is relatively low. The availability of a good social support network likely would ensure help with shopping.

The remaining three IADLs, using transportation, managing finances, and managing medications are critical aspects of everyday competence, but these cannot be managed or supports provided as easily as for the first four IADLs. These are complex behaviors with high cognitive demands that need focused attention from researchers who view them as seriously problematic IADLs for the declining elderly. These IADLs are beginning to be studied with respect to aging, with an increasing emphasis on the cognitive nature of these tasks.

Transportation

The use of public transportation is generally both physically and cognitively demanding, and also has substantial perceptual requirements. It is really not a very feasible alternative for most elderly citizens in this country, even in the rare cases where it is available. I am always struck by how physically difficult and tiring it is to use subways and buses in major cities. The cognitive demands of using an unfamiliar transportation system are also high, although they would be low for an individual who was using a system that he or she had relied on for many years, as he or she would be relying on existing knowledge structures.

The use of private transportation, that is, driving an automobile, is the most feasible and available transportation alternative for most elderly adults in the United States. Driving behavior has been analyzed exhaustively due to the fact that poor driving has consequences for survival of the individual and others in his or her driving trajectory. Driving, relative to the other IADLs, has high perceptual demands, moderate cognitive demands, but low physical demands, so, in fact, it may be less problematic over the long term for elderly adults whose most pressing problem is physical frailty rather than cognitive frailty. Moreover, driving a car for most older adults will have a very high familiarity component, both in terms of the procedural aspects of driving as well as the routes on which they select to drive, rendering the cognitive demands for driving in familiar situations to an acceptable level (Park, 1994b). The driver experience and route familiarity could reduce the cognitive demands of driving for older adults, except in unexpected and ambiguous situations that may occur at any time. It is, of course, essential that older adults have sufficient perceptual resources to determine accurately what is happening and cognitive resources to respond appropriately to these demanding situations. Older adults do have a very high accident rate per mile driven, although they do not drive many miles. Thus their absolute rate of accidents is relatively low.

There is some very exciting work being conducted on aging and driving by Karlene Ball and Cynthia Owsley at the University of Alabama at Birmingham to understand causes and to prevent crashes in older adults. They have determined that useful field of view is an excellent retrospective and prospective predictor of automobile crashes in adults of all ages. Useful field of view, loosely speaking, is one's ability to detect and track static and moving targets in the periphery of vision and can be quantified in a relatively precise manner. Useful field of view is highly correlated with age, such that age predicts poor function. The exciting finding beyond this is that Ball and Owsley have developed a successful training program to improve the useful field of view. They are currently evaluating whether individuals with improved useful field of view are at lower risk of crashes. If this is the case, we may have a critically important intervention that will assist older adults in maintaining competence in they key area of maintaining mobility through driving. In this case, task demands are not reduced through supports, but rather because the individual has been trained to adapt better to the demands of the task.

Managing Medications

Maintaining competence in taking medications in late adulthood is a behavior that is receiving increased attention. Park and Kidder (1996) and Park and Mayhorn (1996) present detailed frameworks in which they discuss the cognitive components of taking medication. The cognitive demands of this task are relatively high, particularly if a medication regimen involves multiple medications. Perceptual requirements are medium and physical strength requirements are low. We have found evidence that older adults have more trouble comprehending medication information and that they have difficulties in remembering medication information (Morrell, Park, & Poon, 1989, 1990). We believe that the working memory component of integrating instructions across multiple medications and developing a plan for medication-taking may pose particular problems for older adults (Park, 1993). We have studied actual adherence to a multiple medication regimen by older adults (Park, Morrell, Frieske, & Kincaid, 1992) using sophisticated electronic monitors and have reported that the oldest-old were significantly more nonadherent than young-old. In a later study, we found them to be more nonadherent than any other age group, followed by middle-aged adults (Park, Morrell, Lautenschlager, & Firth, 1993). When we introduced medication organizers of the type sold in drugstores over the counter as well as organizational charts, we were able to reduce substantially the comprehension and working memory components of medication adherence.

We found these supports significantly improved adherence behaviors in the oldest adults (Park et al., 1992). We are presently working on the role of these devices as with medication bottles that beep at the appropriate time to remind older adults to take medications, thus supporting the prospective aspects of mediation adherence. These aids reduce the cognitive demands, but also relieve the perceptual demands that are associated with adherence. The perceptual demands are reduced because the individuals no longer have to make visual discriminations about what pill they are to take when it is placed in an organizer or when a beeping bottle cap signifies which vial they are to open. These are inexpensive aids that can play an important role in maintaining competence.

Managing Finances

This is a critically important area that has received considerably less attention than driving and medication adherence. Yet it is often poor financial management and decisions that will lead children or other relatives to hold competence hearings or make the decision that an older adult is not competent and may need a guardian. It would appear that this is a very difficult area in which to assess competence. All of us have made financial decisions that in retrospect do not seem competent. And we all know examples of many cognitively intact individuals who have great difficulty managing finances in what would generally be considered a competent fashion. How sensitive financial management is to declining cognitive resources would, of course, partially depend on the complexity of the finances one has available to manage. This is an IADL in need of considerable research and one where perhaps the most important aspect of success involves judgment and decision making. Financial management is such a complex topic that it is beyond the scope of this commentary, but I would suggest that this is a very rich area for future research.

FUTURE DIRECTIONS

One area that has great promise for helping older adults to maintain IADLs is computer technology. There is convincing evidence that older adults can acquire computer skills but that they require somewhat more time to learn (Czaja & Sharit, 1993; P. K. Elias, Elias, Robbins, & Gage, 1987). Roger Morrell, my research associate at the University of Michigan, Kathryn Echt, a student, and I are designing training programs to teach older adults successfully how to acquire rudimentary computer skills. We are also working on a communication system called "Eldercom" that will give older adults access to many information and communication services in an extremely easy-to-use manner. We are implementing the system in a senior center but have very high hopes for its use to maintain social competence in frail elderly, as well as eventually to help physically frail adults that are nondemented to continue to maintain independence. Computers can perform banking functions. They could also be used to order groceries and to shop, and could provide a reminder system for taking medications. In addition, as addicts to the Internet well know, they also can be a major form of entertainment, communication, and social support.

It would appear that in the immediate future some aspects of daily living will be qualitatively improved, particularly for frail elderly, by computer technology. The role of this technology will accelerate rapidly as computer literate adults grow old. Breakthroughs in driving research also indicate that we may be able to provide some training support to maintain this behavior in the immediate future. Finally, there is a burgeoning literature on medication adherence that should result in a much better understanding of this complex behavior. Financial management, however, remains the IADL that is most unexplored from a health perspective and an area where research is critically needed.

In summary, determining how to maintain competent functioning until death is an implicit agenda item for all researchers attempting to understand any aspect of the aging process. More explicit attention to some of the issues raised here on the part of researchers would result in substantial gains for the psychology of aging as well as for our aged citizens.

ACKNOWLEDGMENTS

This research was supported by three grants to the author from the National Institute on aging. Project ROl-AG06265 was awarded for the study of the role of environmental support on the study of memory in the aged; Project ROl-AG09868 focuses on medication adherence in older adults, and Project P50-AG11715 supports research on applications of basic cognitive aging research. The author gratefully acknowledges this support.

REFERENCES

Baddeley, A. (1986). *Working memory.* Oxford: Clarendon Press.

Charness, N. (1987). Component processes in bridge bidding and novel problem-solving tasks. *Canadian Journal of Psychology, 41,* 223–243.

Charness, N. (1989). Age and expertise: Responding to Talland's challenge. In L. W. Poon, D. C. Rubin, & B. A. Wilson (Eds.), *Everyday cognition in adulthood and late life* (pp. 437–456). New York: Cambridge University Press.

Craik, F. I. M., & Byrd, M. (1982). Aging and cognitive deficits: The role of attentional resources. In F. I. M. Craik & S. Trehub (Eds.), *Aging and cognitive processes* (pp. 191–211). New York: Plenum Press.

Craik, F. I. M., & Jennings, J. M. (1992). Human Memory. In F. I. M. Craik & T. A. Salthouse (Eds.), *The handbook of aging and cognition* (pp. 51–110). Hillsdale, NJ: Erlbaum.

Czaja, S. J., & Sharit, J. (1993). Age differences in the performance of computer-based work. *Psychology and Aging, 8,* 59–67.

Elias, P. K., Elias, M. F., Robbins, M. A., & Gage, P. (1987). Acquisition of word-processing skills by younger, middle-age, and older adults. *Psychology and Aging, 2,* 340–348.

Jacoby, L. L. (1992). *Strategic versus automatic influences of memory: Attention, awareness, and control.* Paper presented at the 33rd annual meeting of the Psychonomic Society, St. Louis, MO.

Jacoby, L. L., Jennings, J. M., & Hay, J. F. (1996). Dissociating automatic and consciously-controlled processes: Implications for diagnosis and rehabilitation of memory deficits. In D. J. Hermann, M. K. Johnson, C. L. McEvoy, C. Hertzog, & P. Hertel (Eds.), *Basic and applied memory research: Theory in context* (pp. 161–193). Hillsdale, NJ: Erlbaum.

Jacoby, L. L., Yonelinas, A. P., & Jennings, J. M. (in press). The relation between conscious and unconscious (automatic) influences: A declaration of independence. In J. Cohen & J. W. Schooler (Eds.), *Scientific approaches to the questions of consciousness.* Hillsdale, NJ: Erlbaum.

Lawton, M. P., & Brody, E. M. (1969). Assessment of older people: Self-maintaining and instrumental activities of daily living. *The Gerontologist*, *9*, 179–186.

Lindenberger, U., Mayr, U., & Kliegl, R. (1993). Speed and intelligence in old age. *Psychology and Aging*, *8*, 207–220.

Morrell, R. W., Park, D. C., & Poon, L. W. (1989). Effects of the quality of instructions on memory and comprehension of prescription information in young and old adults. *The Gerontologist*, *29*, 345–353.

Morrell, R. W., Park, D. C., & Poon, L. W. (1990). Effects of labeling techniques on memory and comprehension of prescription information in young and old adults. *Journals of Gerontology: Psychological Sciences*, *45*, 166–172.

Park, D. C. (1994a). Aging, cognition, and work. *Human Performance*, *7*, 181–205.

Park, D. C. (1994b). *Aging, cognition, and driving*. Arlington, VA: Scientex Corporation.

Park, D. C. (1993). Applied cognitive aging research. In F. I. M. Craik & T. A. Salthouse (Eds.), *Handbook of cognition and aging*, 449–493. Hillsdale, NJ: Erlbaum.

Park, D. C., Cherry, K. E., Smith, A. D., & Lafronza, V. N. (1990). Effects of distinctive context on memory for objects and their locations in young and elderly adults. *Psychology and Aging*, *5*, 250–255.

Park, D. C., & Kidder, D. P. (1996). Prospective memory and medication adherence. In M. Brandimonte, G. Einstein, & M. McDaniel (Eds.), *Prospective memory: Theory and applications* (pp. 369–390). Hillsdale, NJ: Erlbaum.

Park, D. C., & Mayhorn, C. B. (1996). Remembering to take medications: The importance of nonmemory variables. In D. Herrmann, M. Johnson, C. McEvoy, C. Hertzog, & P. Hertel (Eds.), *Research on practical aspects of memory, Vol. 2* (pp. 95–110). Hillsdale, NJ: Erlbaum.

Park, D. C., Morrell, R. W., Frieske, D., & Kincaid, D. (1992). Medication adherence behaviors in older adults: Effects of external cognitive supports. *Psychology and Aging*, *7*, 252–256.

Park, D. C., Morrell, R. W., Lautenschlager, G., & Firth, M. (1993, March). *Electronic monitoring of medication adherence hypertensives: Nonadherence is predicted by advanced age*. Paper presented at the meeting of the Society of Behavioral Medicine, San Francisco, CA.

Park, D. C., Puglisi, J. T., & Sovacool, M. (1984). Picture memory in older adults: Effects of contextual detail at encoding and retrieval. *Journal of Gerontology*, *39*, 213–215.

Park, D. C., Puglisi, J. T., & Smith, A. D. (1986). Memory for pictures: Does an age-related decline exist? *Psychology and Aging*, *1*, 11–17.

Park, D. C., Smith, A. D., & Cavanaugh, J. C. (1990). The metamemories of memory researchers. *Memory and Cognition*, *18*, 321–327.

Park, D. C., Smith, A. D., Lautenschlager, G., Earles, J., Frieske, D., Zwahr, M., & Gaines, C. (1996). Mediators of long-term memory performance across the life-span. *Psychology and Aging, 11*, 621–637.

Park, D. C., Smith, A. D., Morrell, R. W., Puglisi, J. T., & Dudley, W. N. (1990). Effects of contextual integration on recall of pictures by older adults. *Journals of Gerontology, 45*, 52–57.

Rhodes, S. R. (1983). Age-related differences in work attitudes and behavior: A review and conceptual analysis. *Psychological Bulletin, 93*, 328–367.

Salthouse, T. A. (1984). Effects of age and skill in typing. *Journal of Experimental Psychology: General, 113*, 345–371.

Salthouse, T. A. (1992). *Mechanisms of age-cognition relations in adulthood.* Hillsdale, NJ: Erlbaum.

Salthouse, T. A. (1993). Speed medication of adult age differences in cognition. *Developmental Psychology, 29*, 722–738.

Salthouse, T. A., Babcock, R. L., Mitchell, D. R., Skovronek, E., & Palmon, R. (1990). Age and experience effects in spatial visualization. *Developmental Psychology, 26*, 128–136.

Weschler, D. (1981). *Manual for the Weschler Adult Intelligence Scale-Revised.* New York: Psychological Corporation.

Commentary: The Social Context
of Competence

Neal Krause

INTRODUCTION

Timothy Salthouse's chapter is first-rate. The emphasis on beginning the study of competence with a clear and unambiguous definition is a vitally important step in conducting meaningful research. However, instead of focusing on this issue, the purpose of this commentary is to elaborate and extend some of the comments that are made toward the end of his insightful chapter. Dr. Salthouse persuasively argues that a key agenda for the future involves assessing the determinants and correlates of competence. As he points out, this kind of knowledge is crucial because in cases where competence declines, it is important to know what is responsible for the loss. This information is essential for the design of effective interventions, especially those that focus on primary prevention.

Dr. Salthouse provides a useful point of departure for the study of the correlates of one crucial dimension of competence—competence for independent living. In particular, he argues that we need to know more about the relative impact of physical health problems and cognitive functioning on the ability of older adults to live independently in the community. The goal of the present chapter is to develop this idea more fully. This will be accomplished by constructing a preliminary model of competence for independent living that includes several potentially useful, social, psychological constructs. In the process, key measurement issues will be discussed that are necessary for evaluating this more complex formulation.

DEVELOPING A MODEL OF COMPETENCE

It may be useful to depict graphically the theoretical specifications provided by Dr. Salthouse because this exercise helps to clarify how the proposed elaborations can contribute to the knowledge base. The simple model he proposes is presented in Figure 2.2. Although this model is consistent with much of the current thinking on this issue, it doesn't go far enough. Stated simply, it is unlikely that there is a one-to-one correspondence between constructs such as physical illness and competence for independent living. Instead, other factors probably intervene. Two constructs that take a decided sociological slant may provide some useful insights. The first involves the expectations and behaviors of significant others, while the second is concerned with the expectations and beliefs of a focal elder.

Initial Elaborations and Extensions

Embedding these two social-psychological domains in the model proposed by Salthouse results in the specification shown in Figure 2.3. It is assumed

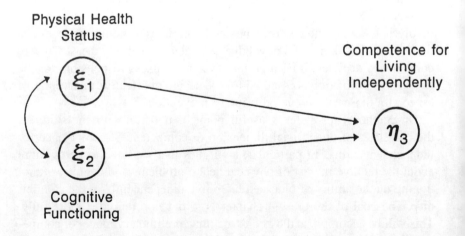

FIGURE 2.2   A simple model of health and competence.

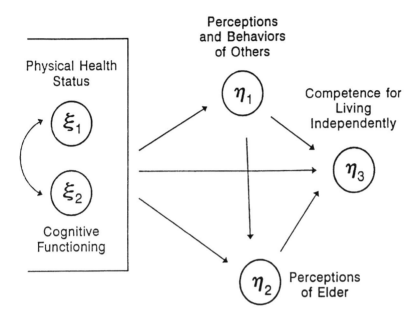

FIGURE 2.3   Incorporating the perceptions of self and others.

in this model that competence for independent living is assessed with self-reported ADL and IADL measures. The selection of the social-psychological constructs depicted in this conceptual framework is governed by two long-standing sociological concepts: the definition of the situation (Thomas, 1951) and the looking glass self (Cooley, 1902).

The two exogenous constructs in Figure 2.3 (i.e., physical health problems and cognitive functioning) are relatively objective phenomena that may be assessed in a reliable way with standard measures. However, as noted previously, competence may not be solely a function of these objective health states. Instead, these behaviors may be determined, at least in part, by the elder's subjective definitions of their objective health status. Often, there is not a perfect match between the two, and there can even be significant slippage between objective health states and subjective interpretations of them (Krause & Jay, 1994). Based on this fundamental realization, Thomas (1951) proposed over half a century ago that subjective definitions should form the focal point of social research because it is these perceptions, rather than relatively objective states, that subsequently determine behavior.

A key issue at this juncture is how subjective definitions of the situation (in this case one's health status) arise. One answer is provided by Cooley (1902). He argued that people make assessments of their worth and capabilities based upon the feedback that is provided by significant others. This is what he meant by the looking glass self. Three concepts may help to adapt the insights provided by Thomas (1951) and Cooley to the study of competence for independent living: the expectations held by significant others, the values they place on the specific ADL or IADL activity in question, and the risks and benefits they believe are associated with engaging in this form of behavior. The basic premise is that these constructs act in concert to determine the feedback provided to older adults, thereby ultimately shaping the elder's subjective definition of their own physical capabilities.

Exploring the Expectations of Others

When a specific physical illness or problem in cognitive functioning arises, significant others are likely to develop clusters of expectations about the behavioral capabilities of a focal elder. For example, if an older adult has arthritis in her shoulder, a significant other is likely to react to this illness by speculating on whether the focal elder is capable of performing standard ADL and IADL functions such as lifting grocery bags.

A key issue for future research is to understand more fully how these expectations emerge. There are a number of possibilities. One is that others compare an elder's current physical state to the state of that elder at an earlier point in time. Another is that the elder's condition is compared to that of other known individuals of a similar age, such as neighbors or other relatives. A third possibility is that the elder is compared to some generalized other, or to some global perception of the performance of most older adults in this condition.

When viewed in isolation, expectations are not likely to explain all of the variance in the feedback provided by others. Social network members not only assess what an elder is capable of doing, they also place a judgment or value on the activity in question. For example, a standard IADL item involves the ability to prepare one's own meals. If significant others believe that an elder is capable of cooking a meal, they will be more inclined to encourage this activity if they also believe that it is important for the elder to prepare his or her own food. In contrast, behaviors not valued highly by others are less likely to be encouraged even if others believe the elder is capable of performing them. For example, an adult daughter may be less inclined to encourage her father to cook for himself if he is living with his wife, who has prepared all his meals for the past 40 years. Moreover, she may not encourage him to do so even though she believes that he can cook for himself.

One final factor that may shape the expectations of significant others comes from the health belief model (Kirscht, 1974), which is closely related to values and may in fact play a role in determining the specific values that are endorsed. According to this view, significant others will encourage an older adult to engage in a specific ADL or IADL activity if they believe the activity will benefit the focal elder and that there are no major risks involved in its performance. For example, a wife may encourage her frail husband to get out of bed each day and walk because she believes that he will benefit from this low level of exercise. However, she may discourage this type of activity if she believes that he would fall, or put undue strain on himself if he were to attempt to walk. Consistent with the perspective developed in this chapter, behaviors that are discouraged are less likely to be performed. This may in turn lead to the atrophy of key skills associated with competence for independent living.

The discussion that has been provided up to this point focuses largely on how the beliefs and expectations of significant others are formed. However, it is important to sketch out how these perceptions are explicitly manifest in interactions between a focal elder and an important social network member. A basic premise in the expanded model shown in Figure 2.3 is that the beliefs held by significant others lead to behaviors that either inhibit or promote those activities that serve as markers of competence for independent living. The work of Baltes and Wahl (1992) on the dependency-support script provides a useful example of how others may inhibit ADL and IADL activities. In particular, the authors maintain that others may reinforce dependent behaviors and discourage or ignore behaviors that promote independence. For example, a social network member may discourage a frail elder from getting out of bed to get himself a glass of water. Instead, the caretaker may tell him to remain where he is and that she will get the water for him. In contrast, the work of Rook, Thuras, and Lewis (1990) provides a useful example of how significant others can promote positive health behaviors, including exercise. The authors argue that group membership and social ties are important because others may pressure a focal person to engage in positive health behaviors. This pressure can take the form of encouragement and positive reinforcement, or it can involve the application of negative sanctions.

To provide a better grasp of the points that have been made so far, it may be useful to expand the segment of Figure 2.3 dealing with the expectations and behaviors of others. This elaborated component of the basic conceptual model is presented in Figure 2.4.

A key issue at this juncture is how to begin to study the behaviors that either inhibit or promote engagement in ADL and IADL activities. There are at least three alternatives, each with its own advantages and limitations. First, consistent with the emphasis on the definition of the situation, researchers should consider focusing on the elder's report of the behavior of the significant other. However, this approach is limited because the influence of others may be expressed in a subtle manner, making it difficult to pinpoint specific instances of where efforts to influence behavior are exercised. For example, disapproval of certain behaviors may be conveyed by facial expressions or by changes in voice intonations. A second way to approach the problem is to rely on behavioral observation. However, this may work best in institutional settings and may, therefore, be less appropriate for the study of behaviors associated with independent living. A third option is to record segments of interaction between an elder and key significant others. These data may subsequently be analyzed by communication specialists who can highlight and enumerate those subtle ways in which things like voice intonations and other fine nuances of the communication process convey feedback to an elder about his or her ability to perform certain activities of daily living (see, e.g., Giles, Coupland, & Wiemann, 1990).

Exploring the Expectations of a Focal Elder

The commentary up to this point has focused largely on the expectations held by significant others and the way these beliefs are communicated to a focal older adult. However, these constructs are of interest only to the extent that they actually shape the subsequent views and behavior of the elderly person. It is for this reason that the beliefs and expectations of the focal elder are regarded as the core element in Figure 2.3. As in the previous section, it is assumed that the beliefs of focal elders are evaluated by assessing their expectations, the value they place on the behavior in question, and the risks and advantages they see in engaging in a particular ADL or IADL activity. Once these data have been gathered, the main

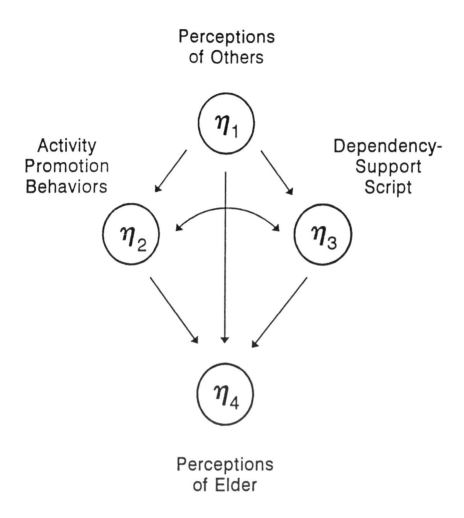

FIGURE 2.4   Elaborating on the expectations held by others.

task is to determine the extent to which the beliefs and behaviors of others help to shape the beliefs and behaviors of the focal elders.

Assessing the interface between these two bodies of data provides a number of challenges. For example, any number of significant others may influence the behavior of an older adult. Evaluating the beliefs and expectations of an entire social network may be prohibitively expensive and time consuming. There are no easy answers to this problem, but one solution may involve focusing solely on the one individual who exerts the greatest influence on the daily activities of a given older adult. Although a number of different approaches may be used to identify this significant other, simply asking the focal elder to identify this person may suffice.

These design issues notwithstanding, assessing the interface between the expectations and beliefs of a significant other and those of a focal elder presents some interesting opportunities for research. An underlying assumption in the model shown in Figure 2.3 is that the beliefs and behaviors of the elder are shaped by the beliefs and behaviors of the influential other. However, this conveys a rather passive image of older adults and creates the impression that their behavior is simply molded by the will of others. This is an unrealistic view. Others may attempt to exert an influence, but the elder may either not respond or may even openly resist. Consequently, an important area for research in the future is the identification of those factors that promote either compliance or resistance to the will of the other. A number of factors may come into play here, including the past history of the relationship between these individuals, the current balance of power between them, and the resources that each brings to their daily social encounters. For example, if the elder is economically dependent upon an adult child, it may be important to determine whether this increases the leverage the child may exert on the elder's behavior.

Additional Areas of Interest

As these examples reveal, the ability and willingness to perform basic ADL and IADL tasks is undoubtedly the result of the complex interplay between many factors. Consequently, a number of constructs can, and should, be added to the relatively simple model depicted in Figure 2.3. Two examples are provided next to illustrate this point.

The model in Figure 2.3 focuses solely on informal social relationships. Even so, it is likely that relationships that arise within the context of formal organizations play an important role as well. In particular, an elder's subjective definition of his or her physical condition is likely to be affected by the feedback from medical personnel. For example, a physician may overtly discourage older adults from engaging in certain kinds of behavior (e.g., lifting heavy objects) because of their current objective health status. But one need only consult the vast literature on noncompliance with a doctor's orders to realize that the behavior of older adults is not shaped solely by formal medical advice (see, e.g., Glasgow, 1991). Instead, the behavior of the elder is more likely to be shaped by the beliefs of significant others, as well as those of medical personnel. The interface between formal and informal sources of influence provides yet another interesting opportunity to expand our understanding of social factors that shape competence for independent living.

The second construct that deserves careful consideration has to do with the scope of the model presented in Figure 2.3. As it stands, this conceptual scheme focuses solely on one informal dyadic relationship. This overlooks the fact that these social ties are embedded in a much broader social context. Although there are many ways to evaluate the social context, examining variations by race and ethnicity may be especially useful. There are a number of ways that race may affect the relationships among these constructs, including definitions of those activities that are deemed essential for independent living. As a result, some of these measures may not be appropriate for the study of people in these groups. For example, the ability to balance a checkbook is frequently included in IADL scales. However, many underprivileged minority group members do not maintain checking accounts. Failure to include culturally relevant indicators of competence may therefore hinder our ability to understand the aging process in all of the cultures that comprise our increasingly diverse society. For example, ignoring cultural variations in scale development may lead to biased estimates of racial and ethnic difference in the competence for independent living.

CONCLUSIONS

The main point in developing a model such as the one shown in Figure 2.3 is to emphasize the notion that neither illness nor the competencies that it affects arise in a social vacuum. Instead, competencies for living independently emerge within the context of ongoing social relationships. Stated somewhat polemically, a number of the behaviors that are considered to be markers of independent living are the products of a jointly negotiated social process where the beliefs and behaviors of others interact with the beliefs and behaviors of elders. The very social nature of this process is reflected in the items that are often used to assess ADL and IADL activities. These indicators are often scored by asking older adults whether they can perform a given activity without the help of others, with the assistance of others, or whether they are unable to do the activity at all. Whether help is requested and whether it is forthcoming may depend, at least in part, upon the social psychological constructs discussed in this chapter.

If the social-psychological perspective that has been discussed here is valid, then some of the principles that have been proposed may have important implications for intervention design. For example, if the goal of a program is to encourage older adults to engage in activities that are essential for independent living, it may not be sufficient to focus solely on the target elders. Instead, practitioners may elect to cast a broader net that explicitly recognizes the potentially important role played by significant others in this process. Involving significant others is not a novel idea in and of itself. However, practitioners may not place a sufficient emphasis on making others aware of the beliefs and expectations they hold, how these perceptions are communicated, and how they ultimately may influence the behavior of the elder in question.

Clearly, this is not the time to provide a well-articulated intervention design. Instead, the goal has been to provide a glimpse of some possibilities that those working in this area may not have considered previously.

REFERENCES

Baltes, M. M., & Wahl, H. W. (1992). The dependency-support script in institutions: Generalization to community settings. *Psychology and Aging, 7,* 409–418.

Cooley, C. H. (1902). *Human nature and the social order.* New York: Scribner's.

Giles, H., Coupland, N., & Wiemann, J. M. (1990). *Communication, health and the elderly.* Manchester, UK: Manchester University Press.

Glasgow, R. E. (1991). Compliance to diabetes regimens: Conceptualization. complexity, and determinants. In J. A. Cramer & B. Spilker (Eds.), *Patient compliance in medical practice and clinical trials* (pp. 209–224). New York: Raven Press.

Kirscht, J. (1974). The health belief model and behavior related to chronic illness. In M. Becker (Ed.), *The health belief model and personal health behavior* (pp. 128–143). Thorofare, NJ: Slack Press.

Krause, N., & Jay, G. (1994). What do global self-rated health items measure? *Medical Care, 32,* 930–942.

Rook, K. S., Thuras, P. D., & Lewis, M. A. (1990). Social control, health risk taking, and psychological distress among the elderly. *Psychology and Aging, 5*, 327–334.

Thomas, W. I. (1951). *Social behavior and personality: Contributions of W. I. Thomas to theory and research*. (E. H. Volkart, Ed.). New York: Social Science Research Council.

CHAPTER 3

Does Being Placed in a Nursing Home Make You Sicker and More Likely to Die?

Fredric D. Wolinsky, Timothy E. Stump, and Christopher M. Callahan

O f all Americans aged 65 or older, 1.3 million, or 4.5%, woke up in nursing homes this morning (Lazenby & Letsch, 1990). This makes nursing homes a key component in the health and health care of older adults. Indeed, in 1991 the total cost of nursing home care was $59.9 billion, or 8% of all health care expenditures (Letsch, Lazenby, Levit, & Cowan, 1992). Because the bulk (69.8%) of nursing home expenditures are financed by public programs, and given the projected increase in the number and proportion of older Americans (Rice & Feldman, 1981), the use of and expense associated with nursing homes has been an issue of considerable national concern. As a result, a substantial amount of research has been conducted on nursing home utilization. See Greene

*Supported by grant R37-AG09692 to Dr. Wolinsky and grant K08-AG00583 to Dr. Callahan from the National Institutes of Health. The opinions expressed here are those of the authors, and do not necessarily reflect those of the funding agency, academic, or governmental institutions involved.

and Ondrich (1990), Kane and Kane (1987), and Wolinsky, Callahan, Fitzgerald, and Johnson (1992) for thoughtful reviews. For the most part, that literature has been concerned with admission rates or lifetime likelihoods of nursing home placement. Among the risk factors identified with some regularity are advanced age, living alone, having difficulties with activities of daily living (ADLs), not being married or living with one's spouse, mental deterioration, being white, having few social supports, living in poverty, being admitted to a hospital, living in senior citizen retirement housing, and needing help with instrumental ADLs (IADLs) (Kane & Kane).

A more intriguing question than who is at risk for nursing home placement, however, is what happens to people after they get there. Put simply, *does being placed in a nursing home make you sicker and more likely to die?* Reports from two provocative studies (Aneshensel, Pearlin, & Schuler, 1993; Wolinsky, Callahan, Fitzgerald, & Johnson, 1992) have recently suggested that nursing home placement is associated with increased mortality risk, even after controlling for a variety of covariates, including health status. Indeed, Wolinsky, Callahan, Fitzgerald, and Johnson report that those who were placed in nursing homes were 2.74 times (adjusted odds ratio; AOR) more likely to die than those who remained in the community, and Aneshensel, Pearlin, and Schuler report that those who were placed in nursing homes were 2.10 times (AOR) more likely to die than those who remained in the community. Neither study reported on the effect of nursing home placement on subsequent morbidity.

Despite their impressive findings, neither report indicted the nursing home industry or the role that it performs as society's agent in caring for people until they die. Methodological limitations involving selection bias and statistical modeling appear to account for this. In terms of selection bias, Wolinsky, Callahan, Fitzgerald, and Johnson (1992) relied on a representative sample of noninstitutionalized older adults, and then followed them for no more than 4 years. Therefore, their sample was biased against those who survived several years after nursing home placement. Aneshensel, Pearlin, and Schuler (1993) relied on a sample of noninstitutionalized older adults with Alzheimer's Disease or related dementias who had primary caregivers and had contacted one of two Alzheimer's Disease and Related Disorders Associations. Thus their sample excluded cognitively intact older adults. Moreover, given the predictable progression from the diagnosis of Alzheimer's Disease to death (an average of 8 years) and the high probability that on the way to death, Alzheimer's patients are placed in a nursing home (Hazzard, Andres, Bierman, & Blass, 1990), the effect of nursing home placement on mortality in Aneshensel, Pearlin, and Schuler's study reflected on the stage of Alzheimer's Disease as well as on exposure to the nursing home.

In terms of statistical analysis, both studies relied on essentially static, baseline models to predict mortality. Indeed, Wolinsky, Callahan, Fitzgerald, and Johnson (1992) used an entirely static multivariable logistic regression approach that included a number of risk factors measured at baseline and an indicator for having been placed in a nursing home thereafter. And although Aneshensel, Pearlin, and Schuler (1993) used proportional hazard models with time-varying covariates, their discrete approach merely substitutes the most proximal (to death) values of the covariates rather than incorporating changes in those covariates over time. Moreover, their measures of health status included only one perceived health question and one marker for having been hospitalized in the preceding year.

Because of these methodological limitations, the critical competing explanation that both institutionalization and death were merely markers of the same underlying process of deteriorating health status could not be ruled out. Nor was it possible for these static baseline models to indicate whether nursing home placement was the sentinel event marking exposure to some causative nursing home agent(s), or merely a marker of preexistent, deteriorating health status trajectories. Therefore, in the end, Wolinsky, Callahan, Fitzgerald, and Johnson (1992) simply stated that

> [w]hether the root cause here is poor health care, poor living conditions, or some other factor(s) that result in an older adult's version of a failure to thrive (including losing the will to live), cannot be determined from these data. Nonetheless, there can be little doubt that nursing home placement is predictive of death. This is entirely consistent with the well known perceptions of older adults and their physicians, as well as a growing body of scientific literature about nursing home experiences, the quality of care provided there, and the desire to avoid nursing homes whenever possible. (p. S181)

and Aneshensel, Pearlin, and Schuler (1993) simply stated that

> [i]nstitutionalization, then, appears to hasten death. . . . Yet, we do not want to suggest increased mortality is an *inevitable* consequence of placement.

Instead, this elevation in risk may reflect more on the quality of institutional care than on the transitional event of placement per se. (p. 66)

The purpose of this chapter is to investigate whether being placed in a nursing home makes you sicker and more likely to die. To do this, we overlay older adults' health trajectories with their movements into and out of nursing homes. This resolves the selection bias and statistical modeling limitations that constrained our (Wolinsky, Callahan, Fitzgerald, & Johnson, 1992) earlier analysis of the nationally representative *Longitudinal Study on Aging (LSOA)*. Five design changes make this possible.

1. We lengthen the catchment period for nursing home placement from 1984 to 1988 to 1984 to 1990.
2. We broaden the focus from the 5,151 respondents selected for the 1986 and 1988 reinterviews to the 7,527 respondents selected for the 1988 and 1990 reinterviews. These first two alterations increase the number of nursing home placement ''events'' from 549 to 934 and reduce the selection bias against those who survive several years after nursing home placement.
3. We use *National Death Index (NDI)* matches rather than collateral reports to document decedent status. This lengthens the catchment period for mortality from 1984 to 1988 to 1984 to 1991, and increases the number of mortality ''events'' from 1,214 to 2,870.
4. We rely on dynamic models that decompose health status trajectories into the sequential pieces occurring before, during, and after nursing home placement. This allows us to directly examine the effect of passing through a nursing home independent of prior and current health status trajectories.
5. We broaden our focus to include the effect of nursing home placement on morbidity as well as mortality.

Our analysis is a bit complicated (some might say tedious) and progresses through five stages. To provide a broad overview of what we are about to do, we briefly summarize those stages here. In the first stage we estimate a baseline model of the risk of nursing home placement using both a logistic regression model similar to our earlier analysis (Wolinsky, Callahan, Fitzgerald, & Johnson, 1992), and a discrete-time hazard model in which each contiguous-person-interval is treated as an independent observation. In the second stage we estimate a baseline model of the risk of dying associated with having been placed in a nursing home after baseline. This involves estimating a logistic regression model similar to our earlier analysis, as well as a proportional hazard model to see if nursing home placement affects the timing of mortality as well as its occurrence. In the third stage of the analysis, we estimate a baseline logistic regression model of the risk of dying at the nursing home among the 934 persons who were placed there after baseline.

The next two stages of the analysis shift to dynamic models. In the fourth stage this involves estimating logistic regression models that reflect the effect of being placed in a nursing home between 1986 and 1988 on dying between 1988 and 1991. This analysis is limited to the 3,118 respondents who were successfully reinterviewed in 1986 and 1988 and who had not been in nursing homes by the time of their 1986 reinterviews. That allows us to statistically control for health status trajectories in the interval before these nursing home placements occurred (i.e., 1984–86), as well as the health status trajectories concomitant with those nursing home placements (i.e., 1986–88), when estimating the effect of those nursing home placements on subsequent death (1988–91). The final stage of analysis uses linear panel methods to estimate the effect of being placed in a nursing home between 1986 and 1988 on changes in five functional status measures between 1988 and 1990. This analysis is limited to the 2,382 respondents who were successfully reinterviewed in 1986, 1988, and 1990, and who had not been in nursing homes by the time of their 1986 reinterviews. That allows us to control statistically for health status trajectories in the interval before these nursing home placements occurred (i.e., 1984–86), as well as the health status trajectories concomitant with these nursing home placements (i.e., 1986–88), when estimating the effect of those nursing home placements on subsequent health status trajectories (i.e., 1988–90).

METHODS

Model

The behavioral model (Andersen, 1968) is the most widely used framework for studying health services utilization (see Wan, 1989), and it has been specifically applied to structure analyses of nursing home placement in general and in the *LSOA* in particular (Greene & Ondrich, 1990; Wolinsky, Callahan, Fitzgerald, & Johnson, 1992). The behavioral model has also been used to structure analyses of morbidity (Wolinsky, Stump, Callahan, & Johnson, 1994) and mortality (Wolinsky, Johnson, & Stump, 1995) in the *LSOA*. Accordingly, the behavioral model need not be discussed here in detail (for a historical review, including its application to the special case of older adults, see Wolinsky, 1990). Basically, the behavioral model views the use of health services as a function of the predisposing, enabling, and need characteristics of the individual. The predisposing component reflects the assumption that some individuals have a greater propensity for using health services. These propensities are characterized by demographics, social structure, and health beliefs. The enabling component reflects the fact that although the individual may be predisposed to use health services, he or she must nonetheless have some means for obtaining them. This involves both familial and community resources. Need, or health status, is specified as the most immediate cause of health services use. It involves both perceived and evaluated health status, with health status frequently taking the form of functional measures and disease histories. Here, we model nursing home placement after baseline, as well as its subsequent effects on morbidity and mortality, as a function of the predisposing, enabling, need, and health services utilization characteristics measured at baseline.

Data

The data are taken from the *LSOA*, which is a 6-year follow-up of 7,527 individuals aged 70 years or more in 1984 who were first interviewed as part of the *Supplement on Aging (SOA)*, which was appended to the *National Center for Health Statistics (NCHS)* 1984 *National Health Interview Survey (NHIS)*. The *SOA* involved the collection of detailed data on the health, social functioning, and living arrangements. Abstracts from the *Medicare Automated Data Retrieval System* (i.e., *MADRS*), as well as the results of matching searches of the *NDI* to document decedent status, were linked on an annual basis through 1991. Follow-up interviews (by telephone if they had one, or by mail if they did not) for the *LSOA* respondents were scheduled in 1986 (except for the 2,376 individuals who, due to budgetary constraints, were not reinterviewed then), in 1988, and in 1990. Based on previous analyses (see Fitti & Kovar, 1987; Harris, Kovar, Suzman, Kleinman, & Feldman, 1989; Johnson & Wolinsky, 1993;

Kovar, Fitti, & Chyba, 1992), we use the unweighted data, and do not adjust for design effects.

Measurement

The means, standard deviations, and coding algorithms of the predisposing, enabling, need, and health services utilization characteristics measured at baseline are shown in Table 3.1 for all 7,527 *LSOA* respondents. Because we have used these variables previously to model health services utilization in the *LSOA* (Stump, Johnson, & Wolinsky, 1995; Wolinsky, Callahan, Fitzgerald, & Johnson, 1992; Wolinsky, Culler, Callahan, & Johnson, 1994; Wolinsky & Johnson, 1991; Wolinsky, Stump, & Johnson, 1995), they shall only be briefly mentioned here. The predisposing characteristics were represented by sex, age, race, education, a set of two dummy variables reflecting living arrangements, nonkin supports, two dichotomous markers for whether the respondent was worried or felt in control of his or her health, and a marker for having a telephone. The enabling characteristics were represented by having private health insurance for *both* physician and hospital expenses, being on Medicaid, population density, residential stability, financial dependence on Social Security, and a set of three dummy variables reflecting geographic region.

There were 27 measures of the need characteristics at baseline. Three were a set of dummy variables decomposing the traditional measure of perceived health status. The next 13 were dichotomous variables indicating whether or not the respondent *had ever had* osteoporosis, a broken hip, atherosclerosis, hypertension, rheumatic fever, rheumatic heart disease, coronary heart disease, angina, myocardial infarction, any other heart attack, stroke, or a cerebrovascular accident, Alzheimer's Disease, or cancer. There were also five dichotomous variables indicating whether or not the respondent had had arthritis, diabetes, an aneurysm, a blood clot, or varicose veins *during the 12 months prior to baseline*. The body mass index (kg/m²) was included as a measure of obesity.

The five remaining measures of health were previously validated and replicated multiple-item scales of functional status (see Clark, Stump, & Wolinsky, in press; Fitzgerald, Smith, Martin, Freedman, & Wolinsky, 1993; Johnson & Wolinsky, 1993, 1994; Wolinsky & Johnson, 1991). The first is called the basic activities of daily living (ADL; alpha = .860). It consists of six items from the traditional ADL (Katz, Ford, Markowitz, Jackson, & Jaffee, 1963), including having any difficulties with such

TABLE 3.1   Means, Standard Deviations, and Coding Algorithms of Predisposing, Enabling, Need, and Health Services Utilization Characteristics Measured at Baseline for All 7,527 *LSOA* Respondents

Variables	*M*	*SD*	Coding Algorithms
Predisposing Characteristics			
Female	.620	.485	1 = yes, 0 = no
Age	76.828	5.594	Actual number of years
Black	.086	.280	1 = yes, 0 = no
Education	9.994	3.651	Actual number of years
Lives alone[a]	.365	.481	1 = yes, 0 = no
Multigenerational family[a]	.176	.381	1 = yes, 0 = no
Kin supports	1.614	.648	2-item scale; 2 = has support for both, 1 = has support for one, 0 = no support
Nonkin supports	2.379	1.363	5-item scale; 5 = support with 5 items, 4 = support with 4 items . . . , 1 = support with 1 items, 0 = no support
Health worries[b]	.453	.498	1 = yes, 0 = no
Health control[b]	.775	.417	1 = yes, 0 = no
Telephone	.970	.172	1 = yes, 0 = no
Enabling Characteristics			
Private insurance	.667	.471	1 = has private physician and hospital insurance, 0 = no
Being on Medicaid	.056	.230	1 = yes, 0 = no
Population density	2.597	2.539	10-point 1980 county adjacency code, ranging from 9 = thinly populated not adjacent to 0 = core SMSA county
Residentially stable	.842	.365	1 = same address for 5 or stable more years, 0 = no
Social Security dependence	.643	.479	1 = yes, 0 = no
Northeast region[c]	.231	.421	1 = yes, 0 = no
Northcentral region[c]	.258	.437	1 = yes, 0 = no
Western region[c]	.176	.381	1 = yes, 0 = no
Need Characteristics			
Ever had . . .			
Osteoporosis	.037	.188	1 = yes, 0 = no
Broken hip	.045	.206	1 = yes, 0 = no

(Continued)

TABLE 3.1 *(Continued)*

Variables	*M*	*SD*	Coding Algorithms
Atherosclerosis	.129	.335	1 = yes, 0 = no
Hypertension	.449	.497	1 = yes, 0 = no
Rheumatic fever	.025	.156	1 = yes, 0 = no
Rheumatic heart disease	.007	.082	1 = yes, 0 = no
Coronary heart disease	.045	.207	1 = yes, 0 = no
Angina	.069	.254	1 = yes, 0 = no
Myocardial infarction	.019	.137	1 = yes, 0 = no
Any other heart attack	.069	.254	1 = yes, 0 = no
Stroke or CVA	.074	.262	1 = yes, 0 = no
Alzheimer's Disease	.006	.074	1 = yes, 0 = no
Cancer	.122	.327	1 = yes, 0 = no
Had . . . in past year			
Arthritis	.541	.498	1 = yes, 0 = no
Diabetes	.098	.298	1 = yes, 0 = no
Aneurysm	.006	.074	1 = yes, 0 = no
Blood clot	.016	.124	1 = yes, 0 = no
Varicose veins	.099	.299	1 = yes, 0 = no
Basic ADLs	.686	.648	6-item scale; 6 = need help with 6 items, 5 = need help with 5 items . . . , 1 = need help with 1 item, 0 = no help needed
Household ADLs	.598	1.123	4-item scale; 4 = need help with 4 items, 3 = need help with 3 items . . . , 1 = need help with 1 item, 0 = no help needed
Advanced ADLs	.149	.493	3-item scale; 3 = need help with 3 items, 2 = need help with 2 items . . . , 1 = need help with 1 item, 0 = no help needed
Lower body limitations	1.849	1.926	5-item scale; 5 = limitation with 5 items, 4 = limitation with 4 items . . . , 1 = limitation with 1 item, 0 = no limitation

Upper body limitations	.422	.804	4-item scale; 4 = limitation with 4 items, 3 = limitation with 3 items . . . , 1 = limitation with 1 item, 0 = no limitation
Body Mass[d]	24.599	4.367	Ratio of weight in kilograms to height in squared meters
Good health[e]	.315	.464	1 = yes, 0 = no
Fair health[e]	.213	.409	1 = yes, 0 = no
Poor health[e]	.118	.323	1 = yes, 0 = no
Baseline Health Services Utilization			
Number of physician visits in past year	4.228	4.102	Actual number of visits, truncated at 13
Hospital contact in past year	.212	.409	1 = yes, 0 = no
Ever placed in a nursing home	.026	.160	1 = yes, 0 = no

Notes:
a. The omitted or reference category is living with another person, such as a spouse or someone else of the same generation.
b. The health opinions questions were not asked of the 747 proxy-respondents. To include these two items *and* the proxy-respondents in the analyses, they were treated as 0s. Further analysis (not shown) excluding the proxy-respondents yielded equivalent effects for the health opinions questions on all outcomes. So, too, did further analysis (also not shown) using alternative imputation procedures. Accordingly, the results reported herein are not likely artifacts of this strategy.
c. The omitted or reference category is living in the South.
d. Data on height and weight were unavailable for 136 respondents. These individuals are excluded from all subsequent analyses.
e. The omitted or reference category is excellent or very good perceived health.

personal activities as bathing, dressing, getting out of bed, toileting, and getting outside, as well as a related item on walking. The second scale is called the household ADL (alpha = .821). It consists of four items taken from the instrumental ADL (Duke University Center for the Study of Aging and Human Development, 1978), including having any difficulties with such household chores as meal preparation, shopping, and light and heavy housework. The third scale is called the advanced (or cognitive) ADL (alpha = .638). It is composed of the three items from the original ADL and IADL scales that do not load with the other items. These are the questions about having any difficulties with managing money, using the telephone, and eating. The 2 other functional health status scales were drawn from Nagi's (1976) disability items. One taps lower body limitations (alpha = .862). It includes having any difficulties in walking a quarter of a mile, walking up 10 steps without rest, standing or being on your feet for 2 hours, stooping, crouching, or kneeling, and lifting or carrying 25 pounds. The other scale taps upper body limitations (alpha = .577). It includes having any difficulties in sitting for 2 hours, reaching up over your head, reaching out as if to shake hands, and using fingers to grasp objects.

Baseline health services utilization was represented by three measures, which are markers for prior patterns of self-reported health behavior. One was a dichotomous indicator of whether or not the respondent had been hospitalized *during the 12 months prior to baseline.* Another was the number of physician visits that occurred *during the 12 months prior to baseline.* The third measure was a dichotomous indicator of whether the respondent *had ever been* placed in a nursing home prior to baseline.

Nursing home placement is a dichotomous measure, indicating whether the respondent was known to have been placed in a nursing home at any time *after* the baseline interviews in 1984 and up through the final reinterview in 1990. Placement status was based on either self-reports ($N = 109$; including reinterviews in the nursing home as well as reinterviews in the community following discharge from the nursing home) or the reports of collaterals ($N = 557$; 302 of whom resided in the same household, and 255 of whom resided elsewhere) that had originally been identified by the respondent at baseline as persons who would know where the respondent was, or what had happened to him or her. This information was supplemented by place of death reports (also obtained from the collaterals) indicating that the respondent had died in a nursing home ($N = 268$).

The two outcome measures are morbidity and mortality. Morbidity is measured by the 5 multiitem functional status scales described previously (basic, household, and advanced ADLs, and upper and lower body limitations). These 5 scales were administered at each reinterview to both respondents and proxy-respondents. Decedent status and date of death between 1984 and 1991 are based on *NDI* determinations. At baseline, all 16,148 *SOA* respondents were asked for permission to link their interview data to the *NDI* on an annual basis, and all but 210 *SOA* respondents (including 68 *LSOA* respondents) consented. Information used to make the match between the *LSOA* and the *NDI* included complete date of birth, full name, father's last name, Social Security Number (SSN), gender, race, marital status, state of residence, and country of origin (Kovar,

Fitti, & Chyba, 1992). *NDI* retrievals were attempted if (a) full name and SSN, or (b) full name and date of birth data were provided at baseline. A scoring system evaluated the quality of the retrievals by assigning predetermined weights to each of the information variables obtained at baseline. The maximum score was 37, and the minimum score was 4. Scores greater than or equal to 28 are considered "good" matches (i.e., presumed dead; $N = 2,464$), scores of 22 or 24 through 27 are considered "fair" matches (i.e., probably dead; $N = 406$), scores less than 22 or of 23 with an exact SSN match were considered "poor" matches (i.e., probably alive; $N = 1,841$), and scores of zero (i.e., no match; $N = 2,748$ [as well as the 68 respondents for whom sufficient information to attempt a match was not available]) are presumed alive. Only the 2,870 "good" and "fair" matches are used to identify decedents in the public use version of the *LSOA*. Date of death is indexed in the number of months since December 1983 for decedents. For survivors, date of death is censored at 97 (representing the end of the 8-year observation period, or January 1992).

RESULTS

Stage One: A Baseline Model of the Risk of Nursing Home Placement

The first column of Table 3.2 contains the adjusted odds ratios (AORs) obtained from the multivariable logistic regression analysis of being placed in a nursing home in the 6 years after the 1984 baseline interviews for the 7,391 *LSOA* respondents for whom complete data were available. The AORs indicate the net change in the odds of being placed in the nursing home given a 1-unit increase in the independent variable, adjusting for all of the other variables in the model. For a dichotomous independent variable, like gender, the AOR indicates the difference in the odds for women versus men. AORs less than 1 indicate a reduction of the odds, AORs with a value of 1 indicate no difference in the odds, and AORs greater than 1 indicate an increase in the odds. For an independent variable with more than two values, like age, the AOR for comparing any two values is determined by multiplying the logistic regression coefficient (obtained by taking the logarithm of the AOR that is shown in the table) by the number of intervals separating the two values (in this case, ages)

TABLE 3.2   Adjusted Odds Ratios (AORs) Obtained from the Multivariable Logistic Regression Models from the First Four Phases of the Analyses of the Effect of Nursing Home Placement on Mortality[1]

Independent Variable	Nursing Home Placement (after the 1984 Baseline Interviews)[2]	Mortality (between the 1984 Baseline Interviews and Dec. 31, 1991)[3]	Dying in the Nursing Home (after the 1984 Baseline Interviews)[4]	Mortality (between 1988 and 1991)[5]
Predisposing Characteristics				
Female		.4383[d]	.4389[d]	.4566[d]
Age	1.0923[d]	1.0845[d]	1.0383[b]	1.0585[d]
Black	.6651[a]			
Lives alone	1.3547[b]			
Nonkin supports	.8925[c]	.8561[d]		.8964[b]
Enabling Characteristics				
Private insurance		.8655[a]		
Social security dependence		.8861[a]		
Population density	1.0360[a]			
Northcentral region	1.3374[b]	1.2030[a]	2.0571[c]	
Need Characteristics				
Hypertension		1.1863[b]		1.2329[a]
Rheumatic fever			2.8594[a]	.3349[a]
Coronary heart disease	.5963[b]			
Any other heart attack	.7191[a]	1.5235[d]		1.4931[a]
Stroke		1.6096[d]		1.6064[a]
Alzheimer's disease	2.3185[a]			
Cancer		1.3760[d]		
Diabetes		1.7541[d]		1.7126[c]
Basic ADLs				1.1947[a]
Household ADLs	1.1309[b]	1.1250[b]		
Lower body limitations	1.0779[a]	1.1063[d]		

TABLE 3.2 *(Continued)*

Upper body limitations		.9185[a]		
Body mass	.9764[b]	.9598[d]	.9562[a]	.9720[a]
Good health		1.2035[b]	.5405[b]	
Fair health		1.2855[b]	.5963[a]	
Poor health		1.5988[d]		
Baseline Health Services Utilization				
Physician visits		1.0150[a]		
Hospital contact		1.2862[c]		1.2863[a]
Nursing home placement	2.0544[d]			
Change (Increases) in Functional Status 1984–86				
Lower body limitations	N/A	N/A	N/A	1.1046[a]
Change (Increases) in Functional Status 1986–88				
Basic ADLs	N/A	N/A	N/A	1.1163[a]
Lower body limitations	N/A	N/A	N/A	1.2042[d]
Health Services Utilization after Baseline				
Nursing home placement 1984–90	N/A	1.9563[d]	N/A	N/A
Nursing home placement 1986–88	N/A	N/A	N/A	1.8463[b]
Model Fit Statistics				
ROC statistic	.751	.763	.704	.754
Hosmer-Lemeshow statistic	13.991	11.277	5.978	4.2093
	($p = .0820$)	($p = .1865$)	($p = .6497$)	($p = .8378$)

Notes:
a. $p \leq .05$.
b. $p \leq .01$.
c. $p \leq .001$.
d. $p \leq .0001$.
1. The following variables were included in the models represented by all four columns: being female, age, being black, education, living alone, living in a multigenerational family, kin supports, nonkin supports, health worries, health control, having a telephone, private insurance, being on Medicaid, population density, residential stability,

(Continued)

TABLE 3.2 *(Continued)*

Social Security dependence, living in the Northeast, Northcentral, or Western regions, having a history of osteoporosis, a broken hip, atherosclerosis, hypertension, rheumatic fever, rheumatic heart Disease, coronary heart disease, angina, myocardial infarction, any other heart attack, stroke, Alzheimer's disease, cancer, arthritis, diabetes, aneurysm, blood clot, varicose veins, basic ADLs, household ADLs, advanced ADLs, lower body limitations, upper body limitations, body mass, good, fair, or poor perceived health, physician visits, hospital contact, and nursing home placement prior to baseline. In addition, the model shown in column 2 also included nursing home placement between 1984 and 1990, and the model shown in column 4 also included changes in basic ADLs, household ADLs, advanced ADLs, lower body limitations, and upper body limitations between 1984 and 1986 and 1986 and 1988, as well as nursing home placement between 1986 and 1988. AORs not significantly different from one at the $p \leq .05$ level are omitted for clarity. Variables with AORs that are not significantly different from one at the $p \leq .05$ level in *any* column are omitted from the body of the table to conserve space.

2. This column represents the multivariable logistic regression analysis of nursing home placement after the 1984 baseline interviews for the 7,391 respondents with complete data.

3. This column represents the multivariable logistic regression analysis of the risk of mortality in the 8 years between the 1984 baseline interviews and December 31, 1991, for the 7,391 respondents with complete data.

4. This column represents the multivariable logistic regression analysis of the risk of dying while residing in the nursing home for the 911 respondents who were placed in a nursing home after the 1984 baseline interviews and for whom complete data exists.

5. This column represents the multivariable logistic regression analysis of the risk of dying between 1988 and 1991 for the 3,073 respondents successfully reinterviewed in 1986 and 1988, and who were not in a nursing home at the time of their 1986 reinterview.

to be compared, and then calculating the AOR associated with that multiplicand. For clarity, AORs not significantly different from 1 (i.e., had no effect) at the $p \leq .05$ level have been omitted. To conserve space, variables whose AORs were never significantly different from 1 in any of the first four phases (i.e., columns) of the analyses have been omitted from the body of the table. Also shown are two model fit indices, the receiver operating characteristics (ROC) and Hosmer-Lemeshow statistics. The ROC statistic indicates that a randomly chosen respondent who was placed in a nursing home was more likely to be predicted as having been placed there than a randomly chosen respondent who had not (Hanley & McNeil, 1982). An ROC statistic $\geq .70$ indicates a good-fitting model, and an ROC statistic of .50 indicates a bad-fitting model (i.e., one that is no better than chance, such as a coin-flip). The Hosmer-Lemeshow statistic is a chi-square goodness of fit measure that assesses, within predicted probability deciles, whether the fitted logistic regression model is correct. A statistically insignificant Hosmer-Lemeshow statistic indicates a model that fits the data well (Hosmer & Lemeshow, 1989).

As shown in column 1 of the table, the logistic regression model fits the data well (ROC statistic = .751, Hosmer-Lemeshow statistic *p* value = .0820). Thirteen variables produced statistically significant effects on nursing home placement. The risk of being placed in a nursing home was greater for older adults, whites, those who live alone, those with fewer nonkin social supports, those who live in less densely populated areas, those who live in the northcentral (versus the southern) region, those not having a history of coronary heart disease or heart attack, those with a history of Alzheimer's Disease, those with more household ADL or lower body limitations, those with leaner body mass, and those who had been in a nursing home at any time prior to baseline. Based on partial *r*'s (not shown), age was clearly the most salient risk factor, followed by previous nursing home placements, nonkin social supports, and living alone. The remainder of the effects were of relatively equal magnitude.

These results are generally consistent with those reported in previous studies (see Kane & Kane, 1987). We offer here our interpretation of these findings. Older adults are more likely to be placed in nursing homes. Whether this reflects a normative decline associated with aging, or serves as a proxy for reduced social and other supports not well measured in the *LSOA*, however, cannot be inferred from these data. The greater risk of whites reflects well-established cultural differences and the institutional discrimination that lingers in the absence of reimbursement strategies comparable to those that have eliminated more socioeconomically based access barriers to hospitals (see Smith, 1990, for an excellent historical review of these issues). Blacks and other minorities consistently have had lower nursing home placement rates than whites. Those who live alone are more susceptible to institutionalization because they do not have someone available in the home to help them remain there. Like those who live alone, those with fewer nonkin social supports have smaller human resources networks to draw upon to maintain their community living status. Those who live in less densely populated areas have both greater per capita access to nursing homes and smaller human resources networks to draw upon. Individuals with a history of coronary heart disease or heart attack are more likely to die, and to die sooner, which censors their opportunity for nursing home placement. Alzheimer's patients (and those with other severe cognitive deficits) are more likely to exhaust the capacity of their social support and human resources networks, and to do so more rapidly. Limitations with household ADLs and lower body functions make it more difficult to maintain independent living and thus increase the likelihood of nursing home placement. Leaner body mass is both a major predictor of the risk of hip fracture (Wolinsky & Fitzgerald, 1994) and a generic marker of deteriorating health status (Hazzard, Andres, Bierman, & Blass, 1990). Prior nursing home stays most likely reflect both underlying medical conditions and the respondent's prior inability to avoid institutionalization. Unfortunately, the extent to which such prior institutional episodes reflect more biomedical than social support issues, or vice versa, cannot be inferred from these data.

Because of limitations in the design of the reinterviews, admission dates are available on only about one-third of those having been placed in nursing homes. As a result, it is not possible to examine the stability of the effects shown in column 1 of Table 3.2 over time with proportional hazard models. Following Allison (1982, 1984), however, it was possible to reconstitute the data on the 7,527 *LSOA* respondents into 19,962 contiguous-person-intervals and estimate a discrete-time hazard model. That is, a respondent's 1984 data can be used to model his or her 1986 nursing home placement status, a respondent's 1986 (or prior) data can be used to model his or her 1988 nursing home placement status, and a respondent's 1988 (or prior) data can be used to model his or her 1990 nursing home placement status. Thus each respondent can contribute up to three contiguous-person-intervals to the discrete-time hazard model. The ability to contribute contiguous-person-intervals is censored when the respondent is placed in a nursing home or dies. These 19,962 contiguous-person-intervals (which still contain only 934 nursing home placements, or "events") then become independent observations for a multivariable logistic regression analysis. The results of that analysis (not shown) are essentially the same as those reported in column 1 of Table 3.2. Further analysis (also not shown) in which two dummy variables are introduced to reflect the three contiguous-person-intervals indicates that the risk of nursing home placement monotonically increases over time, although the rate of that increase is not linear (i.e., the AORs for the second and third contiguous-person-interval markers [compared to the reference category of the first contiguous-person-interval marker] are 1.8797 and 2.0365, respectively, $p < .0001$).

Stage Two: A Baseline Model of the Risk
of Dying Associated with Nursing Home Placement

Column 2 of Table 3.2 contains the AORs, ROC, and Hosmer-Lemeshow statistics obtained from the multivariable logistic regression analysis of mortality in the 8 years between the 1984 baseline interviews and December 31, 1991, for the 7,391 *LSOA* respondents for whom complete data were available. As shown in column 2 of the table, the logistic regression model fits the data well (ROC statistic = .763, Hosmer-Lemeshow statistic p value = .1865). Twenty-one variables produced statistically significant effects on mortality. The risk of dying was greater for men, older adults, those with fewer nonkin social supports, those without private health insurance for physician and hospital services, those who were not financially dependent on Social Security, those who live in the northcentral (versus the southern) region, those having a history of hypertension, heart attack, stroke, cancer, or diabetes, those with more household ADL or lower body limitations, those with fewer upper body limitations, those with leaner body mass, those who perceive their health to be less than excellent or very good, those with more physician visits or having been hospitalized in the year prior to baseline, and those who had been placed in a nursing home at any time after baseline. As reflected in the partial r's, age was the most salient risk factor, followed closely by gender, then by having been placed in a nursing home after baseline, and then nonkin social supports. Further analysis (not shown) deleting the marker for being placed in a nursing home after baseline indicates that nursing home placement makes a substantial unique contribution to the model (chi-square increment = 65.784, $p < .0001$), and that none of the risks associated with the other variables in the model are meaningfully altered by the inclusion of nursing home placement after baseline.

With the exception of the mortality risk associated with having been placed in a nursing home after the baseline interview, a detailed discussion of these results has been presented elsewhere (Wolinsky, Johnson, & Stump, 1995) and need not be repeated. Moreover, the focus here is on the risk of mortality associated with having been placed in a nursing home after baseline. That AOR was 1.9563 ($r = .0873$, $p < .0001$), indicating that those having been placed in a nursing home were about 96% more likely to die than those not having been placed in a nursing home, after adjusting for all of the other variables in the logistic regression model. Thus, the *relative risk* of dying for those placed in a nursing home is substantial. This is remarkably consistent with our previous findings (Wolinsky, Callahan, Fitzgerald, & Johnson, 1992) and those of Aneshensel, Pearlin, and Schuler (1993), despite the differences in samples, observation periods, and covariate specifications. To determine the *attributable risk* of dying (following Selvin, 1991), we multiplied the baseline probability of dying (which was .38 among the 7,527 *LSOA* respondents) by the AOR for nursing home placement (or .9563) 1-minus. This resulted in an absolute difference in the probability of dying associated with nursing home placement (after adjustment for all of the covariates in the model) of .36, which is also rather impressive.

To assess whether the method by which information about nursing home placement after baseline was obtained artificially accounts, in whole or in part, for nursing home placement's relationship with mortality, and additional analyses (not shown) were conducted. These involved replacing the nursing home placement after baseline marker in the multivariable logistic regression model shown in column 2 of Table 3.2 with a set of five dummy variables. These included markers for obtaining nursing home placement information by self-report, in-household collateral reports, out-of-household collateral reports, or by place of death reports, and for collateral reports of death in the absence of any information about nursing home placement. Thus the reference (or omitted) category was having no information about nursing home placement or death. The AORs obtained for all five dummy variables were greater than 1 and highly statistically significant ($p \leq .0048$). As expected, the smallest AOR (1.8990) was for those placed in nursing homes when that information was obtained from self-reports. This indicates that after controlling for all of the other variables in the model, the odds of dying are 90% greater among those with self-reports of a nursing home placement (in the absence of a collateral report of death) versus those for whom no report (from any source) of a nursing home placement exists (also in the absence of a collateral report of death). Accordingly, the substantial risk of dying associated with nursing home placement is not an artifact of supplementing self- or collateral reports with information obtained from place of death reports.

Proportional hazard analysis was used to replicate the multivariable logistic regression model shown in column 2 of Table 3.2 to determine whether the effect of nursing home placement on mortality is altered when the timing of mortality is considered in addition to its occurrence. Those results (not shown) were fundamentally the same. The major difference was that although the unique contribution of nursing home placement remained highly significant (incremental chi square = 14.608, $p < .0001$), both its absolute (AOR = 1.2188) and relative effect appear to have been substantially reduced. This, however, is an artifact of not treating nursing home placement as a time-varying covariate, in that regardless of when the nursing home placement occurred, it is statistically treated as a fixed, baseline trait. Therefore, the logistic regression and proportional hazard analyses yield essentially the same results.

Stage Three: A Baseline Model of the Risk of Dying in the Nursing Home

Column 3 of Table 3.2 contains the AORs, ROC, and Hosmer-Lemeshow statistics obtained from the logistic regression analysis of the risk of dying while residing at the nursing home. Although others (see Greene & Ondrich, 1990) have focused on more successful exits from nursing homes (i.e., live discharges), the *LSOA* is more suited to examining less successful exits (i.e., deaths). This analysis is limited to the 911 *LSOA* respondents who were placed in a nursing home after the 1984 baseline interviews and for whom complete data were available. Of these, only the 367 older adults who were known to have died *at* the nursing home are treated as "events." As shown in column 3 of the table, the logistic regression model fits the data well (ROC statistic = .704, Hosmer-Lemeshow statistic p value = .6497). Seven variables produced statistically significant effects on nursing home mortality. The risk of dying in a nursing home was greater for men, older adults, those who lived in the northcentral (versus the southern) region, individuals with a history of rheumatic fever, those with leaner body mass, and those who perceived their health to be excellent or very good (versus good, fair, or poor [$p \leq .0526$]). Because the ratio (i.e., 7.7) of "events" to variables in the equation is less than the standard rule of thumb (i.e., 10), we used a variety of piecemeal estimation techniques to determine whether these findings were artifacts of overfitting the model (Concato, Feinstein, & Holford, 1993). No such evidence was detected. Thus our confidence in the results shown in the table is enhanced.

With two exceptions, these results are consistent with previous studies, most of which have actually focused on the somewhat different issue of the correlates of live discharges (see Greene & Ondrich, 1990), and with our earlier analysis (Wolinsky, Callahan, Fitzgerald, & Johnson, 1992). The effects of age and gender reflect well-established life expectancy differences. Women outlive men, and the probability of dying increases with advancing age. Mortality rates have been shown to be higher in the northcentral region. Having a history of rheumatic fever has been associated with mortality rates (although this relationship has not been examined in the nursing home). Leaner body mass also generally places older adults at greater risk of mortality.

One of the two exceptions involves the higher mortality risks in the nursing home that are associated with having had better perceived health at baseline. These risks probably reflect two matters. On the one hand, older adults who perceived their health to be better at baseline but were subsequently placed in nursing homes are more likely to have succumbed to unanticipated institutionalizing conditions (e.g., stroke) that are more likely to be terminal, and more rapidly so. This interpretation is compatible with Idler and Kasl's (1991) interpretation of the relationship between perceived health and mortality as an index of survivability. On the other hand, older adults who perceived their health to be poorer at baseline and were subsequently placed in nursing homes are more likely to have a pattern of more frequent hospitalizations, and are thus more likely to die in the hospital, after being transferred there. This is consistent with the results of recent efforts to model hospital utilization patterns over time (Wolinsky, Stump, & Johnson, 1995).

The other exception involves the absence of the protective effects of having lived in multigenerational households at baseline and of having worried about one's health then. In our earlier analysis (Wolinsky, Callahan, Fitzgerald, & Johnson, 1992), we interpreted the former as a marker for an ombudsman effect and the latter as a proxy for identifying the worried well. Although the AORs for both variables are less than 1 (indicating protective effects) in these analyses, neither is statistically significant (p values = .2396 and .3056, respectively). It is possible that their previously marginal statistical significance was diluted by the inclusion of the 2,376 younger, white respondents, in conjunction with the different covariate specification (especially that associated with disease history and perceived health).

Stage Four: A Dynamic Model of the Effect of Nursing Home Placement on Mortality

Column 4 of Table 3.2 contains the AORs, ROC, and Hosmer-Lemeshow statistics obtained from the logistic regression analysis conducted to examine the effect of being placed in a nursing home between 1986 and 1988 on dying between 1988 and 1991. To properly decompose the health status trajectories into their 1984–86 (i.e., before nursing home placement occurred) and 1986–88 (i.e., when nursing home placement occurred) components, this analysis is limited to the 3,073 *LSOA* respondents who were successfully reinterviewed in 1986 and 1988, and who had not been in nursing homes by the time of their 1986 reinterview. Of these 3,073 individuals, 189 were placed in nursing homes between 1986 and 1988, and 703 died between 1988 and 1991. In addition to the 49 predisposing, enabling, need, and prior health services utilization measures included in the previous models, this equation includes 10 indicators reflecting changes in the 5 functional status scales between 1984 and 1986 and 1986 and 1988. The former are markers of the health status trajectory in the period prior to nursing home placement, and the latter are markers of the health status trajectory during the period of nursing home placement.

To the extent that they are comparable, the results shown in column 4 of Table 3.2 are generally consistent with those found in column 2, as well as those reported earlier (Wolinsky, Johnson, & Stump, 1995). Once again, the logistic regression model fits the data well (ROC statistic = .754, Hosmer-Lemeshow statistic p value = .8378). The risk of dying between 1988 and 1991 is greater for men, older adults, those with fewer nonkin social supports, those having a history of hypertension, heart attack, stroke, or diabetes, but not those having a history of rheumatic fever, those with more basic ADL limitations, individuals with leaner body mass, and those having been hospitalized in the year prior to baseline. In addition, increases in the number of lower body limitations between 1984 and 1986 and 1986 and 1988 also increase the likelihood of dying between 1988 and 1991, as do increases in the number of basic ADLs between 1986 and 1988. Finally, the variable of interest, having been placed in a nursing home between 1986 and 1988, also significantly increases the risk of dying (AOR = 1.8463, p = .0044, chi-square increment = 8.071). Indeed, even after controlling for the 49 variables in the baseline model, the five health status trajectory measures prior to nursing home placement, and the five health status trajectory measures during the period when the nursing home placement occurred, being placed in a nursing home between 1986 and 1988 increases the risk of dying between 1988 and 1991 by almost 85%. That translates into a substantial attributable risk of .194 ([703 deaths/3,073 *LSOA* respondents] × .8463). Thus these data provide impressive evidence to rule out the critical competing explanation that both institutionalization (i.e., nursing home placement) and death are merely markers of the same underlying process of deteriorating health status.

That evidence, however, is not definitive. To further clarify the relationship between nursing home placement and mortality, three additional sets of analyses (not shown) were conducted. The first addressed the question of whether those placed in a nursing home between 1986 and 1988 died of different causes during 1989–91 than their counterpart community decedents. Linking the *NCHS Multiple Cause of Death File* for 1989 (data for 1990–91 were not available) to the *LSOA* indicated that 11 (15.9%) of the 69 decedents who had passed through a nursing home had died of pneumonia, compared to only 12 (3.6%) of the 335 community dwelling decedents. This is as expected, given the decreased activity levels of nursing home residents and their increased exposure to opportunistic diseases like pneumonia (Hazzard, Andres, Bierman, & Blass, 1990). In the second set of analyses, the 23 pneumonia deaths were excluded, and the model shown in column 4 of Table 3.2 was reestimated. The effect of nursing home placement remained large and statistically significant (AOR = 1.7786, incremental chi square = 7.037, p value = .0080), suggesting that it goes considerably beyond the increased risks associated with pneumonia. To assess whether the relationship between nursing home placement between 1986 and 1988 and mortality between 1989 and 1991 was an artifact of those about to die being placed in a nursing home, the third set of analyses excluded deaths occurring from any cause in 1989, and the model shown in column 4 of Table 3.2 was again reestimated. The effect of nursing home placement remained large and statistically significant (AOR = 1.77612, incremental chi square = 5.4815, p value = .0192), suggesting that it is not an artifact of nursing home placement immediately prior to death. Thus these three additional sets of analyses do not diminish the substantial effect of nursing home placement on subsequent mortality.

Stage Five: A Dynamic Model of the Effect of Nursing Home Placement on Morbidity

Table 3.3 contains the unstandardized coefficients, their standardized counterparts (betas, in parentheses), and p values (in brackets) obtained from the OLS regression analysis conducted to examine the effect of being placed in a nursing home between 1986 and 1988 on changes in

TABLE 3.3 Unstandardized Coefficients, Standardized Coefficients in Parentheses, and *p* Values in Brackets Obtained from the OLS Regression Analyses of Changes in the Five Functional Status Measures between 1988 and 1990 for the 2,382 *LSOA* Respondents Who Were Successfully Reinterviewed in 1986, 1988, and 1990, and Who Were Not in a Nursing Home at the Time of Their 1986 Reinterview

Independent Variable	Basic ADLs	Household ADLs	Advanced ADLs	Lower Body Limitations	Upper Body Limitations
Change in Functional Status 1984–86					
Basic ADLs	.4452				.0620
	(.2677)				(.0762)
	[.0001]				[.0068]
Household ADLs	.2220	.5017	.0956		
	(.1041)	(.3451)	(.1220)		
	[.0001]	[.0001]	[.0001]		
Advanced ADLs	.1689		.5559		
	(.0450)		(.4033)		
	[.0267]		[.0001]		
Lower body limitations	.1592	.1467		.6313	.0534
	(.1261)	(.1705)		(.4923)	(.0864)
	[.0001]	[.0001]		[.0001]	[.0021]
Upper body limitations			.0466		.4422
			(.0533)		(.3798)
			[.0445]		[.0001]
Change in Functional Status 1986–88					
Basic ADLs	.4057			.0657	.0479
	(.2877)			(.0459)	(.0694)
	[.0001]			[.0319]	[.0066]
Household ADLs	.1393	.3825	.0744	.1072	.0931
	(.0747)	(.3010)	(.1085)	(.0566)	(.1020)
	[.0005]	[.0001]	[.0001]	[.0079]	[.0001]
Advanced ADLs	.1319		.3821		
	(.0405)		(.3190)		
	[.0303]		[.0001]		
Lower body imitations	.1307	.1018		.3976	.0505
	(.0964)	(.1102)		(.2888)	(.0761)
	[.0001]	[.0001]		[.0001]	[.0010]

(Continued)

TABLE 3.3 *(Continued)*

Independent Variable	Basic ADLs	Household ADLs	Advanced ADLs	Lower Body Limitations	Upper Body Limitations
Upper body limitations					.2390
					(.2057)
					[.0001]
Health Services Utilization after Baseline					
Nursing home placement 1986–88	1.3982	−.5891		.5941	
	(.1365)	(−.0844)		(.0571)	
	[.0001]	[.0001]		[.0006]	

Note: The effects of the 49 predisposing, enabling, need, and prior health services utilization measures were included in each of the five OLS regression equations, but are not shown for simplicity. Coefficients not significantly different from zero at the $p \le .05$ level have been omitted for clarity.

the five functional status measures between 1988 and 1990. To properly decompose the functional status trajectories into their 1984–86 (i.e., before nursing home placement occurred), 1986–88 (i.e., when nursing home placement occurred), and 1988–90 (i.e., after nursing home placement occurred) components, this analysis is limited to the 2,408 *LSOA* respondents who were successfully reinterviewed in 1986, 1988, and 1990, and who had not been in a nursing home by the time of their 1986 reinterview. Ninety of these 2,408 reinterviewed survivors had been placed in a nursing home between 1986 and 1988. Although they were included in each of the five OLS regression equations, to conserve space the effects of the 49 predisposing, enabling, need, and prior health services utilization measures included in the previous models are not shown. Under normal circumstances (i.e., linear panel methods), having the baseline assessment of each of the five functional status outcome measures included in each equation makes the effect of each variable shown in the table algebraically equivalent to its effect on changes in that functional status measure between 1984 and 1990 (Kessler & Greenberg, 1980). Because the indicators of change in each of the five functional status outcome measures between 1984 and 1986 and 1986 and 1988 are also included in each equation, however, the effect of each variable shown in the table is algebraically equivalent to its effect on changes in that functional status measure between 1988 and 1990. This permits a direct and conservative test of whether having been placed in a nursing home between 1986 and 1988 has an effect on subsequent changes in functional status that cannot be accounted for by (a) the baseline level of functional status, (b) the other 48 variables taken from the behavioral model, or (c) the 10 indicators of functional status trajectories for the periods before and during nursing home placement.

Before considering the effects of nursing home placement on subsequent morbidity, the effects of the 10 indicators of functional status trajectories warrant brief mention. When the indicators of deteriorating functional status trajectories for 1984–86 or 1986–88 have significant effects, they always have positive effects. That is, prior functional status deterioration predicts future functional status deterioration. Moreover, the effects of prior functional status deterioration on the same functional status outcome measure are always statistically significant and always have the largest relative effects on future functional status deterioration on that outcome measure.

Turning to the effects of nursing home placement on subsequent morbidity reveals further support for the notion that passing through the nursing home increases the risk of adverse outcomes. Even after controlling for the baseline level of functional status, the other 48 variables taken from the behavioral model, and the 10 indicators of functional status trajectories for the periods before and during the nursing home placement, nursing home placement results in statistically significant increases in basic ADL difficulties ($b = 1.3982$, $p < .0001$) and lower body limitations ($b = .5941$, $p = .0006$). These regression coefficients (b's) may be directly interpreted as the regression adjusted mean differences between those placed in a nursing home between 1986 and 1988 and those who remained in the community during that period. In addition, a marginally insignificant ($b = .1398$, $p = .1588$) increase in upper body limitations is also detected. Comparing the standardized regression coefficients shown in the table with those of the 48 other variables (which were included in the equations but are not shown in the table) provides an indication of the relative importance of the effect of nursing home placement. Aside from the baseline and changes in functional health status measures specific to each outcome, nursing home placement always has the second largest effect. These robust results are consistent with our expectations.

Interestingly, nursing home placement results in what appears to be a statistically significant decrease in household ADL difficulties ($b = -.5891$, $p < .0001$), while advanced ADL difficulties are not affected at all ($p = .6886$). The former effect may be an artifact of how the ADL measures are constructed. These measures reflect the number of ADLs for which the respondent has difficulty due to health reasons, but not the number of ADLs that the respondent does not do because someone else does them for him or her. Generally speaking, when respondents are placed in nursing homes, they are no longer responsible for performing household chores such as meal preparation, shopping, and light and heavy housework (which are the four household ADL items). Thus, prior responses indicating difficulties associated with performing these activities due to health reasons become current responses of not engaging in these activities because someone else does them. Therefore, they are no longer counted. Accordingly, the apparent decrease in household ADL difficulties is neither inconsistent with nor contradicts our expectations.

The lack of an effect of nursing home placement on subsequent changes in advanced ADLs is more troubling. We previously hypothesized (Wolinsky, Callahan, Fitzgerald, & Johnson, 1992) that one of the mechanisms that might explain the adverse effect that being placed in a nursing home has on subsequent morbidity and mortality involves an older adult version of the failure to thrive (Braun, Wykle, & Cowling, 1988). If that is the case, then nursing home placement should have adverse effects on cognitive capabilities, which the items in the advanced ADL (especially money management and using the telephone) tap. Thus these analyses would appear not to support the failure-to-thrive explanation.

It is possible, however, that the lack of an effect of nursing home placement on subsequent changes in advanced ADLs is an artifact of what the advanced ADL measure taps. Generally speaking, nursing home residents have an inconsequential amount of money (i.e., their Medicaid mandated allowances) to manage personally. Personal (i.e., private) access to telephones is likely reduced, and nursing personnel may either initiate phone calls for the nursing home resident or be available to provide assistance (this applies to eating as well). Moreover, telephone solicitations and coordination of home services and supports are likely eliminated. Thus the lack of an effect of nursing home placement on subsequent changes in advanced ADLs may simply reflect the diminished load of advanced ADLs confronting the nursing home resident.

DISCUSSION

The purpose of this chapter has been to investigate whether being placed in a nursing home makes you sicker and more likely to die. That is, we have attempted to determine whether nursing home placement was the sentinel event marking exposure to some causative nursing home agent(s), or merely a marker of preexistent, deteriorating health status trajectories. To accomplish this task, we extended our (Wolinsky, Callahan, Fitzgerald, & Johnson, 1992) earlier analysis of the nationally representative *LSOA* five ways.

1. We lengthened the catchment period for nursing home placement from 1984–88 to 1984–90.
2. We broadened the focus from the 5,151 respondents selected for the 1986 and 1988 reinterviews to the 7,527 respondents selected for the 1988 and 1990 reinterviews. These first two alterations increased the number of nursing home placement "events" from 549 to 934.
3. We used *NDI* matches rather than collateral reports to document decedent status. This lengthened the catchment period for mortality from 1984–88 to 1984–91, and increased the number of mortality "events" from 1,214 to 2,870.
4. We relied on dynamic models that decomposed health status trajectories into the sequential pieces occurring before, during, and after nursing home placement. This allowed us to examine directly the effect of passing through a nursing home independent of prior and current health status trajectories.
5. We broadened our focus to include the effect of nursing home placement on morbidity as well as mortality.

Our analyses progressed through five stages in which we made every effort to decompose fully the relationships among nursing home placement, subsequent functional status, and mortality. This included incorporating 49 baseline markers of the predisposing, enabling, need, and prior health services utilization patterns specified in the behavioral model into each equation. Despite these efforts, nursing home placement was almost always significantly associated with getting sicker. Moreover, nursing home placement was always significantly associated with being more likely to die.

It is not possible, however, to unequivocally state that nursing home placement makes you sicker and more likely to die. There are four reasons for this, all of which ironically stem from design limitations that were imposed to rule out the critical competing explanation that both nursing home placement and death are merely markers of the same underlying process of deteriorating health status. These four reasons are best stated as questions.

1. Are the *LSOA* respondents who died late in the 8-year observation window (i.e., 1988–91) a biased sample of those who died over the entire observation window (i.e., 1984–91)?

2. Are the *LSOA* respondents who died at nursing homes a biased sample of those who died as residents of nursing homes but who were transferred to hospitals for their official deaths?

3. Are the *LSOA* respondents who were placed in nursing homes in the middle of the observation window (i.e., 1986–88) a biased sample of all respondents placed in nursing homes?

4. Are the *LSOA* respondents who were successfully reinterviewed at all three follow-ups a biased sample of all *LSOA* respondents?

Of course, the answer to all four questions is yes. Thus, although the baseline components of our analyses (stages 1 and 2) do not bias the national representativeness of the *LSOA* in any way, modeling the risk of dying at the nursing home (stage 3), and the shift to dynamic models of the effect of nursing home placement on subsequent mortality or morbidity (stages 4 and 5), must and do introduce such biases.

There are several additional, although more modest, constraints on the generalizability of these results as well. These constraints are best stated as simple facts. No individual included in the dynamic models (stages 4 and 5) had been in the nursing home for longer than 4 years. None of the analyses included anyone younger than age 70 at the time of their index nursing home placement. The youngest age at which the morbidity or mortality subsequent to nursing home placement could have occurred was greater than 74 years old. Nursing home careers for residents who entered due to acute illnesses (e.g., stroke) were more likely to be followed to completion (i.e., death) than were nursing home careers for residents who entered for rehabilitative purposes (e.g., hip fracture) or due to chronic conditions (e.g., dementia).

These biases and constraints do not diminish the impressive evidence that nursing home placement is significantly and independently associated with getting sicker and being more likely to die. Rather, they merely prevent the assignment of causal attribution for those relationships. Causal attribution, however, is not likely to be attained, because achieving it requires a controlled trial in which pairs of individuals matched on age, gender, race, functional status, and the other salient risk factors identified in Tables 3.2 and 3.3 are randomly assigned to either the treatment (i.e., nursing home) or control (i.e., community-dwelling) group and are then followed until their death. This is unlikely to occur for a variety of reasons, not the least of which are moral and ethical considerations. An alternative but less rigorous design would involve a prospective case-control study in which the cases (those placed in nursing homes) and the controls (those remaining in the community) are matched on age, gender, race, functional status, and the other salient risk factors identified in Tables 3.2 and 3.3. Although the case-control design avoids the moral and ethical problems associated with the randomized controlled trial, the probability of sufficiently precise, simultaneous matching on so many risk factors between those placed in the nursing home and those remaining in the community is not great (Selvin, 1991).

Therefore, for the sake of argument, let us assume that being placed in a nursing home does make you sicker and more likely to die. What might the operative mechanism(s) be? Four rather related possibilities come to mind. The first involves the institutionalized (in the role theory sense; see Parsons, 1951) expectations associated with nursing home placement. As indicated earlier, nursing homes and the nursing home industry perform a societal agency role in that they care for people until they die. Given how well recognized that role is, the concept of the self-fulfilling prophecy (see Merton, 1968) seems appropriate. Upon being placed in nursing homes, residents may simply conclude that this is their twilight role and come to accept (or at least be resigned to) it. As a result, nursing home residents may exhibit an accentuated version of how older adults in general are more accepting than their younger counterparts of deteriorating health status as merely a function of normal aging (Hazzard, Andres, Bierman, & Blass, 1990). In this case, functional deterioration and death are simply seen as normal nursing home life (Kane & Kane, 1987).

A second and related possibility involves the failure to thrive (Braun, Wykle, & Cowling, 1988). When applied to older adults, failure to thrive is usually depicted by altered body weight (typically from undernutrition), impaired or delayed cognitive and physical functioning (sometimes secondary to and sometimes predictive of reductions in dietary intake), and depression (especially that which manifests itself as a generalized mood disturbance and is associated with multiple physical illnesses). According to Braun, Wykle, and Cowling, the failure-to-thrive syndrome is not uncommon:

> Most clinical staff in nursing homes have encountered elderly residents who lose 1 to 2 or more pounds of weight per month, decline gradually in physical function and cognitive ability, and seem to withdraw from food and human contact. At times these dwindlers fade away to death unnoticed. At other times they are thought to be progressing in dementia or giving up the will to live. (p. 809)

For our purposes, two important questions in the failure-to-thrive literature (which among older adults is largely derived rather than empirical) are not yet resolved. One is whether the failure to thrive would be initiated upon placement in a nursing home or at a subsequent time, when it became clear to the older adult that she or he would not be returning to the community. The other is how long it would take, on average, from the onset of undetected failure to thrive to death. If the answer to the first question were the recognition date, and if the answer to the second was more than a year, then the results reported here might be consistent with failure to thrive as the operating mechanism.

The third possibility for the operating mechanism involves the quality of care that is provided to nursing home residents. A growing body of scientific literature (Institute of Medicine, 1986; Ouslander, 1989; Ouslander, Osterweil, & Morley, 1991; Vladeck, 1980) suggests that the quality of care provided to nursing home residents is inadequate at best, and tragic at worst. Although a variety of factors, frequently including negative nursing home personnel attitudes (see Wright, 1988), are cited for the poor quality of health care provided in nursing homes, Kane (1991) lays the blame squarely at the feet of the medical profession:

> Doctors do not like nursing homes. Many physicians go to great lengths to avoid them. They feel uncomfortable there. The lack of staff support and the advanced stages of the patients create a sense that little can be done to make a difference. This perception is both an irony and a tragedy .... Ironically, nursing home residents are probably one of the groups who can profit most from careful attention to both their medical problems and the way their care is rendered. . . . What is missing is . . . leadership. Only a handful of physicians have chosen to invest their energies in improving

nursing home care. A larger group of physicians are reluctant participants in such care, viewing it as unrewarding both medically and fiscally. (p. vii)

Regardless of where the blame is placed for the inadequate quality of the medical, nursing, and social care provided in nursing homes, there is little doubt that it exists. Whether its existence reflects benign or intentional neglect does not matter. What matters is that such neglect places nursing home residents in harm's way. This is, by far, the most negative of the possible operating mechanisms that might account for the association between nursing home placement and subsequent declines in functional status and death.

A final possibility for the operating mechanism involves an extension of the activity theory originally espoused by Havighurst and Albrecht (1953). That theory is based on Mead's (1934) assumption that the social self emerges from and is maintained by meaningful social interaction with other social actors. Adapting Lennon, Bengston, and Peterson (1972), the basic postulates of activity theory relevant to the nursing home context are:

1. the greater the social roles and contacts lost on entry to the nursing home, the less activity one will engage in while there;
2. the greater the activity one engages in at the nursing home, the more role support one is likely to receive;
3. the more support one receives in the nursing home, the more positive one's self-concept is likely to be; and
4. the more positive one's self-concept, the greater one's quality of life in the nursing home is likely to be.

The principal difference between the activity theory and the failure-to-thrive theory is the generally involuntary nature of the former versus the voluntary nature of the latter, although it is possible that activity theory serves as a precursor to the failure to thrive.

Given the impressive evidence of the association between being placed in a nursing home and getting sicker and dying, and assuming that one or more of the four operating mechanisms is involved, it is appropriate to conclude this chapter by briefly speculating about what might be done to enhance the ability of nursing homes to maintain the competence of their older adult residents. Three strategies seem plausible and related, although none of them may be practical in the current context of health care reform and the declining commitment to voluntarism and family and community values. These strategies involve changing the expectations associated with nursing home placement, reducing the social isolation of nursing home residents and thereby increasing their meaningful social interaction, and making nursing homes more resident-friendly.

Changing the expectations associated with nursing homes is likely as difficult a task as changing the social role that has been institutionalized for older adults in American society. Despite provocative essays (Callahan, 1987; Fischer, 1978) that have identified the expectations (including both the lack thereof and the entitlement mentality) associated with growing old as the root of the current crisis in public policy concerning the health and welfare of the aged, little has changed in the past 2 decades. There are two reasons for this. First, changing institutionalized roles is a gradual process that cannot be governmentally mandated. Second, an alternative candidate for the institutionalized role of the nursing home must either exist or be proposed, and aside from preliminary suggestions by Lidz, Fischer, and Arnold (1992), no alternative role has been defined. Thus it is unlikely that noticeable changes in the expectations associated with nursing homes are likely to occur in the short term, although the increasing market share of more vertically integrated nursing homes that include retirement apartments, intermediate care, and skilled nursing facilities suggests the possibility of such shifts in the long term.

Reducing the social isolation and thereby increasing the meaningful social interaction of nursing home residents is an easier task than changing the expectations associated with nursing homes themselves. At the same time, it is likely a less robust buffer to the association between nursing home placement and subsequent morbidity and mortality. Scenarios for reducing social isolation might include adopt-a-parent-or-grandparent programs, or the siting of community activities on nursing home grounds. With regard to the latter, 12-step and other small scale self-help and self-support groups (especially those that emphasize physical as well as social activity) might be most effective. Care must be taken, however, to ensure that such activities create meaningful social interaction for nursing home residents, rather than simply underwrite the operating costs of community activities.

Making nursing homes more resident-friendly may be the most pragmatic approach, especially in the face of a projected increase in the demand for nursing home beds. That is, as new nursing home facilities are constructed, we should capitalize on the opportunity to design them as appropriately as possible (for an extraordinary list of pragmatic suggestions tied to a conceptually driven, goal-oriented model, see Chapter 6 by Victor Regnier and the Commentaries by Neil Charness and Paul Windley). Perhaps the most crucial element here is the emphasis on vertically integrated facilities. This would link independent living with more traditional nursing home services, and thus begin to alter the stereotype of the nursing home as a total institution (Goffman, 1961). The presence of the independent living facilities might also help stem the erosion of autonomy in the more traditional (i.e., intermediate care and skilled nursing facility) long-term care areas (Lidz, Fischer, & Arnold, 1992).

REFERENCES

Allison, P. D. (1982). Discrete-time methods for the analysis of event histories. In S. Leinhardt (Ed.), *Sociological methodology*. San Francisco: Jossey-Bass.

Allison, P. D. (1984). *Event history analysis: Regression for longitudinal data*. Newbury Park, CA: Sage.

Andersen, R. M. (1968). *A behavioral model of families' use of health services*. Chicago: Center for Health Administration Studies.

Aneshensel, C. S., Pearlin, L. I., & Schuler, R. H. (1993). Stress, role captivity, and the cessation of caregiving. *Journal of Health and Social Behavior*, *34*, 54–70.

Braun, J. V., Wykle, M. H., & Cowling, W. R. (1988). Failure to thrive in older persons: A concept derived. *The Gerontologist*, *28*, 809–812.

Callahan, D. (1987). *Setting limits: Medical goals in an aging society*. New York: Simon and Schuster.

Clark, D. O., Stump, T. E., & Wolinsky, F. D. (in press). A race and gender specific replication of five dimensions of functional limitation and disability. *Journal of Aging and Health*, *9*.

Concato, J., Feinstein, A. A., & Holford, T. R. (1993). The risk of determining risk with multivariable models. *Annals of Internal Medicine*, *118*, 201–210.

Duke University Center for the Study of Aging and Human Development. (1978). *Multidimensional functional assessment: The OARS methodology*. Durham, NC: Duke University Press.

Fischer, D. H. (1978). *Growing Old in America* [o.p.]. Oxford, England: Oxford University Press.

Fitti, J. E., & Kovar, M. G. (1987). *The supplement on aging to the 1984 National Health Interview Survey*. DHHS Publication 87-1323. Washington, DC: U.S. Government Printing Office [hereafter USGPO].

Fitzgerald, J. F., Smith, D. M., Martin, D. K., Freedman, J. N., & Wolinsky, F. D. (1993). Replication of the multidimensionality of activities of daily living. *Journal of Gerontology: Social Sciences, 48,* S28–S31.

Goffman, E. L. (1961). *Asylums: Essays on the social situation of mental patients and other inmates.* Garden City, NJ: Anchor Books.

Greene, V. L., & Ondrich, J. I. (1990). Risk factors for nursing home admissions and exits: A discrete-time hazard function approach. *Journal of Gerontology: Social Sciences, 45,* S250–S258.

Hanley, J. A., & McNeil, B. J. (1982). The meaning and use of the area under a Receiver Operating Characteristic (ROC) curve. *Radiology, 143,* 29–36.

Harris, T., Kovar, M. G., Suzman, R., Kleinman, J. C., & Feldman, J. J. (1989). Longitudinal study of physical ability in the oldest-old. *American Journal of Public Health, 79,* 698–702.

Havighurst, R., & Albrecht, R. (1953). *Older people.* New York: Longmans, Green.

Hazzard, W. R., Andres, R., Bierman, E. L., & Blass, J. P. (1990). *Principles of geriatric medicine and gerontology* (2nd ed.). New York: McGraw-Hill.

Hosmer, D. W., & Lemeshow, S. (1989). *Applied logistic regression.* New York: Wiley Interscience.

Idler, E. L., & Kasl, S. (1991). Health perceptions and survival: Do global evaluations of health status really predict mortality? *Journal of Gerontology: Social Sciences, 46,* S55–S65.

Institute of Medicine. (1986). *Improving the quality of care in nursing homes.* Washington, DC: National Academy Press.

Johnson, R. J., & Wolinsky, F. D. (1993). The structure of health status among older adults: Disease, disability, functional limitation, and perceived health. *Journal of Health and Social Behavior, 34,* 105–121.

Johnson, R. J., & Wolinsky, F. D. (1994). Gender, race, and health: The structure of health status among older adults. *The Gerontologist, 34,* 24–35.

Kane, R. M. (1991). Foreword. In J. G. Ouslander, D. Osterweil, & J. Morley (Eds.), *Medical care in the nursing home.* New York: McGraw-Hill.

Kane, R. A., & Kane, R. L. (1987). *Long-term care: Principles, programs, and policies.* New York: Springer.

Katz, S., Ford, A. B., Moskowitz, R. W., Jackson, B. A., & Jaffee, M. W. (1963). Studies of illness in the aged. The index of ADL: A standardized measure of biological and psychosocial function. *Journal of the American Medical Association, 185,* 94–101.

Kessler, R. C., & Greenberg, D. F. (1980). *Linear panel analysis: Models of quantitative change.* New York: Academic Press.

Kovar, M. G., Fitti, J. E., & Chyba, M. M. (1992). *The longitudinal study of aging; 1984–1990.* DHHS Publication 92-1304. Washington, DC: National Center for Health Statistics.

Lazenby, H. C., & Letsch, S. W. (1990). National health expenditures, 1989. *Health Care Financing Review, 12*, 1–26.

Lennon, B., Bengston, V., & Peterson, J. (1972). An exploration of the activity theory of aging: Activity types and life satisfaction among in-movers to a retirement community. *Journal of Gerontology, 17*, 180–185.

Letsch, S. W., Lazenby, H. C., Levit, K. R., & Cowan, C. A. (1992). National health expenditures, 1991. *Health Care Financing Review, 14*(2), 1–30.

Lidz, C. W., Fischer, L., & Arnold, R. M. (1992). *The erosion of autonomy in long-term care.* New York: Oxford University Press.

Mead, G. H. (1934). *Mind, self, and society.* Chicago: University of Chicago Press.

Merton, R. K. (1968). *Social theory and social structure.* New York: Free Press.

Nagi, S. Z. (1976). An epidemiology of disability among adults in the United States. *Milbank Memorial Fund Quarterly, 54*, 439–468.

Ouslander, J. G. (1989). Medical care in the nursing home. *Journal of the American Medical Association, 262*, 2582–2590.

Ouslander, J. G., Osterweil, D., & Morley, J. (1991). *Medical care in the nursing home.* New York: McGraw-Hill.

Parsons, T. P. (1951). *The social system.* New York: Free Press.

Rice, D. P., & Feldman, J. J. (1981). Living longer in the United States: Demographic changes and health needs of the elderly. *Milbank Memorial Fund Quarterly, 61*, 362–396.

Selvin, S. (1991). *Statistical analysis of epidemiologic data.* New York: Oxford University Press.

Smith, D. B. (1990). Population ecology and the racial integration of hospitals and nursing homes in the United States. *Milbank Quarterly, 68*, 561–596.

Stump, T. E., Johnson, R. J., & Wolinsky, F. D. (1995). Changes in physician utilization over time among older adults. *Journal of Gerontology: Social Sciences, 50*, S45–S58.

Vladeck, B. (1980). *Unloving care: The nursing home tragedy.* New York: Basic Books.

Wan, T. T. H. (1989). The behavioral model of health care utilization by older people. In M. Ory & K. Bond (Eds.), *Aging and health care.* New York: Routledge.

Wolinsky, F. D. (1990). *Health and health behavior among elderly Americans: An age-stratification perspective.* New York: Springer.

Wolinsky, F. D., Callahan, C. M., Fitzgerald, J. F., & Johnson, R. J. (1992). The risk of nursing home placement and subsequent death among older adults. *Journal of Gerontology: Social Sciences, 47*, S173–S182.

Wolinsky, F. D., Culler, S. D., Callahan, C. M., & Johnson, R. J. (1994). Hospital resource consumption among older adults: A prospective analysis of episodes, length of stay, and charges over a seven-year period. *Journal of Gerontology: Social Sciences, 49*, S240–S252.

Wolinsky, F. D., & Fitzgerald, J. F. (1994). The risk of hip fracture among noninstitutionalized older adults. *Journal of Gerontology: Social Sciences, 49*, S165–S175.

Wolinsky, F. D., & Johnson, R. J. (1991). The use of health services by older adults. *Journal of Gerontology: Social Sciences, 46*, S345–S357.

Wolinsky, F. D., Johnson, R. J., & Stump, T. E. (1995). The risk of mortality among older adults over an eight-year period. *The Gerontologist, 35*, 150–161.

Wolinsky, F. D., Stump, T. E., Callahan, C. M., & Johnson, R. J. (1994). Consistency and change in functional status among older adults over time. In *Journal of Aging and Health.*

Wolinsky, F. D., Stump, T. E., & Johnson, R. J. (1996). Hospital utilization profiles among older adults over time: Consistency and volume among survivors and decedents. *Journal of Gerontology: Social Sciences, 50*, S88–S100.

Wright, L. K. (1988). A reconceptualization of the 'negative staff attitudes and poor care in nursing homes' assumption. *The Gerontologist, 28*, 813–820.

Commentary: The Role of Physical Health in Understanding Societal Mechanisms for Maintaining Competence in Old Age

Ilene C. Siegler*

The role of a discussant at a conference such as the Penn State Conference reported in this volume is to be provocative and to generate discussion on site and to encourage the major presenter to write a better chapter after the comments than before. Thus, the excellent preceding chapter by Wolinsky, Stump, and Callahan serves as the stimulus for this commentary. A consideration of the role of nursing homes in the life of the elderly when their competence is impaired raises questions of social importance that challenge our research paradigms to make a contribution to something that remains personally frightening in a way that most other topics in aging do not. There has been tremendous progress in gerontology in the past 50 years. The aging population and those of us who study "them" are victims of our own successes. That is, more and more older people live long enough to get frail, and we have, with our findings, convinced the scientific community that behavioral and risk factor interventions can improve the health and the quality of life for all

*Dr. Siegler's work has been supported by grants HL36587 and HL45702 from the National Heart Lung and Blood Institute and by AG09276 and AG12458 from the National Institute on Aging.

131

(see Abeles, Gift, & Ory, 1994; Cassel, Rudberg, & Olshansky, 1992; Kaplan, 1994; Kaufmann, Parker, & Lenfant, 1994).

Wolinsky, Stump, and Callahan challenge this optimistic notion by their finding that nursing home placement, controlling for physical health and other alternative explanations, increases mortality approximately two-fold. They then go on to offer some sociological explanations for their findings:

1. Self-fulfilling prophecy—nursing homes are the societally sanctioned places to die;
2. Failure to thrive as a kind of response to abandonment;
3. Poor quality of care—medical, nursing, and social—in nursing homes; and
4. Activity theory.

The authors then point out that the nursing home is the place where people end up when they have no more choices left and suggest that a hospice is a place to die with a better reputation. They further point to the crux of the matter: nursing homes have a hospicelike function as well as a rehabilitative function, and the LSOA data are inadequate to test this most important hypothesis.

What is one to make of all this? First, how adequate are the data to answer the critically important questions that the author asked? Discussants are invited to comment from the perspective of their own work (see Siegler, 1989; Siegler & O'Keefe, 1992). My first contribution is to push the envelope on the quality of the data to test the model further. Look at Table 3.1. What is missing? First, there are all of the unmeasured variables, the most important being depression and mental status, which have a major impact on nursing home populations (see Gatz & Smyer, 1992; Burns & Taube, 1992). If we assume, for purposes of argument only, that mental status is not part of health, then how well is health controlled? Look at the need characteristics under "ever had" and "had in the past year." This is a very odd way to conceptualize physical health in the elderly. For example, what kinds of heart attacks are not myocardial infarctions? What about the fact that hypertension, atherosclerosis, coronary heart disease, angina, myocardial infarctions, and diabetes often occur in the same person at the same time? And what about the fact that the prevalence for the conditions listed are lower than would generally be expected, even given the odd way they are classified?

Given at baseline, that all LOSA persons are noninstitutionalized data from the National Health Interview Survey for men and women age 75 and older (see Cassel, Rudberg, & Olshansky, 1992, Ex. 1, p. 91) would suggest that 44.67% of men and 58.85% of women report arthritis. This compares favorably to the 54.1% reported in Table 3.1; 29.4% of men and 42.3% of women report hypertension compared to 44.9% in Table 3.1—44.9% seems high; 37.1% of men and 34.2% of women report heart disease, which is significantly higher than even all of the various manifestations of heart disease summed up in Table 3.1. The prevalence of Alzheimer's Disease at .6% seems low as well. So even if the statistics and the modeling procedures control for health data, the techniques cannot be better than the data they are given to work with. Thus, how can the models control for health when it is so poorly measured? Given this, it is difficult to interpret the coefficients for the adjusted odds ratios for the health factors that appear in the models that report the results.

When the data aren't there, there is no way to argue that there was or was not bias introduced in comparing those who did and did not enter nursing homes and those who did and did not die; but the fact that those groups did not differ on the health measures indexed does not prove that they didn't differ in depression as either a chronic condition or as a response to their institutionalization, or that the degree of disease present wasn't a major explanation for the findings. Thus the authors of chapter 3 may or may not have real findings. That is not to say their analyses are incorrect. However, if they had had better measures of health, they might have found differences in models that controlled for health when they included measures of mental health that could account for a twofold mortality difference.

But, assume their findings are correct and that my concerns about the measurement of health, while not unreasonable, are nonetheless insufficient to change the basic findings of the analyses. In response to the indictment of medical care, I ask these questions: What difference would be made if it were perfect? What would perfect medical and nursing care provide? What about things that can't be fixed? Since we aren't yet in a bionic universe and can't replace most parts of the central nervous system, what is the best that could possibly be done? At the end of life, what should happen? When and how should people die? A very thoughtful book provides part of the answer, for which I thank my friend and colleague Howard C. Eisner.

Sherwin B. Nuland (1995) is a very wise and caring physician who has written a best seller called *How We Die: Reflections on Life's Final Chapter*. And when we consider the fate of those in nursing homes—or as Nuland would suggest, the fate of all of us who live long enough to be elderly is basically that no matter what—with time, we wear out. Thus what is to be studied and conquered is disease at ages where cure is possible and premature mortality—but in the very old, perhaps nothing should be done. I don't think that Wolinsky et al.'s findings would surprise Nuland very much [see chapters 1–3 of *How We Die*]. He might even have the courage to ask if the findings are not reasonable. Perhaps by having an earlier mortality, given equivalently poor health, the nursing home is providing a benign function to the elderly by reducing the time of disability and suffering. When none of the options left are good ones, reducing the time spent in the bad ones may not be such a bad deal.

However, if we argue that the findings are correct and that there is no reason that nursing home placement should have any effect on mortality—because, after all, those who don't go to nursing homes are just as old, and if the statistical controls work, they are just as worn out as those who don't, then what of the explanations?

Failure to thrive and self-fulfilling prophecy may be related to depression, and we know that depression is related to mortality and especially to mortality in those with disease (see Anda et al., 1993; Frasure-Smith, Lespearance, & Talajic, 1992; Kaplan & Keil, 1993; Williams & Chesney, 1993). Furthermore, activity theory may be related to its parent— disengagement theory (Cumming & Henry, 1961) or to the findings that suggest that social support and economic resources also predict mortality controlling for health (when the controls for health were state of the art; see Williams et al., 1992). Thus, findings from our own studies of coronary patients that have been replicated by others suggests that it is likely that a combination of poor economic resources, low social support, and depression combined to increase the mortality among those who were institutionalized compared to their peers who were not. While these findings have been on noninstitutionalized persons who are somewhat younger than those under discussion in this commentary, there is little reason to believe that the same mechanisms may not be operative. Furthermore, data on social support, health and the elderly can be found in the excellent chapter by Antonucci and Akiyama, and in the commentary by Carstensen and Lang in this volume. See chapters 13 and 14.

REFERENCES

Abeles, R. P., Gift, H. C., & Ory, M. G. (Eds.). (1994). *Aging and the quality of life.* New York: Springer.

Anda, R., Williamson, D., & Jones, D. (1993). Depressed affect, hopelessness and the risk of ischemic heart disease in a cohort of U.S. adults. *Epidemiology, 4,* 285–294.

Burns, B. J., & Taube, C. A. (1990). Mental health services in general medical care and in nursing homes. In B. S. Fogel, A. Furino, & G. L. Gottlieb (Eds.), *Mental health policy for older Americans: Protecting minds at risk* (pp. 63–84). Washington DC: American Psychiatric Press.

Cassel, C. K., Rudberg, M. A., & Olshansky, S. J. (1992). The price of success: Health care in an aging society. *Health Affairs, 11,* 87–98.

Cumming, E., & Henry, E. W. (1961). *Growing old: The process of disengagement.* New York: Basic Books.

Frasure-Smith, N., Lespearance, F., & Talajic, M. (1993). Depression following myocardial infarction. *JAMA, 164,* 1541–1545.

Gatz, M., & Smyer, M. A. (1992). The mental health system and older adults in the 1990s. *American Psychologist, 47,* 741–751.

Kaplan, G. A. (1994). Reflections on present and future research on bio-behavioral risk factors. In S. J. Blumenthal, K. Matthews, & S. M. Weiss (Eds.), *New research frontiers in behavioral medicine* (pp. 119–134). Washington DC: National Institute of Health, NIH Publication No. 94-3772.

Kaplan, G. A., & Kiel, J. E. (1993). Socioeconomic factors and cardiovascular disease: A review of the literature. *Circulation, 88,* 1973–1993.

Kaufmann, P. G., Parker, S. B., & Lenfant, C. (1994). Behavioral and biomedical research: A partnership for better health. *Psychosomatic Medicine, 56,* 87–89.

Nuland, S. B. (1995). *How we die: Reflections on life's final chapter.* New York: Vintage Books-Random House.

Siegler, I. C. (1989). Developmental health psychology. In M. Storandt & G. R. Vanden Bos (Eds.), *The adult years: Continuity and change* (pp. 119–142). Washington, DC: American Psychological Association.

Siegler, I. C., & O'Keefee, J. E. (1992). *Aging and health.* Invited address presented at the meetings of the American Psychological Association, Washington, DC.

Williams, R. B., Barefoot, J. C., Califf, R. M., Haney, T. L., Saunders, W. B., Pryor, D. B., Hlatky, M. A., Siegler, I. C., & Mark, D. B. (1992). Survival in patients with angiographically documented coronary artery disease: Prognostic importance of social and economic resources in medically treated patients. *Journal of the American Medical Association, 267*(4), 520–524.

Williams, R. B., & Chesney, M. A. (1993). Psychosocial factors and prognosis in established coronary artery disease: The need for research on interventions. *Journal of the American Medical Association, 270,* 1860–1861.

Commentary: Nursing Home Placement and Subsequent Morbidity and Mortality

Laurence G. Branch

W olinsky, Stump, and Callahan (1996) have prepared a most interesting analysis addressing the question "What risks does passing through a nursing home create for those who are placed there?" These authors succinctly summarize the literature that clarifies the risk factors associated with placement in a nursing home, an issue of dominant importance during the past decade. As they point out, however, any rigorous examination of the influence of nursing home placement on subsequent morbidity and mortality has been scant, in large measure attributable to a dearth of appropriate longitudinal data. These investigators rely on multiwave data from the *Longitudinal Study on Aging* (*LSOA*) from 1984 through the 1990 reinterviews, with augmentation from the *National Death Index* (*NDI*) through 1991. They therefore had 934 nursing home placement "events" as the core of their analytic activity, and data to assess "health status trajectories into the sequential pieces occurring before, during, and after (these) nursing home placements" (Chapter 3, p. 97).

When reviewing the previous literature on the influence of nursing home placements on subsequent morbidity and mortality, meager as it is, Wolinsky, Stump, and Callahan note that a prior study by Wolinsky, Callahan, Fitzgerald, and Johnson (1992) reported that those placed in nursing homes were 2.74 times more likely to die than those who remained in the community, based on an adjusted odds ratio, and another study by Aneshensel, Pearlin, and Schular (1993) reported that those placed in nursing homes were 2.10 times more likely to die than those who remained in the community, based on an adjusted odds ratio. However, it appears to me that the generalizability of those analyses is hindered by the possibility of severe selection bias among those individuals who chose to enter a nursing home compared to those who did not. In long-term care, the selection process itself is so little understood that selection bias itself cannot be ruled out as a plausible rival hypothesis to explain adjusted odds ratio differences such as those reported by Wolinsky et al. (1992) and Aneshensel et al. (1993).

THE STAGES OF ANALYSIS

The first stage of their analysis documents the adjusted odds ratio of various predictors of subsequent nursing home placement. The goodness of fit of their models is not appreciably better than the fit of other models in the literature, all of which have been disappointing to this reader of the literature, including my own study published well over a decade ago (Branch & Jette, 1982). Our ability to predict nursing home placement by the configuration of predisposing, enabling, and need characteristics so often measured in our national surveys is simply disquieting. From my own perspective, it seems to me that precipitating events such as a significant change in the health status of the individual or a substantial change in the configuration of support systems may be triggering events that force a decision concerning long-term care, and that decision may be nursing home placement. To the extent that the hypothesis of a precipitating stimulus applies, the periodicity of our typical multiyear longitudinal data systems (e.g., reinterviewing respondents every year or 2 as is the usual case) simply will not tap the critical precipitating events. An entirely different longitudinal design would be necessary in my opinion to learn more about the factors that are truly related to the decision concerning institutional placement. Fortunately, the present analysis is not trying to fill this void in the literature, but rather trying to clarify another void, namely, the implication of nursing home placement once made on subsequent morbidity and mortality.

The second and third stages of this creative analysis quantify the risk of dying associated with nursing home placement over the 8 years of follow-up (i.e., between the 1984 baseline interviews and the end of calendar year 1991). These investigators identified 21 variables that produced statistically significant associations with mortality in this cohort of 7,351 *LSOA* respondents, including the variable of placement in a nursing home any time after baseline. In fact, they report that placement in a nursing home is associated with a 96% increase in the likelihood of dying compared to those not having been placed in a nursing home, after adjusting for all the other covariates in the multiple logistic regression model. This finding is impressive indeed. As they show in their Table 3.3, age was the most salient risk factor for death in this cohort, followed closely by gender, and in third place in their model was the variable of interest for this investigation—having been placed in the nursing home after baseline. Determining the attributable risk of dying to nursing home placement, Wolinsky, Stump, and Callahan calculated an absolute difference in the probability of dying associated with nursing home placement after adjustments for all of the covariates in the model at 0.36, which they describe as "rather impressive as well." I concur. This result is startling to me and may be important for the continuing development of public policy.

One variable missing from their model that would seem to be particularly important for a fuller understanding of the role of institutional long-term care on subsequent morbidity and mortality is the availability and use of community-based long-term care as an alternative to institutional long-term care. Unfortunately, it appears that the *LSOA* data set did not have an appropriate measure that would have allowed a comparison of the role of institutional long-term care use versus community long-term care use on subsequent morbidity and mortality. If such a measure had been available, perhaps the selection bias problems could have been attenuated with a focused analysis on the subset of *LSOA* respondents who chose one form of long-term care over the other (i.e., institutional long-term care compared to community long-term care). The analysis I propose unfortunately will have to wait until another time.

The fourth stage of their analysis is interpreted by Wolinsky, Stump, and Callahan as "provid[ing] impressive evidence to rule out the critical competing explanation that both institutionalization (i.e., nursing home placement) and death are merely markers of the same underlying process of deteriorating health status" (Chapter 3, p. 122). They acknowledge, however, that their evidence is not definitive. The implications of this analysis are among the most far reaching of this stimulating report. More definitive findings will be welcomed by all serious readers. However, it is worth noting that these authors have placed some confidence in these preliminary findings.

Stage five examines whether nursing home placement has an independent and significant effect on subsequent morbidity, as defined by decreasing functional status trajectories after controlling for all the relevant covariates. The authors state that ''even after controlling for the baseline level of functional status, the other 48 variables taken from the behavioral model, and the 10 indicators of functional status trajectories for the periods before and during the nursing home placement, the nursing home placement results in statistically significant increases in basic ADL difficulties and lower body limitations'' (Chapter 3, p. 119). Again, the authors' interpretation of this analysis is unequivocal: nursing home placement itself is associated with significant morbidity defined in terms of decreasing functional status.

INTERPRETATIONS OF THE ANALYSIS

In their discussion, Wolinsky, Stump, and Callahan present four intriguing possible interpretations for their finding that nursing home placement is significantly associated with subsequent functional status decline and mortality. The first hypothesized mechanism is a variant of the self-fulfilling prophecy hypothesis, namely, that nursing home placement per se can lead the nursing home staff to assume that culturally defined stereotypical behavior of institutionalized patients will occur, and these cultural stereotypes include functional decline and death.

The second hypothetical mechanism suggested is an adaptation of the failure-to-thrive hypothesis originally offered in pediatrics, but in this instance applied to older adults. In this adaptation, the failure-to-thrive hypothesis seems to rest on the assumption of self-fulfilling expectations held by the residents themselves that they will fail to thrive. This failure-to-thrive hypothesis rests on expectations of the residents, in contrast to the previous hypothesis of the self-fulfilling prophecy, which rests on expectations of the nursing home staff that nursing home residents deteriorate in function.

The third hypothesized mechanism is predicated on the assumption that the quality of care provided to nursing home residents is inadequate at best and perhaps tragic at worst. The responsibility underlying this plausible operating mechanism previously had been placed squarely at the feet of the medical profession by Kane (1991).

The fourth hypothesized mechanism is based on the activity theory/ disengagement theory offered in various ways in gerontologic literature. This theory would suggest that individuals placed in nursing homes have reduced opportunities to be active because of the nature of the environment; consequently, their activity levels erode and functional limitations replace their prior levels of activity. The authors point out that a primary difference between this fourth hypothesized mechanism of activity theory and the second hypothesized operation mechanism, or failing to thrive, is based on the generally involuntary nature of the former compared to the voluntary nature of the later.

CONCLUSION

In summary, Wolinsky, Stump, and Callahan have presented a most inter- esting hypothesis, namely, that nursing home placement itself is associated with increased mortality and morbidity. I commend them for the thorough- ness of their analytic model; very few colleagues if any could analyze the secondary data better than they have. The data available to them were from the *Longitudinal Study on Aging* (*LSOA*), a data set with both strengths and weaknesses. Their analyses offer compelling data to support their hypothesis that nursing home placement becomes a separate and important stimulus for subsequent functional decline in mortality of its residents for other variables, rather than the more benign hypothesis that nursing home placement is yet another step in a longer trajectory of decline of people at the end of their lives. The data that support this thesis should demand the attention of all serious students of gerontology and long-term care policy. Further investigation of this thesis with other data sets—data sets that include indicators for the availability and use of community long-term care and whose reference population is more com- prehensible than the by-product of the *LSOA*'s complex sampling strat- egy—are indeed warranted. Wolinsky, Stump, and Callahan have offered an interesting hypothesis and provided the first preliminary test.

REFERENCES

Aneshensel, C. S., Pearlin, L. I., & Schular, R. H. (1993). Stress, role captivity, and the cessation of caregiving. *Journal of Health and Social Behavior*, *34*, 54–70.

Branch, L. G., & Jette, A. M. (1982). A prospective study of long-term care institutionalization among the aged. *American Journal of Public Health*, *72*(12), 1373–1379.

Kane, R. M. (1991). Foreword. In J. G. Ouslander, D. Osterweil, & J. Morley (Eds.), *Medical care in the nursing home*. New York: McGraw-Hill.

Wolinsky, F. D., Callahan, C. M., Fitzgerald, J. F., & Johnson, R. J. (1992). The risk of nursing home placement and subsequent death among older adults. *Journals of Gerontology: Social Sciences*, *47*(4), S173–S182.

CHAPTER 4

Long-Term Care Institutions and the Maintenance of Competence: A Dialectic between Compensation and Overcompensation

Margret M. Baltes and Ann L. Horgas

Loss of autonomy, lack of competence, and increasing dependency in old age is of long-standing interest to gerontologists from different disciplines. Dependence is often used as a criterion in deciding about a person's living situation; that is, whether to be institutionalized or not. The purpose of this chapter is twofold: (1) to summarize our research on the role of the social environment of institutions in fostering dependency and on interventions in the social environment to promote independence, and (2) to discuss dependency in relation to the more general concept of everyday competence.

The best-known types of dependency in old age are structured and physical dependency. The former is a research object of sociologists; the latter the subject of epidemiologists. In our work, *behavioral dependency* has been the focus. It is defined as a "characteristic of individual behavior" (e.g., asking for help, accepting help from others, being passive) and is analyzed in terms of the social environment in which it takes place. As such, our research on dependency is focused at microsocial structures.

THEORETICAL BACKGROUND

To date, there are two theoretical paradigms, supported by sizable bodies of empirical research, that address the environmental conditions of behavioral dependency in old age: the model of learned helplessness (Seligman, 1975) and the model of learned dependency (Baltes, 1982, 1988, 1995, 1996). Both models are grounded in social learning theory and consider dependency as the outcome of a learning process. The etiologies and consequences of dependency in the two models are, however, antithetical.

Seligman (1975) and his collaborators have demonstrated that when there is a lack of systematic, predictable connections between behavioral and environmental events (i.e., when there is noncontingency), animals and humans learn that their behaviors have no differential consequences. Repeated experience with such noncontingency results in negative outcomes, such as cognitive deficits, motivational and emotional deficits. In turn, these deficits lead to lower performance, passivity and depression, respectively. Later ''cognitive'' reformulations of the original model have added attributional perspectives (Abramson, Seligman, & Teasdale, 1978). People in this situation perceive the lack of behavioral consequences as failure and attribute it to personal incompetence, an unresponsive environment, or both. Depending on one's attributional style, noncontingency is believed to lead to the experience of lack of control and, in turn, to learned helplessness and dependency. Thus noncontingency between behavior and environmental response is at the root of learned helplessness, and loss is the salient definition of learned helplessness-based dependency (e.g., loss of control over contingencies or responses).

In contrast to Seligman's model of learned helplessness, the model of *learned dependency* assumes *differential environmental contingencies for dependent versus independent behaviors as well as differential (or multifunctional) outcomes for dependency* (M. Baltes, 1988, 1995, 1996; M. Baltes & Skinner, 1983). Therefore, differential contingency is the basis of learned dependency, and the dynamic between gains and losses is the most salient definition of ''learned dependency'' (see also M. Baltes & Skinner). Thus, theoretically, the two models differ in their specification of the two sources of dependency (e.g., noncontingency versus contingency) and their evaluation of the resulting outcome (e.g., dependency as only loss or also as gain). Practically, they differ in their implications for intervention (i.e., whether to intervene and in which direction to intervene).

FINDINGS FROM THE LEARNED DEPENDENCY MODEL

To analyze the social environmental system producing dependency, my collaborators and I have employed three convergent methodological strategies: experiments, sequential observation, and ecological intervention (Baer, 1973). With regard to the experimental work and findings, suffice it here to conclude that dependent behavior is not always the consequence of incompetence due to physical or mental impairment; rather, environmental factors are at least coresponsible in its development and maintenance. Of specific importance in the present context are the findings from sequential observation and ecological intervention research. These will be described next.

Sequential Observation

The sequential observation research approach established the impact of social environmental consequences on dependent behaviors in everyday life. In particular, we examined the interactive stream of behaviors between elderly persons and their social partners during morning care situations. By the term "social partners" we mean other persons such as staff members who interact with the focus person. This research was conducted in a variety of living environments, including long-term care institutions and private dwellings. In specific, the behaviors of both the elderly target person and his or her social partner were observed. To record the stream of behavior or the interaction between these two actors, we used an electronic device that allowed the recording of the elders' behavior along five categories and of the partners' behavior along six categories. The five categories for the elderly were sleeping, constructively engaged, destructively engaged, nonengaged, independent self-care and dependent self-care behaviors. The six categories for social partners' behaviors were engagement supportive, nonengagement-supportive, independence-supportive, dependence-supportive behavior, no response, and leaving. Any behavior could follow any other behavior. Consequent events could result from staff or from self. Responses by staff were labeled congruent (dependence-supportive behavior following dependent behavior) or incongruent (independence-supportive behavior following dependent behavior) aside from not reacting at all (no response) or leaving the room. Responses from self could refer to any behavior of the focus resident (i.e., independent behavior following an independent act, independent behavior following a dependent act or vice versa, or constructively engaged behavior following sleeping). In Figure 4.1, only the continuation of the antecedent behavior with the same type of behavior is presented as well as responses from others.

We demonstrated that the dominant interaction pattern in these microsocial systems is one in which dependent behaviors of the elderly are immediately attended to, while independent behaviors are ignored. *In other words, it was dependent behavior rather than independent behavior on the part of the elderly that "produced" social responses* (see Figure 4.1, two left columns). Dependent behaviors of elderly adults, more than any other actions in their behavioral repertoire, resulted in immediate and congruent reactions from social partners. As a consequence, dependent behaviors initiated and provided social contact (for a review, see M. Baltes, 1982, 1988, 1995; M. Baltes & Reisenzein, 1986; M. Baltes & Wahl, 1987), whereas *independent* behaviors did *not* prompt responses from others. In fact, independent self-care behaviors were mostly ignored and independent prosocial (constructively engaged) behaviors were followed by a congruent, supportive response with only a 25% probability. There were practically no incongruent behavior interactions, that is, independent behavior followed by dependence-supportive or dependent behavior by independence-supportive behaviors of staff.

The observed patterns relating to dependent and independent behaviors of older adults are highly robust and replicable across cultures (e.g., Germany and the United States), nursing homes, gender, length of institutionalization, and health status, but they are old-age specific. Because of the high predictability and reliability of these behavioral patterns, we have labeled them the "dependency-support script" and the "independence-ignore script."

Moreover, a study of elderly adults and their partners in private dwellings (M. Baltes & Wahl, 1992; Wahl & M. Baltes, 1990) showed that the dependency-support script was not specific to institutions (see Figure 4.1, middle and right two columns). Even in their homes, interactions

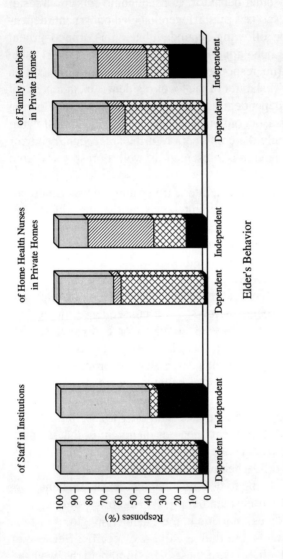

FIGURE 4.1   Dependency-support script in response to elders' antecedent self-care behavior across three settings.

between elders and their social partners, whether home health nurses or family members, were dominated by the dependency-support script. There was, however, greater diversity in interaction patterns in the home setting. Elders' independent and dependent behaviors were followed by both congruent and incongruent responses. This is particularly noticeable in the case of independent behavior of the elderly person (see Figure 4.1). In contrast to the institutionalized elderly adults, community-dwelling elders could not be 100% certain which consequence would follow their independent behavior, although the likelihood was greater for dependence-supportive behavior or punishment to occur.

For the most part, the social environment accepts dependent behavior as appropriate and congruent with normative expectations of aging. Reichert (1993) was able to confirm this suggestion in a laboratory study that compared nurses and educators' interactions with elderly people in problem-solving situations. Nurses' interactions with elders were characterized by significantly more direct and immediate helping behaviors, a finding that may be a product of the medical helping model in which responsibilities are taken over by the medical environment and the caregivers. Thus social expectations and stereotypes of aging are likely to contribute to the production of a ''dependency-support script.''

This view is further confirmed by the attributional styles held by elderly persons and their social partners with regard to dependent and independent behaviors. When confronting elders and their social partners with their respective observed behaviors, Wahl (1991) found that partners ascribed responsibility for dependent behaviors to the elderly persons but took credit for elders' independent behavior. In contrast, elderly persons ascribed responsibility to themselves for their independent behavior, but attributed their dependent behavior either to illness or to their environment (i.e., the behavior of social partners).

In sum, the dependency-support script describes an environment that is overresponsive and overprotective, thereby fostering dependent behaviors at the cost of independent behaviors. This overprotective environment is insensitive to the old person's strengths and competencies and tends to compensate for weaknesses that are not there; that is, it overcompensates. Negative social expectations about old persons are, indeed, a major factor in the production of the ''dependency-support script.'' Therefore, intervention geared at changing this seemingly dysfunctional interaction pattern appears to be the only plausible conclusion. Qualifications are needed, however, before proceeding with any intervention (see also Horgas, Wahl, & Baltes, 1996).

We have to realize that, in the context of the "dependency-support and independence-ignore script," dependent behaviors are instrumental in securing social consequences, attention, and contact; that is, in exerting control (albeit passive control) over the social world. In this sense, dependent behaviors are highly functional and adaptive. They represent not only a *loss* in the form of reduced autonomy but also a *gain* through control over social contact. This fact makes at least the goal of intervention controversial. Clearly, the goal of making everyone independent at any cost is neither realistic nor appropriate. In the case of learned helplessness, intervention is usually warranted. In the case of learned dependency, intervention can be the desired avenue if change is geared primarily at increasing the independence-support script. In other words, the goal of intervention cannot be to ignore dependent behavior but instead to reinforce independent behavior, that is, to tie social contact and social interaction more to *independent* behavior rather than to dependent behavior. Thus the target of intervention is increasing the independence-support script and decreasing the independence-ignore script rather than eliminating the dependence-support script.

Ecological Intervention

With this in mind, we designed a training program for social partners, that is, the caregiver, that stresses responsiveness to autonomy and independence. To date, we have implemented the intervention approach in the social world of institutions (M. Baltes, Neumann, & Zank, 1994) and demonstrated the intended effects of the training program (see Figure 4.2). Following training, caregivers exhibited more independence-supportive behaviors both in response to (that is, contingent on) independent behaviors as well as in response to dependent behaviors of the elderly residents when compared to nontrained caregivers (see Figure 4.2). In addition, dependence-supportive behavior declined in response to independent behavior in the experimental group and also in response to dependent behavior, albeit in both the experimental and control groups (see left side of Figure 4.2). As a consequence of the increase in independence-supportive behaviors among the staff, independent behaviors among the residents also increased (not shown in Figure 4.2). In principle, then, it is possible

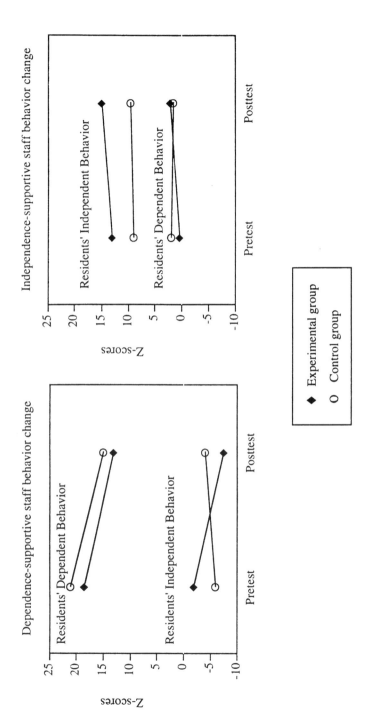

FIGURE 4.2 Intervention training effects.

to alter the prevalent dependency-support and independence-ignore script of the social world of elderly nursing home residents. The resulting environment is one that stimulates and fosters independent behavior and continues, albeit less frequently, to be responsive to dependency. In other words, the environment can be fitted to both the strengths and the weaknesses of elderly adults, which creates a balance between security (dependence-supportive behavior) and stimulation (independence-supportive behavior; see also Parmalee & Lawton, 1990).

Because of the losses that come with age, there is often little doubt that support is needed. The question is, who or what decides when there is to be support for dependency and when there should be demand for or stimulation of independence? The answers to these questions depend, to some extent, on elderly individuals' desires and capabilities. At a more general level, the decision of the extent to which independence and dependence should be supported depends on the *competence* level of the older person. This seems particularly important because dependency, even in very circumscribed areas, is often generalized by the staff to signify general incompetence of the elderly person (Collopy, 1988). Questions arise as to what factors influence the competence level of elders in everyday life? Where and how can we intervene prior to the occurrence of dependency? These issues and questions have led us to consider the concept of everyday competence in late life to enrich, broaden, and complement our work on dependency.

Everyday Competence in Late Life

During the past several years, we have made an attempt to tackle conceptual and measurement issues of everyday competence. We will first present a theoretical rationale for a recently proposed two-component model of everyday competence. Second, we will present some empirical evidence regarding this multidimensional model of everyday competence and factors, including institutions, which influence it.

THE MEANING OF EVERYDAY

The study of everyday competence must first address the concept of *every day* and of *competence*. The entity of every day can be characterized by three dimensions: a temporal, a social, and a geographical or physical one (Braudel, 1992; Lehr & Thomae, 1991). Thus, the day, the social roles, and the physical environment set the scene for opportunities for and restrictions on the occurrence of behaviors. The more often these occurrences are repeated, the more likely it is that they become a behavioral norm or a typical day, thus representing a structure and a characteristic way of behaving. This approach to the study of every day requires the assessment of all the activities that elderly persons engage in during a typical day, as well as the context in which they occur.

THE MEANING OF EVERYDAY COMPETENCE

Inferring from the preceding paragraph, everyday competence is the orchestration of efforts and skills in the management of daily life within multiple domains. How competently one organizes or orchestrates one's life depends on his or her resources as well as the environmental demands. As such, the assessment of how competently a person handles a typical day of his or her life requires us to consider the sequence of activities done on an average day *and* their social and physical embeddedness. Competence in our approach and, we would argue in any approach, is measured via performance. We agree with Lawton (1983) that "these capacity-oriented constructs, however, are usually not directly measurable. Therefore, one way to measure competence is to define behaviors that imply the presence of some element of competence" (p. 350). Granted, measurement can be closer or further away from tapping capacity or reserves. For instance, a measurement procedure using a testing the limits approach yields performance data that more closely reflect reserves and capacities than a one-time baseline assessment. In our work, a multidimensional assessment of everyday competence via the Yesterday Interview was used.

The *Yesterday Interview*, first developed by Moss and Lawton (1982), is an instrument that allows us to measure or quantify the complexity and richness of the activities completed during one day in an elderly person's life. The frequency and duration of activities engaged in by the participant during the day preceding the interview are assessed, as well as the location, the social embeddedness (e.g., presence of social partners), and the experienced difficulty level of the performed activities (e.g., the effort it takes to conduct the activity and whether assistive devices are used). From these data, activity profiles can be developed that reflect different levels of social, cognitive, self-care, and leisure activities. In addition, the variability in activities within activity styles can be determined. By assessing the contextual dimensions of the activities (i.e., the location and the presence of social partners), we can also get a flavor of the richness and complexity of participants' social roles and social engagement. In addition, the level of perceived difficulty associated with the reported activities provides a measure of self-efficacy regarding the activities in which elders are engaged.

A TWO-TIERED MODEL
OF EVERYDAY COMPETENCE: BACO AND EXCO

Recently, we proposed a classification of everyday competence in late life in two components: a *ba*sic level of *co*mpetence (BaCo) and an *ex*panded level of *co*mpetence (ExCo) (M. Baltes, Mayr, Borchelt, Maas, & Wilms, 1993; M. Baltes, Maas, Wilms, & Borchelt, 1996). Our multidimensional and contextual perspective of everyday competence is consistent with earlier attempts in the literature to differentiate between Activities of Daily Living (ADL), Instrumental Activities of Daily Living (IADL), and Advanced Activities of Daily Living (AADL) (see, for instance, Lawton, 1983; Fitzgerald, Smith, Martin, Freedman, & Wolinsky, 1993). It is new in that it proposes a theoretical argument for the differentiation in two components.

First, we argue, that basic level of competence (BaCo) is related to activities that are necessary for survival and are largely automated and normative for independent living in adulthood in Western societies. One can expect these activities to be more or less universal and less affected by cultural variations. In contrast, expanded level of competence (ExCo) relates to activities that reflect preferences, motivations, and specific skills of people and that influence the overall quality of life.

Second, we propose that both components will be differentially affected by contextual and personal resources. Because of the universal nature of BaCo, we expect it to be less affected by sociocultural, psychological, and economic factors but more highly influenced by health-related factors. On the other hand, ExCo reflects discretionary and leisure activities and should be more heavily influenced by variability in behavioral and social resources (see Figure 4.3).

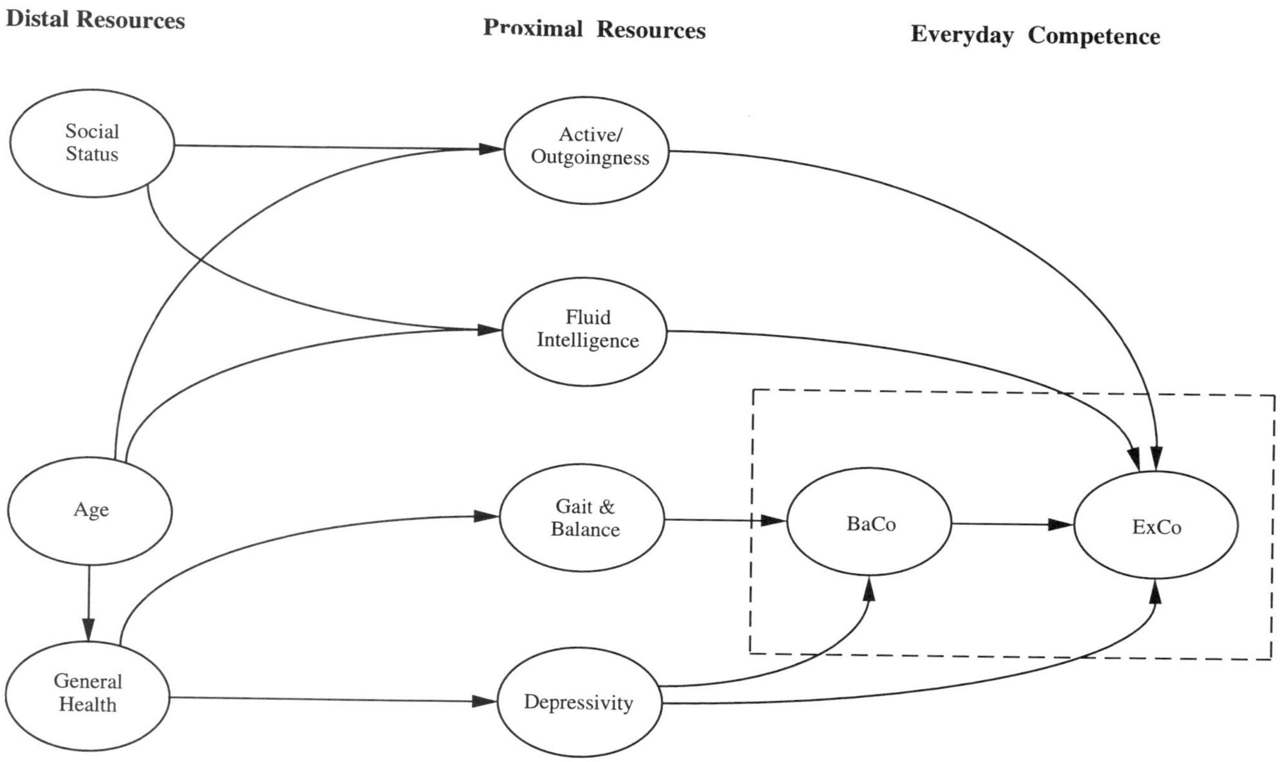

Distal Resources   Proximal Resources   Everyday Competence

FIGURE 4.3   Two-component model of everyday competence.

Empirical Findings on Everyday Competence

We have tested this two-component model of everyday competence that is differentially predicted by various health and psychosocial factors within the Berlin Aging Study (BASE), an interdisciplinary study of a representative sample of 70- to 103-year-old residents of West Berlin (see P. Baltes, Helmchen, Mayer, & Steinhagen-Thiessen, 1993, for more detailed information about BASE). A structural equation model was fitted to test the differential prediction of BaCo and ExCo from health-related and social-psychological factors (see Figure 4.3). The results support our main hypotheses that (a) there are two distinct, but interrelated, components of competence, basic and expanded competence, and (b) these two components are differentially predicted by health, fluid intelligence, personality factors, and social resources. BaCo was most strongly predicted by gait and balance and depressivity; ExCo was most strongly related to fluid intelligence and active/outgoingness. (These analyses have been described more fully in M. Baltes et al., 1993 and M. Baltes et al., 1996).

The system of resources considered in this model explains a total of 85% of the reliable variance in BaCo and 91% of the reliable variance in ExCo. Thus we have good evidence to support our two-component model of everyday competence and its differential association with other person and contextual variables. The reader has probably noticed that no contextual variables were included in the model. This is the case because socioeconomic status indicators statistically outperform the contextual variables, such as setting, that we have available in BASE.

For this reason, however, we have begun to explore the influence of institutionalization and context on BaCo and ExCo using separate analyses. In this context, we have also begun to examine the role of social support in general in maintaining BaCo and ExCo. Empirical findings in each of these domains will be described next.

THE INFLUENCE OF CONTEXT ON BACO AND EXCO

How are BaCo and ExCo activities influenced by context? We examined the role of context in two ways. First, we assessed whether or not the amount of time spent and the variability in BaCo and ExCo activities differed across residential context (i.e., institutionalized versus community-dwelling). Here, institutionalization was defined as residing in a nursing home or sheltered care setting. Second, we investigated the relationship between the social and the immediate physical context of activities and the two domains of competence.

Residential Context

Using analyses of covariance models, we assessed whether the amount of time spent in basic and expanded competence activities differed by residential status, controlling for functional limitations, marital status, gender, and age. The results indicated that institutionalized persons spent significantly less time doing ExCo activities than the noninstitutionalized elders (about 7 hours versus 10 hours per day), but there was no effect of residential status on the amount of time spent in BaCo activities (see Figure 4.4). Both groups spent about 3 hours per day with these activities. Similar analyses examining the variability in activities revealed that institutionalized elders did fewer different BaCo and ExCo activities, although the magnitude of the difference was more pronounced for ExCo activities. Thus it appears that elderly subjects residing in institutional settings spent the same amount of time doing basic self-care activities as community-dwelling elders, but did fewer different basic activities during that time. In addition, institutionalized older adults spent less time in and had a more restricted range of ExCo activities.

Social and Physical Context

Due to the richness of the *Yesterday Interview* data, we can obtain a closer look at the social and physical context of daily activities within the broader context of where the person resides. In particular, we can examine whether activities are done alone or with others and whether they are done inside or outside of one's private quarters for both community-dwelling and institutionalized subjects.

Again, analysis of covariance models were conducted to determine whether the amount of time spent in basic and expanded competence activities in different social and geographic contexts differed by residential status, after controlling for functional impairment, sex, marital status, and age. Differences between institutionalized and community-dwelling elders emerged only with regard to time spent doing indoor BaCo and ExCo activities alone (see Figure 4.5).

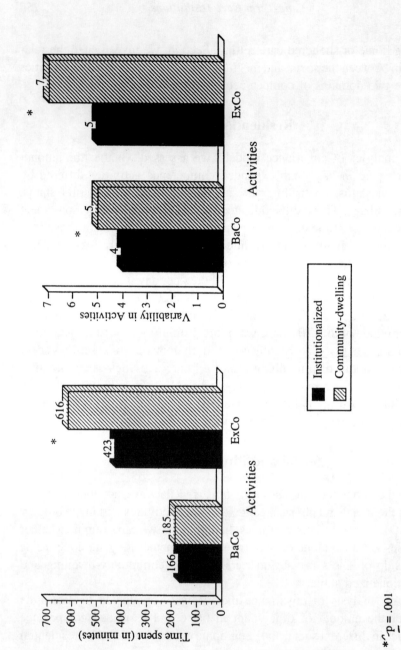

FIGURE 4.4 Effect of residential context on time and variability in basic and expanded competence activities (covariate adjusted means).

*ʌp = .001

156

The following interpretations are possible when considering social, physical, and residential context and time spent in activities (see Figures 4.4 and 4.5). In the case of BaCo, less time spent alone indoors may very well be the result of a compensatory, albeit often an overcompensatory effect by social partners, indicating that others are providing assistance with or actually taking over basic self-care tasks. This is corroborated by the finding that nursing home residents spent more time in BaCo activities with others. In the case of ExCo activities, a positive interpretation of less time alone indoors would consider social partners as stimuli to engage in ExCo activities. Such an interpretation loses its credibility, however, when considering that institutionalized elders spent overall less time in ExCo activities. Thus, spending less time alone indoors in ExCo activities might just be due to the very environment in which the older people are living. Institutions are places where a group of people lives together, which means that people may represent figures but not necessarily meaningful contacts.

THE ROLE OF SOCIAL SUPPORT IN MAINTAINING COMPETENCE

Accordingly, we examined the role of social support in relation to BaCo and ExCo more explicitly by examining the social networks of the participants in the BASE study. In particular, we assessed the relationship between instrumental and emotional support, functional status (i.e., limitations in ADL and IADL), and time spent in BaCo and ExCo activities (Marsiske et al., 1994). With regard to instrumental and emotional support, participants were asked who provided assistance with a variety of instrumental and emotional support tasks, and how much help they provided. These analyses showed that subjects with no functional limitations who received high amounts of instrumental support spent *less* time in ExCo activities. Conversely, at low levels of functioning, high levels of instrumental support were related to more time in ExCo activities.

Thus, it appears that help, when it is not explicitly needed, may have an inhibitory effect on activity participation. In contrast, help appears to have a compensatory or facilitating effect among those with measurable needs for assistance. As such, we again see evidence to support the dependency-support script among older adults. These findings point to the need to consider the influence of context on everyday competence

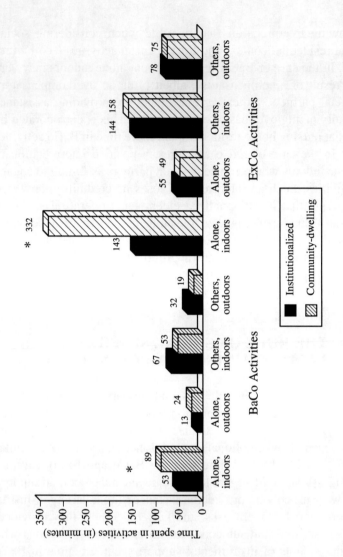

FIGURE 4.5 Effects of physical, residential, and social contexts on time spent in basic and expanded competence activities (covariance adjusted means).

*$p = .001$.

activities in yet another way. By examining not only the residential, social and physical context, but also the immediate context of caregiving needs, we can gain a richer, more multidimensional understanding of everyday competence in late life and factors that foster and hinder it.

Summary and Conclusions

From the results presented here, it is clear that long-term care institutions play an important role in promoting and maintaining both dependency and independence or incompetence and competence in late life. First, there is considerable evidence that too much physical assistance, that is, overprotection or overcompensation, by nursing home caregivers can induce and maintain behavioral dependency. This phenomenon has been labeled the ''dependency-support script.'' Although this interactional pattern has been shown to extend beyond the nursing home to other caregiving situations, it is most exclusive in long-term care settings. There is a tendency to regard elderly people as incompetent and in need of help that is given even when not needed. The environment tends to overcompensate and overprotect. Though not explicitly examined in our work, this over-compensation could result in a number of adverse physical and psychological consequences. Some of these could include increased physical frailty (because of disuse), depression, and hopelessness, which may, in turn, contribute to the high rates of mortality among newly admitted nursing home residents (see Wolinsky, Chapter 3 in this volume).

In contrast, however, nursing homes play an important compensatory role that becomes necessary when competence level has been reduced below a level necessary for adequate daily functioning. By providing needed assistance in basic self-care activities (BaCo) when needed, nursing home residents are able to maintain levels of engagement in social and leisure activities (ExCo) that are comparable to noninstitutionalized elders. In particular, nursing home residents spend less time doing solitary, indoor activities and spend approximately the same amount of time with others and going outdoors as noninstitutionalized elders. Thus there is a differential effect of institutionalization on everyday competence depending on the social (with others versus alone) and physical context (indoors versus outdoors) and the type of activity (BaCo versus ExCo) considered.

As such, the nursing home context represents an environment with low demands and thereby yields an important adaptive strategy for dealing with physical, mental, and social incompetencies often associated with advanced old age (P. Baltes & M. Baltes, 1990). In this sense, dependency and institutionalization may become an integral part of successful aging that helps individuals to maintain the highest level of competence possible. One model of successful aging, *selective optimization with compensation*, argues that dependency or other forms of performance or activity reductions may have positive, adaptive value (P. Baltes & M. Baltes, 1990). With regard to behavioral dependency, the elderly person faced with increasing losses in reserves and strength has several choices:

1. to give up the domains and activities hampered by functional loss;
2. to compensate for losses by searching for new means to maintain activities; or
3. to become increasingly dependent in those weakened or threatened domains to free energy for the pursuit of other activities that have higher personal priority.

In the latter strategy, the person acknowledges losses and delegates some control to others as a form of proxy control.

The model of selective optimization with compensation (P. Baltes & M. Baltes, 1990) highlights the possible adaptive potential of lowered performance such as behavioral dependency. This model argues that effective coordination of three processes, *selection, compensation*, and *optimization*, facilitates successful aging despite the losses encountered and a reduction in reserve capacities. *Selection* refers to the fact that age-related losses often require a reduction in the range of activities and domains of functioning. The remaining domains are of higher personal priority and involve a convergence of environmental demands, individual motivations, skills, and biological capacities. The second component, *compensation*, becomes important when life tasks require a level of performance beyond that currently possible. Compensation becomes operative when losses and reductions of behavioral capacities are experienced by older adults, particularly in regard to situations or goals that demand high levels of physical or mental functioning for adequate performance. The third component, *optimization*, is derived from the argument that it is also possible to maintain high levels of functioning in old age in some selected domains through practice and acquisition of new bodies of knowledge and technology. Consideration of this model of successful aging with its emphasis on increased selection and compensation in late life suggests that dependency may not represent only helplessness, lack of control, dysfunction, or passive control of social contact. Instead, dependency may represent self-selection and the outcome of a process of active selection and compensation.

More broadly, this model illustrates the potential importance of nursing homes as an important compensatory mechanism for some older adults that minimizes the losses associated with aging and maximizes well being and functioning. By compensating for physical, mental, social, and functional losses, nursing homes provide support for functioning in both basic self-care and expanded social and leisure domains. The evidence presented here indicates that, in terms of the time spent doing basic self-care and expanded social and leisure activities, nursing home residents do not differ dramatically from community-dwelling elders. The major difference between the activities of elderly adults in the two residential contexts was in terms of the time spent alone: those residing in long-term care settings spent less time alone. This lends support to the notion that moving to a long-term care setting can be an important compensatory mechanism for coping with late-life losses and can help elders to maintain some level of competence in their everyday lives, which may contribute to the quality of life and well being.

In sum, nursing homes have to be highly sensitive to the competence levels of its residents. The same kind of assistance can be compensation or overcompensation depending on the competence level of the resident it is given to. In this sense, assistance has to be tailor-made not to over- or underestimate the strengths of a resident. Nursing homes have the difficult task of walking on a tightrope and keeping balance between compensation and demands.

At least two caveats should be mentioned. In this chapter, we have focused on selected aspects of context such as the immediate social, residential, and geographic contexts of activities. We have not considered more macroecological contextual factors of living spaces that impact the lives and activities of older adults. Certainly, there is great heterogeneity among nursing homes and other long-term care contexts, with possible differential consequences for dependency and competence among its residents.

Further, we consider competence only in terms of the actual performance of activities throughout the day. Despite the richness of the data from the *Yesterday Interview*, we are only able to assess the types of activities, the amount of time spent doing them, and the variability within activity types. Certainly, there are likely to be differences in the quality of actual behavioral competence between those who live in nursing homes and those who do not. In addition, we only considered time spent in activities, not the time spent in resting. If we considered the latter, the greater amount of resting in nursing home residents' profiles of daily activities becomes glaringly obvious. Even so, it will be necessary to know the spacing of resting periods throughout the day's activities before judging it as an indicator of incompetence or competence.

In conclusion, we believe we have highlighted the difficult task with which nursing homes, in particular, and caregiving contexts for the aged, in general, are faced. The line between compensation and overcompensation is a fine one, and caregivers must tailor their level of assistance to each resident's needs and be sensitive to changes in the resident's competence level over time. This is not always an easy task, especially given the realities of nursing home caregiving work with its generally high ratio of residents to staff, high staff turnover rates, and relatively low levels of staff education and training. Nonetheless, nursing homes are an important context of aging for many older adults, and one that can play a vital compensatory role in maintaining some level of competence. The challenge for nursing homes is to create a caregiving context that promotes individually appropriate levels of compensation and stimulation among the residents and to provide the caregiving staff with the necessary resources and skills to help achieve this goal.

REFERENCES

Abramson, L. Y., Seligman, M. E. P., & Teasdale, J. Y. (1978). Learned helplessness in humans: Critique and reformation. *Journal of Abnormal Psychology, 87,* 49–74.

Baer, D. J. (1973). The control of developmental processes: Why wait? In J. R. Nesselroade & H. W. Reese (Eds.), *Life-span developmental psychology: Methodological issues* (pp. 187–193). New York: Academic Press.

Baltes, M. M. (1982). Environmental factors in dependence among nursing home residents: A social ecology analysis. In T. A. Wills (Ed.), *Basic processes in helping relationships* (pp. 405–425). New York: Academic Press.

Baltes, M. M. (1988). The etiology and maintenance of dependency in the elderly: Three phases of operant research. *Behavior Therapy, 19,* 301–319.

Baltes, M. M. (1995). Dependency in old age: Gains and losses. *Current Directions in Psychological Science, 4,* 14–19.

Baltes, M. M. (1996). *The many faces of dependency in old age.* New York: Cambridge University Press.

Baltes, M. M., Maas, I., Wilms, H. U., & Borchelt, M. (1996). Alltagskompetenz in Alter: Theoretische Überlegungen und empirische Befunde [Everyday competence in old age: Theoretical overview and empirical findings]. In K. U. Mayer & P. B. Baltes (Eds.), *The Berlin aging study* (pp. 525–542). Berlin: Akademie Verlag.

Baltes, M. M., Mayr, U., Borchelt, M., Maas, I., & Wilms, H. U. (1993). Everyday competence in old and very old age: An inter-disciplinary perspective. *Ageing and Society, 13,* 657–680.

Baltes, M. M., Neumann, E. M., & Zank, S. (1994). Maintenance and rehabilitation of independence in old age: An intervention program for staff. *Psychology and Aging, 9,* 179–188.

Baltes, M. M., & Reisenzein, R. (1986). The social word in long-term care institutions: Psychological control toward dependency. In M. M. Baltes & P. B. Baltes (Eds.), *The psychology of control and aging* (pp. 315–343). Hillsdale, NJ: Erlbaum.

Baltes, M. M., & Skinner, E. A. (1983). Cognitive performance deficits and hospitalization: Learned helplessness, instrumental passivity, or what? Comments on Raps, Peterson, Jonas, and Seligman. *Journal of Personality and Social Psychology, 45,* 1013–1016.

Baltes, M. M., & Wahl, H. W. (1987). Dependence in aging. In L. L. Carstensen & B. A. Edelstein (Eds.), *Handbook of clinical gerontology* (pp. 204–221). New York: Pergamon Press.

Baltes, M. M., & Wahl, H. W. (1992). The dependency-support script in institutions: Generalization to community settings. *Psychology and Aging, 7,* 409–418.

Baltes, P. B., & Baltes, M. M. (1990). Selective optimization with compensation. In P. B. Baltes & M. M. Baltes (Eds.), *Successful aging: Perspectives from the behavioral science* (pp. 1–34). New York: Cambridge University Press.

Baltes, P. B., Mayer, K. U., Helmchen, H., & Steinhagen-Thiessen, E. (1993). The Berlin Aging Study (BASE). Overview and design. *Ageing and Society, 13,* 483–515.

Braudel, F. (1992). *The structure of everyday life (Vol. 1).* Berkeley: University of California Press.

Collopy, B. J. (1988). Autonomy in long-term care: Some crucial distinctions. *The Gerontologist, 28,* 10–27.

Fitzgerald, J. F., Smith, D. M., Martin, D. K., Freedman, J. A., & Wolinsky, F. D. (1993). Replication of the multidimensionality of activities of daily living. *Journal of Gerontology: Social Sciences, 48,* S28–S31.

Horgas, A. L., Wahl, H.-W., & Baltes, M. M. (1996). Dependency in late life. In L. L. Carstensen, B. A. Edelstein, & L. Dornbrand (Eds.), *The practical handbook of clinical gerontology* (pp. 54–75). Thousand Oaks, CA: Sage.

Lawton, M. P. (1983). Environment and other determinants of well-being in older people. *The Gerontologist, 23,* 349–357.

Lehr, U. M., & Thomae, H. (1991). Alltagspsychologie: Aufgaben, Methoden, Ergebnisse [Everyday psychology: Problems, methods, and results]. Darmstadt: Wissenschaftliche Buchgesellschaft.

Marsiske, M., Lang, F. R., & Baltes, M. M. (1994). *Beyond routine: Competence and social support in the daily lives of older adults.* Paper presented at the thirteenth biennial meetings of the International Society of Behavioral Development, Amsterdam, The Netherlands.

Moss, M., & Lawton, M. P. (1982). Time budgets of older people: A window on four lifestyles. *Journal of Gerontology, 37,* 576–582.

Parmalee, P. A., & Lawton, M. P. (1990). The design of special environments for the aged. In J. E. Birren & K. W. Schaie (Eds.), *The handbook of the psychology of aging* (3rd ed., pp. 464–488). New York: Academic Press.

Reichert, M. (1993). *Hilfeverhalten gegenüber alten Menschen: Eine experimentelle Überprüfung der Rolle von Erwartungen* [Helping behavior towards elderly people: An experimental analysis of expectations]. Essen: Blau Eule.

Seligman, M. E. P. (1975). *Helplessness: On depression, development, and death.* San Francisco: Freemann & Co.

Wahl, H. W. (1991). Dependence in the elderly from an interactional point of view: Verbal and observational data. *Psychology and Aging, 6,* 238–246.

Wahl, H. W., & Baltes, M. M. (1990). Die soziale Umwelt alter Menschen: Entwicklungsanregende oder hemmende Pflegeinteraktionen? [The social environment of the elderly: Development-enhancing or inhibiting care interactions?]. *Zeitschrift für Entwicklungspsychologie und Pädagogische Psychologie, 22,* 266–283.

Commentary: Dependency Scripts and Competencies: New Direction or More of the Same?

Steven H. Zarit

T he empirical work on dependency-support scripts described by Baltes and Horgas represents the most significant advance in recent years in understanding the interactions between elders and staff in nursing homes. Anyone who has spent any time in nursing homes will recognize the processes Baltes and Horgas describe of how dependency is reinforced and independence discouraged. These processes sometimes occur in passive or unspoken ways, and sometimes with aversive or punishing practices. The effort of their chapter to expand upon the notion of dependency scripts by including a broader perspective on competencies and of describing more fully the complex processes of adaptation is an exciting direction.

Yet reading the chapter produced a sense of déjà vu, or as the great sage Yogi Berra is reputed to have said, "Déjà vu all over again." These issues have been raised before, although not so eloquently, nor with the type of compelling empirical evidence of the process by which dependencies are reinforced. In the past, however, efforts to call attention to the inadvertent production of dependencies by institutional settings have largely been ignored, or incorporated into empty slogans about quality of life that do little to change the basic reality of living in a nursing home. More recently, this issue has slipped into the background, as public debate has mainly been concerned with controlling costs. Do Baltes and Horgas revive this important issue, or will their work be just another footnote in the history of long-term care?

The gerontological field has long been divided between those who believe that minor reforms can make nursing homes function adequately and advocates of more basic changes in the underlying models and assumptions of institutional care. In 1974, Kahn and I published a paper in which we reviewed what was known at that time about treatment of the mentally ill and frail elderly. In that paper we called attention to the bias toward institutional care that was found among clinicians and, indeed, in public policies that both openly and inadvertently encouraged institutionalization. We questioned the adequacy of institutional care, but not on the usual grounds. While recognizing that issues such as staff ratios, training, programming, and environmental design are all important, we felt that attention to these features of institutional settings, without appropriate goals or concepts of care, could actually have a regressive effect. Instead, we drew upon a broader critique that argued that settings such as nursing homes were characterized by "institutionalism," which produces considerable pressure on residents toward dependency and incompetence (e.g., Ochberg, Zarcone, & Hamburg, 1972).

We saw two processes as having deleterious effects. The hierarchical structure of nursing homes and their accompanying routines, which are organized for the convenience of staff, rob elderly residents of a sense of personal control over their lives. Even such a basic issue as having a say over who you share a room with (not to mention the indignity of having a roommate imposed on you) is decided by institutional imperatives, not personal choice. The importance of personal control, of course, has been dramatically demonstrated in Rodin and Langer's 1977 (see also Rodin, 1986) classic study, in which they found that giving people even small measures of control such as taking care of a plant can make a large difference in their functioning, and perhaps even survival.

Second, we believed, as Baltes and Horgas demonstrate so effectively, that institutional settings reinforce dependence, not independence. We did not identify specific reinforcement patterns with the precision of Baltes' recent work. Instead, we emphasized contextual issues that create pressures for dependency. Staff tend to conceptualize their role of "caring" in a one-dimensional and unreflective way. Wanting to give "tender loving care" (an old cliche in the nursing home field), they provide too much assistance at times, thereby undermining independent activities. Coupled with this tendency is institutions' aversion of risk. It is preferable to take over activities for residents than to take the chance they might injure themselves. Thus a person who walks with some difficulty may be encouraged to go into a wheelchair to avoid a fall. These processes lead, in the end, to what Kahn (1975) called "excess disabilities," that is, increases in functional disabilities not warranted by the person's underlying impairment.

In our 1974 paper, Kahn and I looked at studies that tried to improve the quality of life in nursing homes and other institutional settings for the elderly. We examined a wide range of interventions from group therapy to changes in environmental design. While some amelioration was possible, the results of these diverse studies proved that institutions were highly resistant to change. Although it was not difficult to produce some positive benefits in the short run on a wide variety of measures, it proved virtually impossible to sustain any positive changes over time. The basic forces toward dependency remained strong and persistent, even after staff training and other efforts to sustain innovative care.

There have been many changes in nursing homes in the past 20 years. Overall, the quality has risen and many of the worst homes have been improved or eliminated. These meliorations have occurred while the population in nursing homes has changed dramatically. People in nursing homes are sicker and more severely disabled than in the past. Part of these changes are due to Medicare policies that discharge patients sooner from acute hospitals. Another trend is that people with chronic, debilitating conditions such as dementia are living longer than before (Olshansky, Rudberg, Carnes, Cassel, & Brody, 1991). Despite these challenging conditions, nursing home staff often do a remarkable job in meeting complex demands with very limited resources.

Under these circumstances, it is perhaps not surprising that dependency scripts prevail in nursing homes. Nor should it be surprising that the experience of other researchers is that nursing homes remain remarkably resistant to some kinds of change, even in the face of overwhelming evidence of the efficacy of new approaches.

An area of research where this resistance can be seen very clearly is in management of incontinence. In recent years there have been considerable innovations in management of incontinence. Research programs by Louis Burgio, Jack Schnelle, and others have demonstrated the effectiveness of strategies for reducing incontinence in many nursing home residents currently in diapers (e.g., K. Burgio & L. Burgio, 1991; Schnelle et al.,

1993). But despite the demonstrated success of these trials, efforts to sustain the intervention beyond the period of the experimental trial have been thwarted. Once the researchers leave, staff revert to their old habits. It is simply easier to manage incontinence by putting people in diapers than to adopt toileting schedules and related procedures for keeping someone dry and a bit more independent.

More general efforts to train nursing home staffs in ways that may sustain more positive approaches have also been discouraging. The efforts of my colleagues Smyer, Brannon, and Cohn (1992) have utilized the best practice models of training in mental health and aging for nursing home staffs. Training interventions have been organized in innovative ways, including a recent project in which supervisors, rather than ordinary staff, have been the primary focus. While this research has shown that knowledge of practices can be changed, there is little evidence that new behaviors can be sustained (Smyer, Brannon, & Cohn, 1992; also L. Burgio & K. Burgio, 1990).

These interventions, of course, have not touched the main fabric of institutional resistance, the dependency scripts. I avidly await reports from Baltes and Horgas on the staff training programs they describe, which focused directly on dependency scripts. Perhaps that type of direct effort will be more effective and lead to long-lasting changes.

Baltes and Horgas extend the basic work on dependency scripts in two important ways. First is the finding that dependency scripts are not limited only to institutional settings. Families often respond in similar ways, as do nursing home staff. The main difference is that independent behaviors are also likely to be supported to a greater extent in home settings. One reason for the difference is there is usually less aversion to reasonable risks at home. The older person and family can make decisions about taking risks that are consistent with their values, rather than institutional policy. Concern about litigation and bad publicity prevents nursing homes from taking even reasonable risks. It is far worse to have one patient fall than to restrict mobility of many. But the prevalence of dependency scripts among families of the elderly reveals a great deal about some basic, societal attitudes about aging.

Over the years, interest in research on attitudes about aging has declined. Students first discovering the field are often intrigued by the notion that many of the social difficulties of older people are due to stereotypes about aging, and they want to study and change these beliefs. I have often found myself in the position of discouraging this type of intervention as too unfocused, and instead directing these students to conduct more promising (perhaps more fashionable) lines of inquiry. In light of the pervasiveness of dependency scripts, perhaps these students have been right after all. The search for a linkage between conceptual schemes about aging and dependency scripts would be an exciting line of inquiry. That type of inquiry would help us learn more about our basic conceptualizations of aging and how those beliefs may inadvertently cause excess disabilities.

The other major contribution that Baltes and Horgas make is their differentiation between Basic (BaCo) and Expanded (ExCo) competencies. This distinction between the activities necessary to sustain life and those pursuits that are discretionary and more likely to add zest and individual-ization to our lives may prove to be a very useful way of profiling residents in long-term care. Rather than just examining Activities of Daily Living, this formulation takes us into a realm in which we consider the things people do for personal pleasure and when they have choices. This approach also makes it possible to consider specific trade-offs in care and in living situations. In a sense, then, it takes us closer to that ephemeral concept, ''quality of life.'' In long-term care settings, routines concern only BaCo. Opening up the possibilities implied in ExCo could result in dramatically different ways of structuring daily routines and activities by providing more attention to individual lifestyles and preferences.

A real strength of this conceptualization is its underpinning from data using a microanalytic approach to social interactions. The 24-hour diary format of the *Yesterday Interview* (Moss & Lawton, 1982) has provided Baltes and Horgas with the kind of detailed information on behavior patterns that is needed to go beyond simple characterizations of daily life. This data collection strategy is especially appropriate when new conceptual frameworks are being developed. Questionnaires and checklists all too often narrow the choices prematurely, before an adequate theoretical model and understanding of social processes and exchanges has been developed. Other approaches to finding out about activity patterns, such as retrospec-tive estimates, are probably unreliable, given the heavy load they place on memory.

An obvious next step is to put together dependency scripts with this model of competency, and while Baltes and Horgas took some steps in that direction, the results seemed forced. In particular, I am not convinced that the balance of BaCo and ExCo they found in institutional settings represents evidence of successful aging or ''selective optimization with compensation.'' That concept implies an active process by which people make meaningful trade-offs to maintain important activities (P. Baltes & M. Baltes, 1990). As M. Baltes and Horgas described, however, dependency in nursing homes is, in part, imposed. It is difficult to reconcile "optimization" with a process by which necessary dependencies are encouraged. Although some useful strategies for measuring quality of life are likely to come from this framework for evaluating competency, issues of choice and preference must also be taken into account.

What, then, are the implications of these contributions for improving long-term care? Do these conceptual advances, understanding dependency scripts and the distinction of BaCo and ExCo, give us tools for improving quality of life in institutional settings in meaningful ways? Or is the unremitting institutionalism that Kahn and I described 20 years ago going to overwhelm these penetrating advances?

Interventions based on changing dependency scripts, along with new and better ways of training staff and changing the work environment may go a long way to modifying some of the deleterious processes in institutional settings. I would like to suggest a different approach, however, one that is consistent with the powerful findings provided by Baltes and Horgas but that changes the basis of interactions between residents and staff in long-term care settings. The starting point is the recognition that long-term care settings should be organized as places to live rather than as minihospitals with routines organized around concepts of medical care, or primarily for the staff's ease, or because that is how things have always been done. To the extent possible, people should have autonomy and control over their lives, including the right to refuse care, if they are competent to make that decision.

Perhaps surprisingly, most of the advances in programming and design in recent years have been made for dementia patients. Special units in nursing homes for dementia care have burgeoned. What constitutes a special unit varies considerably, and some may offer little more than a locked door. But at their best, these programs provide greater autonomy to dementia patients. Because of having a safe and secure environment, residents do not have to be restricted as much. A major collaborative study is currently underway, which should provide a better indication of how well these programs are performing (e.g., Holmes, Splaine, Teresi, Ory, Barrett, Monaco, & Ramirez, 1994).

One very interesting approach to dementia care is the Group Home, which has been developed widely in Sweden (Malmberg & Zarit, 1993). Characterized as an alternative to traditional nursing homes, Group Homes are organized explicitly on a social model. Group Homes consist of five to seven ordinary apartments that are linked together by a hallway and secured to the outside. There are common areas for activities, eating, preparing food, and other household chores. Residents sign a lease for their apartment, receive a key to the door, and may close and lock the door as they choose. While staff have a key to each apartment, they do not infringe on privacy, except when necessary. The program of activities stresses familiar, household tasks, to the extent that residents can perform them. Staff do not perform activities for residents, but instead assist and encourage them to do as much for themselves as possible in everything from dressing and bathing to housework and preparing meals. In other words, staff are specifically trained to implement an "independence script." On the downside, staff often feel frustrated that residents cannot be more active and that most activities are one-on-one, rather than in small groups.

What is most striking about this setting is the degree to which a person's autonomy and dignity are supported, compared to a typical nursing home. Residents are remarkably calm, with little of the agitated and restless quality typically seen in nursing home patients (Malmberg & Zarit, 1993). A comprehensive evaluation of group homes has not been done, so it is not possible to determine if residents' good adaptation is related to the amount of autonomy and control they have or to some other factor. Who gets selected into group homes in the first place may be an issue, since a highly agitated person would be more likely to be routed to a psychogeriatric hospital. On the other hand, surprisingly few people are moved out because they prove to be too difficult to manage (Malmberg & Zarit). While group homes and similar programs warrant careful study, preliminary observations suggest that this type of situation may support autonomy and competency better than when people with dementia live in a facility run on a medical model, where they are patients, and not really residents.

In conclusion, the concepts presented by Baltes and Horgas, dependency scripts and the distinction between basic and expanded competencies, is more than déjà vu. While reviving an important stream of thought about functioning of older people in long-term care, their article takes us to a new level of understanding of how these facilities work and gives us tools for rethinking, and possibly reshaping typical patterns of care. We should not, however, underestimate the forces that resist change in institutional settings, nor should we naively believe we are doing the best possible. There are growing numbers of people who spend the last years of their lives with profound disabilities. The challenge is to move beyond platitudes about good care to a more basic conceptualization of supporting autonomy and dignity to the extent possible.

REFERENCES

Baltes, P., & Baltes, M. (1990). Selective optimization with compensation. In P. B. Baltes and M. M. Baltes (Eds.), *Successful aging: Perspectives from the behavioral sciences* (pp. 1–34). New York: Cambridge University Press.

Burgio, K. L., & Burgio, L. D. (1991). The problem of urinary incontinence. In P. A. Wisocki (Ed.), *Handbook of clinical behavior therapy with the elderly* (pp. 317–336). New York: Plenum.

Burgio, L. D., & Burgio, K. L. (1990). Institutional staff training and management: A review of the literature and a model for geriatric, long-term-care facilities. *International Journal of Aging and Human Development, 30*, 287–302.

Holmes, D., Splaine, M., Teresi, J., Ory, M., Barrett, V., Monaco, C., & Ramirez, M. (1994). What makes special care special: Concept mapping as a definitional tool. *Alzheimer's Disease and Associated Disorders, 8*, S41–S53.

Kahn, R. L. (1975). The mental health system and the future aged. *The Gerontologist, 15*(1, Pt. 2), 24–31.

Kahn, R. L., & Zarit, S. H. (1974). Evaluation of mental health programs for the elderly. In P. O. Davidson, F. W. Clark, & L. A. Hamerlynck (Eds.), *Evaluation of behavioral programs: In community, residential and school settings* (pp. 223–252). Champaign, IL: Research Press.

Malmberg, B., & Zarit, S. H. (1993). Group homes for people with dementia: A Swedish example. *The Gerontologist, 33*, 682–686.

Moss, M., & Lawton, M. P. (1982). Time budgets of older people: A window on four lifestyles. *Journal of Gerontology, 37*, 576–582.

Ochberg, F. M., Zarcone, V., & Hamburg, D. A. (1972). Symposium on institutionalization. *Comprehensive Psychology, 13*, 91–104.

Olshansky, S. J., Rudberg, M. A., Carnes, B. A., Cassel, C. K., & Brody, J. A. (1991). Trading off longer life for worsening health: The expansion of morbidity hypothesis. *Journal of Aging and Health, 3*, 194–216.

Rodin, J. (1986). Aging and health: Effects of the sense of control. *Science, 233*, 1271–1276.

Rodin, J., & Langer, E. (1977). Long-term effects of control-relevant intervention with the institutionalized aged. *Journal of Personality and Social Psychology, 35*, 897–902.

Schnelle, J. F., Newman, D. R., White, M., Abbey, J., Walston, K. A., Fogerty, T., & Ory, M. G. (1993). Maintaining continence in nursing homes through the application of industrial quality control. *The Gerontologist, 33*, 114–121.

Smyer, M., Brannon, D., & Cohn, M. (1992). Improving nursing home care through training and job redesign. *The Gerontologist, 32*, 327–333.

Commentary: Quality Improvement and the Management of Dependency in Nursing Facilities

Diane Brannon and Theresa Barry

In keeping with the focus on social structure as the context for aging, our response to Baltes and Horgas' chapter will be on the role of institutions in managing dependency. It is the potential adaptiveness of dependency behaviors that are of particular interest here. The observation that, depending on the elderly person's functional status, the institutional environment can be inhibiting or liberating, is an important one. It is one that also has implications for regulatory policy and management of nursing facilities. How can long-term care institutions meet the challenge of caring for without diminishing the capacity of residents? To address this question, we will review quality improvement adaptations currently occurring in U.S. nursing facilities. These changes have the potential to alter the context that institutions provide for residents.

DEPENDENCY VERSUS INCOMPETENCE

One of the most important conclusions from this and related work is that it suggests that the expression of dependency may indeed be an adaptive form of control over the elder's social environment. It is fascinating that the strategy we use so effectively in childhood to get what we want and need and that we must shelf for most purposes in adulthood, becomes a viable modus operandi again in late life. Help-seeking behavior is an expression of dependency; it is also a critical life skill.

In the institutional setting, the nurses' call bell embodies the expression of dependency and the tool with which to elicit a response from the environment. Competent use of the call bell is an elegant example of behavioral principles at work. An objective observer might, in fact, conclude that residents practice behavior management in their interactions with staff far more effectively than staff use such techniques. Is the value attached to autonomy for the disabled elder, then, one of ''I can do things for myself'' or ''I can get things done when and how I want them done''?

What would happen, for example, if we were successful in training nursing home staffs to practice behavior management principles such that residents were responded to only when they exhibited independence rather than dependence. What would be the effect on residents? Assuming such a strategy was employed universally, some residents would lose their primary strategy for influencing the world around them. No one, one might argue, would advocate a universal prescription for treatment of all residents. Yet regulatory policy tends to create incentives for uniform treatment.

According to Baltes and Horgas' findings, institutions serve to support expanded competencies of functionally impaired residents by liberating them from the basic tasks of living, but they, as well as family caregivers, may inhibit such competencies in less impaired elders by providing too much or inappropriate support. In investigating the causes of poor care outcomes, Alverno, Mattson, and Rudman (1992) found that elements of physical, psychosocial, and clinical care rather than resident characteristics accounted for most of the variance in malnutrition, decubiti, and functional status. How do nursing home staffs differentiate between appropriate dependency and nonproductive dependency, and how can care plans and services be tailored accordingly?

EFFORTS TO DIFFERENTIATE CARE

Individualization of care has never been easy to implement in nursing homes because of the relatively low levels of clinical expertise available in caregiving roles. The complexity implied by true individualization is incompatible with common expectations regarding use of nonprofessional staff, though completely compatible with the diversity displayed in the nursing home population. In his early writing on the management of complexity, the Nobel-prize-winning economist Herbert Simon (1957) noted two opposing strategies for delegating complex tasks—by blueprint and by recipe. In the blueprint approach, managers specify in detail the expected outcome and hire people who have the skills to put together a workable sequence of steps to produce that outcome. Using the recipe approach, management must focus on defining the sequence of steps, making them understandable and workable by just about anyone. In this case, it is assumed that the outcome will be acceptable if this series of steps is followed. For the most part, nursing homes rely on nonprofessionals and focus on specifying the processes of care using the recipe approach. Nonprofessionals, it is assumed, cannot be trusted to know the sequence of steps involved in caring for residents; therefore, protocols must be developed and enforced.

Clinical guidelines for several types of treatments in nursing facilities have been issued in conjunction with implementation of the Minimum Data Set/Resident Assessment Protocol (MDS/RAP) system in U.S. facilities. While the RAPs do contribute to the goal of differentiating care, they are too general to produce individualized care. Choices and modifications of the "recipe" must be made, and it is not yet clear the extent to which these should be made by professional care planners or nonprofessional caregivers. It is clear, however, that there is no longer just one "care routine" applied to all residents. Increasingly, these facilities are making themselves more complex organizationally and clinically to differentiate care. There are currently strong regulatory and market incentives resulting in both clinical and organizational strategies geared toward providing appropriate levels and types of care.

Both the needs and demands of the resident population of U.S. nursing facilities have changed. After prospective payment for acute-care hospitals was implemented, the acuity level of long-term care patients began to increase (Shaughnessy & Kramer, 1989). These "sub-acute care" patients, as well as in some states long-stay Medicaid reimbursed residents, are increasingly enrolled in some sort of managed care system. Central to managed care is the function of the case manager who shops for cost-effective care.

TOTAL QUALITY MANAGEMENT

An increasing demand for evidence of cost effectiveness of services has led the long-term care industry to seek new ways to increase productivity while maintaining quality care in a cost-effective manner (Dimant, 1991). Recently, the concept of total quality management (TQM) has been considered as a solution to the quality control problems in nursing homes. Total quality management (TQM), a training and management system identified with the work of Deming (1986), has been adopted by the health care industry to address cost and quality problems (Kritchevsky & Simmons, 1991). It is grounded in a philosophy of meeting and exceeding customer-defined requirements and working toward continuous improvement (Gaucher & Coffey, 1993) and, as such, is a systems level approach to differentiating care.

TQM can be summarized by several basic components that have been found to be applicable to health care (Deming, 1986). Experts agree that quality improvement cannot be effective without a commitment to pursue an organization's mission from both managers and employees (Joint Commission on Accreditation of Healthcare Organizations, 1991). It involves having top management's commitment to provide an environment where TQM can flourish. This includes the empowerment of employees through the provision of training and necessary resources to improve the process (Gustafson, 1992). According to Gaucher and Coffey (1993), the basic belief should be that employees want to do their best, they know the most about their specific jobs, and they should be involved in any planned improvements or changes within an organization. Further, attributing organizational problems to system processes rather than individual employees, as well as committing to the use of data to improve and manage processes, is essential to TQM (Gustafson, 1992). The integration of the analytical knowledge of processes involved with interpersonal skills is another vital component of TQM, especially in health care. Prior difficulties have arisen when human resources staff and top management have encouraged participative management styles and involvement of staff in organizational development, but have failed to quantitatively demonstrate the effects of these approaches (Gaucher & Coffey, 1993). Nevertheless, subsequent efforts to quantify specific processes in health care have been successful with the employment of statistical quality control methods. These methods record process and outcome data via flow charts, cause and effect diagrams, histograms, scatter diagrams, and Pareto charts (Joint Commission on Accreditation of Healthcare Organizations, 1993).

This process can be performed by those actually rendering the tasks rather than by surveyors or managers not directly involved in caregiving. This ongoing feedback not only helps to quickly identify problems, it empowers the nursing home staff. The process can be evaluated by gathering data on the outcome measure as well as through resident and family satisfaction. Such work processes and outcome measures can be developed for clinical conditions such as falls, sleep disruption, and restraint use (Schnelle, Ouslander, Osterweil, & Blumenthal, 1993). Finally, TQM entails enlisting the entire organization to work toward a goal of continuous improvement and to capitalize on the cumulative effects of numerous small improvements (Gustafson, 1992).

These concepts of TQM have been applied extensively in many health care settings. For example, studies have used nursing staff and physicians as functional units and operationalized quality as the number of nosocomial infections (Lynch & Jackson, 1985) and postsurgical hospital mortality rates (Kritchevsky & Simmons, 1991). Using the tenets of TQM, hospitals have not only improved the quality of care rendered to patients, they have also increased employee job satisfaction and opinions regarding their organizations (Counte, Glandon, Oleske, & Hill, 1992). Although many published examples have supported the virtues of applying TQM to health care (Al-Assaf & Schmele, 1993; Krater-Wood, 1990; Kritchevsky & Simmons, 1991), few studies have focused on using these concepts in nursing homes. Recently, however, some have recognized the potential for employing TQM to address the cost-quality dilemma faced by nursing homes.

Clinical Management

One aspect of TQM, statistical process control, has been applied to clinical care in nursing facilities to identify and alter dependency-producing staff behaviors. A statistical quality control method was used to assess the effectiveness of a prompted-voiding toileting procedure on urinary incontinence (Schnelle, Newman, Fogarty, Wallston, & Ory, 1991). Standards were set to specify how dry residents should be if toileted on a 2-hour schedule. Using random samples of residents, supervisors monitored control charts to assess continuously maintenance of standards by nursing assistants. The study found that the use of statistical quality control allowed supervisors to determine if nursing aides were changing residents at the appropriate time within acceptable zones of variability (Schnelle, Newman, & Fogarty, 1990). Statistical quality control has also aided in the maintenance of improved continence care over time (Schnelle et al., 1993). Similarly, ongoing staff feedback and self-monitoring forms were shown to improve incontinence care using a prompted-voiding technique (Burgio, Engel, et al., 1990; Burgio, McCormick, et al., 1994; Palmer, Bennett, Marks, McCormick, & Engel, 1994). Moreover, Palmer and her colleagues noted the importance of identifying extrinsic rather than intrinsic factors contributing to urinary incontinence.

Schnelle et al. (1992) developed a quality control management system to improve staff adherence to federal regulations regarding restraint use. The process was implemented to assure that staff released, exercised, and repositioned residents every 2 hours. The management system resulted in fewer restrained residents, and residents were released and repositioned by nursing assistants more consistently than before the intervention, though long-term effects were not realized probably due to lack of administrative commitment. Since the implementation of new regulations and inspection survey standards in 1990, real changes have occurred in the way resident care is conducted in U.S. nursing homes. The use of restraints has been significantly reduced (Zinn, Aaronson, & Rosko, 1993). In their place, less restrictive and dependency-producing interventions, such as behavior management programs, are being instituted.

Finally, the Minimum Data Set (MDS), the federally mandated periodic assessment system, holds great potential for supporting continuous improvement as a standardized approach for nursing home staff to identify patterns of symptoms, behaviors, treatments, and clinical outcomes (Spuck, 1992). When fully computerized, these data will help staff adjust individual care processes as well as clarify facility norms and clinical outcomes (Glass, 1992).

Organizational Management

These concepts of TQM have become more appealing to the long-term care industry, and some researchers have begun to investigate the efficacy of its application in solving administrative problems that affect quality in nursing homes. Dimant (1991) applied the principles to administrative work processes using monitoring systems for podiatry care, physician medication orders, and dementia assessment in one nursing facility. Using suggestions from staff members rather than management, the system measured how well physicians followed specific policies, procedures, and practice guidelines. A computerized pharmacy software system was installed and provided feedback to physicians regarding resident medications. Reducing the number of steps required of nurses and physicians, the system helped to virtually eliminate medication errors in the nursing home. To monitor ongoing customer satisfaction, resident and family satisfaction questionnaires were maintained throughout the resident's stay in the facility. The use of TQM in this nursing home resulted in improvements in the specific work processes identified.

Long-term care industry leaders recently reported in a Delphi study (Brannon, Castle, & Zinn, 1995) on changes currently taking place in nursing homes that they view as most significant. Overall, three trends emerged:

1.   Nursing facilities are becoming more internally complex through diversification into specialty care units for a range of service needs from personal care to subacute rehabilitation and postsurgical care.

2.   The external affairs of the nursing home have also become more complex as integrated health systems and managed care have begun to incorporate long-term care.

3.   Finally, there is a heightened need to manage information with greater sophistication than has been done in the past (e.g., TQM) to demonstrate the cost effectiveness of clinical care.

While it is always speculative to anticipate the real impact such changes may have on the appropriateness of care, it seems likely that these organization-level changes will produce more options for elders and greater accountability for facilities. While most progressive service organizations now define quality as "meeting or exceeding customer expectations" (Dean & Evans, 1994), the Institute of Medicine and subsequently the Omnibus Budget Reconciliation Act of 1987 (OBRA) expanded this definition by stating that quality in nursing homes requires that the functional, medical, social, and psychological needs of residents be individually determined and met by periodic assessments and care planning (Coleman, 1991; Institute of Medicine, 1986). This is clearly a challenge to individualize care to the extent possible in the institutional setting. There are numerous contingencies regarding the effectiveness of periodic assessment, quality improvement, and other changes, however. Longitudinal process-outcome studies currently underway will eventually clarify the effectiveness of these approaches to managing dependency in institutional settings.

REFERENCES

Al-Assaf, A. F., & Schmele, J. A. (1993). *The textbook of total quality in healthcare*. Delray Beach, FL: St. Lucie Press.

Alverno, L., Mattson, D. E., & Rudman, D. (1992). Indicators of adverse somatic outcome in three Veterans Affairs nursing homes. *Hospital and Community Psychiatry*, *43*(12), 1223–1226.

Brannon, D., Castle, N., & Zinn, J. (1995). Current innovation in the nursing home industry: Results of a Delphi study. *Nursing Home Economics*, *2*(1), 8–12.

Burgio, L. D., Engel, B. T., Hawkins, A., McCormick, K., Scheve, A., & Jones, L. T. (1990). A staff management system for maintaining improvements in continence with elderly nursing home residents. *Journal of Applied Behavior Analysis*, *23*(1), 111–118.

Burgio, L. D., McCormick, K. A., Scheve, A. S., Engel, B. T., Hawkins, A., & Leahy, E. (1994). The effects of changing prompted voiding schedules in the treatment of incontinence in nursing home residents. *Journal of the American Geriatrics Society*, *42*(3), 315–320.

Coleman, B. (1991). *The Nursing Home Reform Act of 1987: Provisions, policy, and prospects*. Boston: University of Massachusetts at Boston Gerontology Institute.

Counte, M. A., Glandon, G. L., Oleske, D. M., & Hill, J. P. (1992). Total quality management in a healthcare organization: How are employees affected? *Hospital and Health Services Administration*, *37*(4), 503–518.

Dean, J. W., & Evans, J. R. (1994). *Total quality: Management, organization and strategy*. Minneapolis: West Publishing Company.

Deming, W. E. (1986). *Out of the crisis*. Cambridge, MA: Massachusetts Institute of Technology.

Dimant, J. (1991). From quality assurance to quality management in long-term care. *Quality Review Bulletin*, *17*(7), 207–215.

Gaucher, E. J., & Coffey, R. J. (1993). *Total quality in healthcare*. San Francisco: Jossey-Bass Inc.

Glass, A. P. (1992). Resident assessments: A new toll for measuring and improving nursing home quality. *Journal of Healthcare Quality*, *14*(3), 24–25, 28–30.

Gustafson, D. H. (1992). Lessons learned from an early attempt to implement CQI principles in a regulatory system. *Quality Review Bulletin*, *18*(10), 333–339.

Institute of Medicine. (1986). *Improving the quality of care in nursing homes*. Washington, DC: National Academy Press.

Joint Commission on Accreditation of Healthcare Organizations. (1991). *An introduction to quality improvement in health care*. Oakbrook Terrace, IL: JCAHO Publications.

Krater-Wood, R. E. (1990). How to use continuous quality improvement theory and statistical quality control tool in a multispecialty clinic. *Quality Review Bulletin, 16,* 391–397.

Kritchevsky, S. B., & Simmons, B. P. (1991). Continuous quality improvement: Concepts and applications for physician care. *Journal of the American Medical Association, 266*(13), 1817–1823.

Lynch, P., & Jackson, M. M. (1985). Monitoring: Surveillance for nosocomial infections and uses for assessing quality of care. *American Journal of Infection Control, 13,* 161–173.

Palmer, M. H., Bennett, R. G., Marks, J., McCormick, K. A., & Engel, B. T. (1994). Urinary incontinence: A program that works. *Journal of Long-Term Care Administration, 22*(2), 19–25.

Schnelle, J. F., Newman, D. R., & Fogarty, T. E. (1990). Statistical quality control in nursing homes: Assessment and management of chronic urinary incontinence. *Health Services Research, 25*(4), 627–637.

Schnelle, J. F., Newman, D. R., Fogarty, T. E., Wallston, K., & Ory, M. (1991). Assessment and quality control of incontinence care in long-term care facilities. *Journal of the American Geriatrics Society, 39*(2), 165–171.

Schnelle, J. F., Newman, D. R., White, M., Abbey, J., Wallston, K. A., Fogarty, T., & Ory, M. G. (1993). Maintaining continence in nursing home residents through the application of industrial quality control. *The Gerontologist, 33*(2), 114–121.

Schnelle, J. F., Newman, D. R., White, M., Volner, T. R., Burnett, J., Cronqvist, A., & Ory, M. (1992). Reducing and managing restraints in long-term care facilities. *Journal of the American Geriatrics Society, 40*(4), 381–385.

Schnelle, J. F., Ouslander, J. G., Osterweil, D., & Blumenthal, S. (1993). Total quality management: Administrative and clinical applications in nursing homes. *Journal of the American Geriatrics Society, 41*(11), 1259–1266.

Shaughnessy, P., & Kramer, A. (1989). The increased needs of patients in nursing homes and patients receiving home health care. *New England Journal of Medicine, 322,* 21–27.

Simon, H. (1957). *Models of man.* New York: John Wiley.

Spuck, J. (1992). Using the long-term care Minimum Data Set as a tool for CQI in nursing homes. In J. Dienemann (Ed.), *Continuous quality improvement in nursing* (pp. 95–105). Washington, DC: American Nurses Association.

Zinn, J., Aaronson, W., & Rosko, M. (1993). Variations in the outcomes of care provided in Pennsylvania nursing homes. *Medical Care, 31,* 475–487.

CHAPTER *5*

Social Support and the Maintenance of Competence

Toni C. Antonucci and Hiroko Akiyama

A long-standing goal of life-span developmental psychology is to address practical problems of development faced by individuals at different points in the life span. As psychologists we seek to understand the basic principles underlying behavior, but as developmental psychologists we are also concerned with linking those principles to the resolution and solution of problems that individuals face as they develop both intraindividually and interindividually. Our present focus on Societal Mechanisms for Maintaining Competence in Old Age can best be served by applying basic principals of behavior and recent empirical evidence to the problem at hand. In this chapter, we do so within the context of social relations and their function to help or hinder the individual's ability to cope with the challenges of age.

We begin with a very brief introduction and overview of some of the classic works in the field of social relations. We provide a succinct summary of the generally accepted findings in the field. By way of introduction we believe it is also important to review the conceptual and methodological limitations of previous work. To provide a theoretical overview, we present two conceptual models that have guided much of the empirical investigations reported in this chapter. These are the life-span developmental framework of Convoys of Social Relations (Kahn &

Antonucci. 1980) and the Support/Efficacy Model of Social Relations (Antonucci & Jackson, 1987). Using these theoretical perspectives as a base, we suggest how interpersonal relationships might allow for proactive interventions that will help people maintain competence as they age. Finally, we speculate about how these theoretical perspectives might be used to design and develop interventions. In short, we believe that using these theoretical perspectives and the available empirical data, it is possible to help people engage in proactive activities that will facilitate the maintenance of competence in the domains of physical and mental health throughout old age.

INTRODUCTION

Although there probably has always been a folklore that friends and family help an individual feel better, scientists never really formally attended to this view until empirical evidence began to demonstrate a direct link between social support and health. In the 1970s Cassel (1976) and Cobb (1976), two well-known epidemiologists, argued that social relations led to increased host resistance. They proposed that people who had a sense of belongingness or closeness with others were less likely to get sick. Large empirical studies followed. Two bodies of research concerning the effect of social relations on mortality and morbidity were particularly persuasive. The first indicated that the presence of social ties decreased the risk of mortality.

Social Relations and Mortality

These findings have been replicated in Alameda County, California; Tecumseh, Michigan, Evans County, Georgia, Sweden, and Finland (e.g., Berkman & Syme, 1977; Blazer, 1982; House, Robbins, & Metzner, 1982; Kaplan et al., 1988; Schoenbach, Kaplan, Fredman, & Kleinbaum, 1986; Orth-Gothmer & Johnson, 1987). Using large epidemiological longitudinal studies, the data consistently showed that people who reported the existence of better quality of social relationships were less likely to have died at the time of follow-up. These longitudinal follow-ups ranged from as little as 2 years to as long as 11 years. The association between social relations and mortality is impressive, but there have also been numerous studies demonstrating the relationship between social support and morbidity.

Social Relations and Morbidity

The studies of social relations and morbidity examined a wide range of health-related activities and illnesses. In each of the following cases the existence of or the quality of social ties was associated with reduced morbidity. For example, Antonucci, Kahn, and Akiyama (1989) found that people who spoke with supportive others about their cancer symptom were much more likely to seek treatment for that symptom than those who did not; Medalie and Goldbourt (1976) found reduced incidence of angina and heart disease among men who reported fewer family conflicts and strains in a 5-year study of Israeli men. Other impressive associations between social relations and morbidity include recovery from heart disease (Ruberman, Weinblatt, Goldberg, & Chaudhary; 1984), reduction in number of symptoms (Cohen, Teresi, & Holmes, 1985), hospitalizations (Wan & Weissart, 1981), use of emergency rooms (Coe, Wolinsky, Miller, & Prendergast, 1985), prevention or postponement of institutionalization (Lindsey & Hughes, 1981), help-seeking behaviors (Brody, Poulschock, & Masciocchi, 1978; McKinlay, 1980; Rundall & Evashwick, 1982), maintenance of health behaviors (Berkman & Breslow, 1983; Langlie, 1977), and adherence to medical regimens (Caplan, Robinson, French, Caldwell, & Shinn, 1976; Doherty, Schrott, Metcalf, & Iasiello-Vailas, 1983).

These findings, though only briefly mentioned, are impressive and persuasive. This accumulation of evidence clearly indicates the existence of an association between social relations and health. The next question to consider is whether this information can be useful for improving the competence of the elderly. The goal is to convert what is known about the association between social support and health to practical application and the design of proactive, interactive and reactive programs to aid the elderly. But before taking that step, it is critical to evaluate the quality of the empirical evidence. To do this, we examine the conceptual and methodological strengths of the field thus far.

CONCEPTUAL AND METHODOLOGICAL ISSUES

Conceptual Issues

There have been a number of conceptual problems identified in this field over the years. The most fundamental problem is the lack of distinction among different social relations constructs. The concepts of social network, social support, and support quality have been intermeshed. Many researchers have not distinguished among these concepts and have simply assumed they all represent the same thing. The result is often the lack of distinction among measures that are assessing different characteristics of social relations. It is now much more clearly understood that social networks, social support, and support quality are each very different aspects of the broad concept of social relations. For example, it is not difficult to grasp that being married does not necessarily mean your spouse provides you with support, nor does it mean that all the people who are married are fortunate enough to be involved in high quality relationships.

Conceptually, these variables are linked. For example, it is hard to have a high quality marital relationship unless you are actually married. And it is not likely that you would rate your marriage as being of high quality unless there is some exchange of social support, though the type of support that is provided and received might vary considerably. An additional factor is that these relationships are likely to be confounded in large studies. Although each individual has only one spouse, it is clear that having more people in your network increases the likelihood that there is someone who provides any one or a number of types of support. These additions also may increase the likelihood that you are satisfied with the quality of at least some of your relationships.

There has also been a theoretical ambiguity that has plagued the field and may, in fact, be related to the conceptual ambiguity. The goal has not always been clear with respect to the association between social relations and health. Is the goal simply (1) to describe the association, and be able (2) to predict how certain social relationship configurations might affect health outcomes, or is it (3) to explain and understand the association? Perhaps the answer depends partly on the disciplinary background of the person asking the question. For our purposes, it is useful to answer yes to all three. It is useful to be able to describe, predict, and explain the association between social relations and health. At the practical level, information on each of these points should greatly enhance our ability to help the individual, for example, to maintain competence throughout old age.

Methodological Issues

Originally, there were serious methodological problems in the field of social networks and social support (Antonucci & Depner, 1982; Antonucci,

1985). For example, everybody had their own idea of how to measure social support. Some focused on role status: are you married?, Do you have children? Others asked about feelings and focused on the affective aspects of the relationship: is there somebody you love/who loves you? do you have somebody to confide in? Still others focused on tangible support or what others do to help you: somebody to lend you money? provide sick care? drive you to the airport or the doctor's office? Another type of question focused on what might be called negative support or the negative aspects of social relations: somebody who gets on your nerves? makes too many demands on you? doesn't understand you? Still another issue is the degree to which provider and receiver agree on the amount and direction of support exchanges. It is easy to recognize that these questions, each of which taps specific aspects of social relations, clearly do not provide information that could be considered unifying or singular in nature. Although all of these are, of course, potentially important aspects of social relations, they each tap slightly different aspects of relationships.

Another problem involved sample quality. Samples varied considerably in composition and in quality. For example, studies might involve small clinical samples, regional samples, patients with a particular diagnosis or disease, or people who belonged to a certain organization. The generalizability across these studies was certainly limited, though investigators did not always limit their generalizations from these biased samples.

Other methodological problems involved the ways in which the data were actually collected. Most studies relied on self-report. Of course, this is potentially a problem since it was not clear how accurately or objectively the individuals perceived their social relations. The type of data collection also varied considerably. It might be face-to-face interviews, telephone interviews, or mail questionnaires. If respondents were unable to answer for themselves because of language or health problems, responses were often accepted from proxies, that is, close relatives or friends who were assumed to be able to answer for the targeted respondent. The ability of these proxy respondents to answer as accurately as the original targeted respondent would in such personal and private matters should not automatically be presumed.

Although what we were learning about social relations and the additional clarity being achieved both conceptually and methodologically was impressive, there remained the lack of an overall theoretical model that might integrate what was being learned about social relations. To this end, Kahn and Antonucci developed the Convoy Model of Social Relations.

CONVOY MODEL OF SOCIAL RELATIONS

The Convoy Model of Social Relations (Kahn & Antonucci, 1980) can best be summarized as follows: Characteristics of the individual and the situation influence the kinds of social relations, including social network, social support, and support satisfaction, that the individual experiences. These factors combine to influence overall health and well-being. The individual is surrounded by this Convoy of Social Relations, people who protect and socialize them, and optimally help to improve their life situation. It was recognized, however, that relations could be negative and have a negative influence on the individual. Instead of protecting people, helping them to feel good about themselves, helping them sustain their own health and well-being, these relationships could make the individual more vulnerable. This is fundamentally a life-span theory, which focuses on the development and accumulation of these interactions over time. Three characteristics of the Convoy Model reiterate this emphasis.

Convoy Model—Hierarchical Model

The Convoy model is basically a hierarchical one. Individuals are surrounded by potentially large numbers of people, but the degree to which these relationships are close and important varies considerably. We have conceptualized and operationalized this concept through the use of three concentric circles, with a still smaller circle in the middle representing the individual and having the word "you" written in it. People have had little trouble conceptualizing their relationships this way or using the concentric diagram to provide data about their convoy of social support (see Antonucci, 1986, for more details). It is important to note that relationships are hierarchical because it helps to understand why specific interactions with certain individuals have very powerful effects, whereas the same interactions with less hierarchically close individuals might have essentially no effect. Closeness is not necessarily role-based. Thus although spouses are frequently mentioned as the person so close and important to you that it would be hard to imagine life without them, this closeness is not assumed. Nor is it assumed that all relationships, close and otherwise are uniformly positive in nature. A spouse or child might be very close to you but also might be the source of much stress and strain.

Convoy Model—Antecedent/Consequent Effects

Similarly, relations are hypothesized to have a cause and effect quality. One antecedent event or action can and often does lead to a consequent reaction. Interrelationships are not random but build upon each other in a causal, consistent, and often predictable manner. Receiving supportive interactions often leads to feelings of gratefulness and enrichment. Individuals on the receiving end of the supportive transaction feel positive about the actions of others and the investment of those people in them. They are also much more likely to the provider of support to the same or other individuals at a later date.

Convoy Model—Life Span Perspective

Most important to this conceptualization of social relationships is the life-span perspective. Individuals grow and mature both intraindividually and interindividually. As capabilities and comprehension develop, the individual has a better understanding of both what one's own needs as an individual are and what it means to be the recipient of support from others. Babies do not understand much about the support provided by their mothers, but as they develop they have a much better understanding of the significance of support and its importance to their own development. Similarly, as these supportive interactions accumulate, individuals develop a personal history both with specific others, such as their parents, as well as with global others, for example, authority figures like teachers or employers, and with friends or coworkers who are peers. Relations can be cumulative in both a positive and negative direction and with specific others as well as categories of others. They are also likely to change as new people are added and others are lost, for example, through marriage or death. Since old age often involves losses through death, divorce, illness, and other limitations, how the elderly compensate for these losses is very important. While one might not argue that the death of a spouse disrupting a marriage of 50 years can easily be replaced by a substituting relationship, it may be the case that individuals who have experienced high quality marital relations are better able to make functional, if limited, substitutions, than are others whose marriages were of lesser quality. In general, however, as social relations evolve in specific special relations, such as mother and child or husband and wife, there also appears to be the development of overall patterns of social interaction that have life-span and developmental generalizability.

This theoretical construction helped in the description and perhaps even the prediction of the relationship between social support, health, and well-being but did very little to explain the mechanisms through which these results might be achieved. To this end, James Jackson and Toni Antonucci proposed the Support/Efficacy Model of Social Relations.

SUPPORT/EFFICACY MODEL OF SOCIAL RELATIONS

The Support/Efficacy Model (Antonucci & Jackson, 1987) was developed to explain the processes and mechanisms through which social relations might have the observed positive effect on health and well-being. It was argued that through continual interactions with a successive array of significant or supportive others, individuals develop the belief that they have the ability to meet the demands of the situation, to meet successfully the challenges they face. In short, it might be said that these interactions provide the individual with the ability to achieve and maintain competence. The Support/Efficacy Model assumes the characteristics of the Convoy Model outlined previously, that is, that relationships are hierarchical, have cause and effect associations, and are life-span in nature. Thus the continual interactions that people have with convoy members over their lifetimes have cumulative effects. The importance of these interactions vary depending upon the past history of the dyad and on relative importance of the ''supporter'' to the ''supportee.'' Thus help or advice from someone who has always provided good support in the past will be more valued than from someone who is an enemy or has a history of bad judgment. Similarly, support from a close friend or relative is perceived differently than support from a stranger or an enemy. Continual interactions with close supportive others providing the target person with encouraging feedback or support is thought to have a cumulative positive effect. Similarly, it should be recognized that the opposite might be true, and individuals without such support or with ''supportive'' others who express doubt in the individual's ability will serve to undermine that person's goal setting. In the context of maintaining competence throughout old age, the

Support/Efficacy Model would predict that supportive others can help older people set and meet goals that will maximize adaptation to the challenges of aging. This might mean adaptation to changes in physical surroundings, physical limitations, or illnesses. Given the nature of aging, these adjustments would not be singular but are likely to be continual and cumulative. The process must therefore be understood to be dynamic in nature.

This model is proposed as a useful guide toward understanding the demonstrated association between social relations and health. The model is consistent with data thus far available. Next, we consider the application of these theoretical perspectives to maintaining competence.

SOCIAL RELATIONS AND MAINTAINING COMPETENCE

In this section we propose to link the theory, the known data, and the pressing problem of helping the elderly to maintain competence. To begin, we introduce the Health/Disease Continuum as a useful conceptualization for the experience of the elderly regarding their health. Next, the constructive linking of the health/disease continuum to the maintenance of competence is considered.

Health/Disease Continuum

Health is one of the most pressing concerns of the elderly. Everyone, and especially older people, move along a health continuum from very healthy to experiencing health crises to recovering from health crises. At each point on the health continuum, different behaviors on the part of the individual are warranted as are different kinds of interactions with others. Thus, for example, when the individual is predisease or very healthy, it is most useful to engage in preventive health behaviors such as appropriate exercise, nutritious diets, or fastening of seat belts. Also during this period it is important to avoid aversive health behaviors such as overeating, excessive drinking, and smoking. As one moves along the health continuum, one is more likely to experience an acute health crises. At this point the individual might need to deal with a number of types of crises, for example, a heart attack, a broken hip, or being diagnosed with a significant illness. And finally, at the postcrises or recovery phase, lifestyle changes or rehabilitative behaviors are often required to achieve and maintain recovery.

Health Continuum and Social Relations

It is already known that certain mechanisms seem to operate at different points on the health continuum. Other work in this field (Silverstein & Bengtson, 1991) has noted that it is useful to think of individuals as requiring and benefiting most from different types of social relations and interactions, depending upon specific circumstances. In this case the specific circumstance might be seen as their location on the health continuum. At the prevention level, the effect of supportive others on maintaining appropriate (and sometimes inappropriate) life styles or health behaviors has been documented (Rakowski, Julius, Hickey, Verbrugge, & Halter, 1988; Umberson, 1987; Krause, Goldenhar, Liang, & Jay, 1993). The activities referred to previously as important at the predisease end of the health continuum can be minimized or maximized through relations with others who either encourage or reinforce specific types of health behaviors. Examples might include friends who go walking with you or relatives who insist on fastened seat belts while they are driving, but others might also reinforce aversive health behaviors by urging you to drink or smoke a cigarette when they are having one. These might be considered more normative, noncrises behaviors. The social interactions occurring around these events are generally of a nonemergency nature.

At the point of a specific health crises, it is often most useful to have supportive others available. Here, when the individual is actually coping with the acute aspects of the crises, there may be very specific needs. Examples include someone to perform CPR, someone to help the older patient make critical and urgent treatment choices, or someone to simply reassure the elderly person at the time of an operation, for example, hip replacement (compare Litwak & Messeri, 1989). However, as you move into the rehabilitation period when you need psychological support, different aspects of the social relations become critical. You need somebody who makes you feel like you can achieve your goal of a lifestyle change or who provides you with the basic motivation to recover. Bandura's (1986) finding indicating that the successful recovery of postmyocardial infarction husbands was significantly related to their wives' beliefs in their recovery is an interesting example. Data are also available now that address the issue of direct effects of social relations either on immune response or neuroendocrinal functioning (Dorian & Garfinkle, 1987; Jemmott & Magloire, 1988; Kiegolt-Glaser et al., 1987). Both of these functions can influence the individual's susceptibility to and recovery from health crises. With this perspective and assuming the evidence presented thus far is convincing, the next step is to take a proactive view of social relations. Social relations obviously involve both the target person, in this case the older person, and his or her supportive others. If we think of the individual as moving along the health continuum, both parties must feel that their role is to maximize the factors associated with health at all points on the continuum and minimize those factors that interfere or negatively influence outcome.

We turn now to an overview of empirical evidence that may help us understand social relations among the elderly as well as a consideration of the evidence already available concerning the link among social relations, health, and well-being. An impressive amount of data are now available. Consequently, we are beginning to achieve a better understanding of how social relations affect health and well-being. Outlined in the next section are some preliminary thoughts on this matter. Empirical supporting evidence is also provided.

EMPIRICAL EVIDENCE:
SOCIAL RELATIONS AND COMPETENCE

Social Networks among the Elderly

Perhaps the most basic questions concern descriptive characteristics of the support networks of older people. What kinds of social relations do the elderly have? Who are their close and intimate network or convoy members? Over the last several years, good empirical evidence has been accumulating. It is now possible to construct the social networks of the elderly based on large nationally representative samples. As Shanas (1979) noted from data collected in the late '60s, elderly people are not left alone or isolated. They often report significant close social relations. If we are interested in using supportive others to help maintain competence, it is important to document who are the supportive others to whom older people might turn and what is the nature of these relationships. We use data collected as part of our program of research at the Survey Research Center to outline what is already known and consider how this information might be used to maintain competence in old age.

We begin with data from our project on Social Relations and Mental Health over the Life Course (Akiyama & Antonucci, 1994). These data include 1,702 people from 8 to 93 years of age. Interviews were conducted by trained interviewers in 1 hour face-to-face meetings. The data were collected from a tricounty area of metropolitan Detroit. The study itself is unique because it contains parallel data on the social relations of a community based on a random sample of people that covers most of the life course. The study is also unique because an exactly parallel study was conducted in Japan, providing the interesting opportunity to compare the findings between the vastly different cultures. The Japanese study includes 1,842 people from age 8 to 96. The Japanese data were collected in the Yokohama metropolitan area, an industrial city chosen because of its similarity to Detroit. The Japanese data were collected by trained staff from Central Research Services, a Tokyo-based survey organization in a 1 hour face-to-face interview.

Our data indicate that people across all ages have a considerable number of individuals they consider close and important to them. While there are significant age differences, people of all ages report, on the average, between 8 and 11 network members. Since the data for children, those between the ages of 8 and 12, were collected in a slightly different fashion to account for their limited cognitive capacities, we focus here on the data from a subsample who received the adult interview, those between the ages of 13 and 93.

There are significant age differences in the number of people who are listed as very close, somewhat close, and close. The pattern is curvilinear. The youngest and oldest age groups report the fewest people in their networks, while the middle-aged group, that is, people from 35 to 49, report the most. Similarly, there is a great deal of overlap in the role relationships of people who are included in the network. The overwhelming majority of people are family members. The youngest age group is most likely to include parents, siblings, and friends, while the oldest tends to include spouse (when alive), children, grandchildren, and friends. The middle-age groups include spouse, children, siblings, and friends. Clearly, the old, like the young, have a great number of social relationships they consider important. And although these are only cross-sectional data, it is clear that the relationships are predominantly with the same people over time. Of course, age differences are not the same as age changes; nevertheless, it does seem likely that in this case age differences give us some indication of age changes.

Since the inner circle consists of spouse, children, and siblings, it is clear that except in the case of major family disruptions such as death and divorce, these people are likely to remain the same over time. Since our focus here is on the elderly, it is useful to note that the greatest source of loss of network members among the elderly is likely to be death. For example, while spouse is listed as the closest person in the network for most married people, we know that with age and among older women, in particular, the probability of being married declines radically.

As we develop long-term strategies for maintaining competence, it is important to recognize that the people who will be critical to the maintenance of competence are likely to be consistent, longtime members of the older person's close personal network. These data also have implications for Carstensen's socioemotional selectivity theory (1992). However, some significant members of the network will be lost, so individuals must make adjustments. Younger adults may have marginally larger networks, but it is useful to note that the number of inner circle members varies by less than one at any point in the life span. It is probably true that younger people have a wider array of contacts, but the really close and important ones appear to remain substantially the same. Perhaps, consistent with Carstensen's socioemotional selectivity theory, older people simply do not bother to maintain those more extensive, but clearly less important, ties.

Social Support among the Elderly

We also know a great deal about the exchanges people experience. We have documented the degree to which older people give to and receive support from their network members. Information is available about a relatively wide array of instrumental and affective support exchanges. Detailed information concerning support provided and received from a random sample of older American adults is available from the Supports of the Elderly Study (Kahn & Antonucci, 1984). The data were obtained from a national representative sample of 718 individuals, 50 years of age and older. People aged 70 and above were oversampled by including all members of the household over 70 once the household was selected into the sample. The Supports of the Elderly was the first study to focus exclusively on the elderly and their social relations, including social network, social support, and what we then called support adequacy. The data were collected in 1980 and included a 1-hour face-to-face interview of people aged 50 to 95. Several additional characteristics about this sample should be mentioned. Interviews were also conducted with a subsample of network members mentioned by the original sample. Sixty-nine couples are part of that special subsample.

We asked about six types of support exchanges in this study, both giving and receiving. The six types of support were confiding, reassurance, respect, sick care, talk about problems, and talk about health. The data indicate that a great deal of giving and receiving of each of the six types of support is reported. Three types of data documenting these exchanges are interesting:

1. the total amount of support exchanged;
2. the degree of reciprocity; and
3. the veridicality of support exchanges.

Antonucci and Akiyama (1987) found that all six types of support are provided and received at every age. They examined the exchanges by age and circle placement, that is, the degree of reported closeness of the network member. As one might predict, there are circle placement differences in both providing and receiving support. More exchange of support is reported among inner circle members than middle or outer circle members. Their examination of age differences, however, indicated that there is no age difference in the reported receipt of support, but there is an age difference in the provision of support. In other words, there was no difference in the amount of support that an individual reported receiving regardless of age. Younger people, on the other hand, reported providing more support to their network members than older people. The second point of interest concerning reciprocity focuses on the role of relationship to exchange. The greatest role relationship link is between two types of support, confiding and sick care. As Ingersoll-Dayton and Antonucci (1988) indicate, the greatest amount of reciprocity is between spouses, less among children and friends.

Another interesting aspect of the exchange of social support concerns the degree to which each of the support partners agrees in his or her report of the support that has been exchanged, that is, the perceived veridicality of the exchanges. Antonucci and Israel (1986) examined this question specifically. Using the data collected from the network members of the original respondents, as previously described, it was possible to explore the degree to which each person agreed that he or she had received whatever support the other had reported providing and vice versa. Specific veridicality ranged from 49% to 60%, with an overall veridicality rate reaching a high between closest network members of 86%. Veridicality was clearly related to closeness; spouses had the highest rate of agreement concerning support exchanges, and friends had the lowest. Veridicality was not significantly related to life satisfaction, happiness, or negative effect, but perception of support was. Ingersoll-Dayton and Antonucci (1988), using the same data but only the original respondents' perception of nonreciprocity in close relationships, found that their perception was related to well-being, especially perception of the network as too demanding and negative affect. Thus one might conclude that any intervention should target the focal person's perception rather than agreement with others or even objective reality.

Two things should be emphasized about these data. The first is that the greatest agreement is among the people to whom you feel most close, and the second is that whether or not you agree about the support that you exchange with another is not as fundamentally important to your well-being as your satisfaction with the relationship.

And finally, Acitelli and Antonucci (1994) conducted another set of analyses using couple data from the Supports of the Elderly Study. They found that no reciprocity measure reported by the husband, including both actual and perceived reciprocity reports, was significantly related to the husband's well-being. On the other hand, each assessed measure of actual and perceived reciprocity was significantly related to the wife's well-being.

It might also be useful to note that there are clear cultural differences in the perception and report of reciprocity. In another study that included data from white and African Americans as well as a sample of French elderly (Antonucci, Fuhrer, & Jackson, 1990), while 47% of African Americans and 38% of white Americans reported that they received less support than they provided, only 4% of the French respondents felt this was the case. On the other hand, 59% of the French but only 46% of the white Americans and 36% of the African Americans felt their relationships were equally reciprocal. These findings suggest that there may be differences in cultural norms and expectations.

The results just summarized seem particularly important as we begin to think about designing interventions that will maximize the role of interpersonal relationships in the maintenance of competence in old age. It may not be the objective reality of the relationship or even the agreement between the two parties about their supportive exchanges that is important, but rather the identity of the target person as well as the target individual's perception of the support exchanged.

Remember the original link that made the concept of social support interesting to epidemiologists and health professionals is that people who reported "better" social relations were healthier, less likely to die, had fewer illnesses, had better psychoimmunological functioning, and generally better mental health. In developing the link between social relations and competence among the elderly, one more facet of the data is especially useful. Next, we examine the degree to which different aspects of social relations appear to affect differentially or be significantly associated with outcomes. These data will directly impact proactive and reactive interventions.

LINK TO DIFFERENT TYPES OF COMPETENCE

Maintaining competence is a life-span phenomenon. For the most part, maintaining competence is best achieved through interactions with others, especially in old age. The relevant types of interactions are those most commonly alluded to as social support. This is not only to say that others help them maintain competence but that competence itself is a moving target. As health status changes, competency goals are likely to change as well. Successfully walking 5 miles might signal competence to the healthy 60-year-old, but walking 50 feet might also signal a successful and important competency achievement to the same 60-year-old, 6 months poststroke.

Interpersonal interactions that maximize competence are likely to vary by the criteria of interest. Although we are interested in old age, it is not age that is the defining characteristic that earmarks the unique features that optimize competence. Rather, it is the specific domain of competence being targeted that determines the important characteristics of the relationship. Baltes and Baltes (1990) have considered a similar point in their work on selective optimization with compensation. Next, we expand on this idea with a specific focus on old age. Nevertheless, there is every reason to believe that these principles are operative at any age.

In the most simple case, when the individual is not confronted by any pressing major problems (such as illness, poverty, or bereavement), it appears to be the case that satisfaction with support relationships has a positive, generalized effect on well-being. On the other hand, when the individual is confronted with a specific problem, supportive behaviors that directly address the problem are extremely useful, especially when the outcome assessed is specific to the problem. Next, several examples from current studies are provided.

The PAQUID Study

Recent data from a unique epidemiological study of a representative sample of the elderly in southwestern France have examined related information and enabled us to specify further the effects of different characteristics of support relationships. The study of Personnes Agees Quid (PAQUID) is a longitudinal study of 3,777 people aged 65 and over. Data were collected in the Gironde and Dordogne departments of France by specially trained staff in 1-hour interviews. A series of analyses on the first wave survey data examined the relative effect of support network or structure measures such as size and composition of network and quality of social support, including positive and negative evaluative measures, on depressive symptomatology (Antonucci, Fuhrer, & Dartigues, 1995). The sample of the first wave survey consists of largely healthy individuals who, we might say, are at the predisease end of the health continuum. Findings indicate that while both types of support significantly reduce depressive symptomatology, quality of support measures account for almost twice the variance as network measures. One might argue that the maintenance of competence in the form of mental health among relatively healthy older persons is best explained through the quality of interactions with others.

The Supports of the Elderly Study

In another set of analyses based on the Supports of the Elderly study, mentioned earlier, it is clear that support measures are differentially related to outcome measures. Examination of support variables predicting happiness of this generally healthy sample indicates that qualitative or evaluative measures of support as well as the perception of reciprocity in close relationships are related to happiness, whereas quantitative variables are much less related (Antonucci & Akiyama, 1987). Once again, maintaining competence through mental health is significantly related to the quality of social relations of the healthy elderly.

Cancer Symptom Study

Another study addresses health issues and maintenance of competence through an examination of the performance of appropriate health care behaviors. In a follow-up study of the Supports of the Elderly study, we asked people about the experience of specific symptoms. The follow-up study involved the reinterview 4 years later of 404 respondents from the previous study. In 1984, people were contacted by telephone and asked about social relations that were specific to the goal of seeing a health professional about the symptoms they had experienced. Antonucci, Kahn, et al. (1989) were interested in what factors influence seeking a medical opinion about a cancer-suspicious symptom. This question is important since the elderly often die of treatable cancers because they do not have their symptoms evaluated in a timely manner. As one might predict, severity of symptom clearly influences seeking a doctor's advice. In addition, however, the number of supportive others the respondent has talked to about the symptom and having network members who do something helpful for the respondent about the symptom were also both significantly predictive of seeing a doctor about the symptom.

As ever more varied data concerning support relations become available, some generalized inferences can be drawn. In the absence of major, specific problems, general satisfaction with social relations seems to have a significant effect on well-being. However, when individuals are facing specific problems, as is the case with symptoms, functional limitations, or illness, the receipt of specific types of support is more significantly related to outcome than generalized satisfaction with relationships. Although we cannot yet claim a causal relationship, it is clear that one type of relationship becomes more important than another depending upon the situation at hand. In the case of the study involving cancer symptoms, having people specifically address issues related to the symptom is related to getting that person to seek health care.

These data suggest that specificity is required in the model to maintain competence in the face of specific challenges or threats that confront the elderly. The cancer symptom data indicate that specific support from others directed at the health problem, in this case the symptom, is most useful in getting the individual to seek professional help. Other data are less direct but also suggestive.

These are preliminary thoughts and a brief review of findings, some of which are very new, others of which are old but have not been considered in light of this particular issue of maintaining competence. As an overview, it might be added that work in several nations leads to still another observation. While there may be some universals in these relationships, there are also some cultural differences either in the basic relationships or how they are expressed. Although in the next section we speculate broadly, on the more cautious side, we want to add that it is necessary to be careful about overgeneralizing to other cultures, countries, or ethnic groups. Nevertheless, we would like to speculate about how these observations may have an impact upon an intervention program proactively aimed at helping the elderly maintain competence.

INTERVENING TO MAINTAIN COMPETENCE

A lifetime integration of the Social Relations and Health Continuum and the Support/Efficacy Model seems especially appropriate for our consideration of the question of maintaining competence.

Proactive Planning

If we begin with the recognition that everyone moves along the Health Continuum, the need to plan for changing needs as one moves along the continuum is clear. One can plan proactively. Individuals can think of those characteristics of their interactions with their close and supportive others, which are most helpful, or least helpful, at each stage. One might target increased interaction with specific others who could help an older person maintain a healthy lifestyle, while avoiding interactions with those who might influence the older person to engage in health aversive behaviors. Examples of the former might be walking buddies, of the latter (excessive) eating buddies. In anticipation of specific crises, one could outline how supportive others might be informed or made knowledgeable enough to help at the moment of crises. Examples that might be useful would be specific contacts with experts to recognize problems such as numbness in the left arm as a possible indication of heart problems. Another possibility would be daily calls or signals (lifting of the shades or opening of the blinds) from informal supportive others to signal health. Other possibilities include more formal supports such as Life Line, an auxiliary health care service allowing the elderly to press a device worn around the neck to call for emergency help.

Similarly, at the point of rehabilitation, each individual might consider which characteristics of their relationships or which persons in their network might be most beneficial to achieving their rehabilitative goals. But this should not be considered singularly unidirectional. Supportive others also should be actively engaged in this process, and they should take a long-term, bidirectional view as well. Plans can be developed for both parties helping each other if and when they need help. As one moves along the Health Continuum there are likely to be potential issues such as declining health and increasing limitations. Significant supportive others can plan to help each other in proactive ways. These might include encouraging regular checkups so that impairments can be minimized through early identification. Proactive planning might also target physical surroundings and life circumstances. Supportive others might encourage the elderly to move to more appropriate housing (e.g., to single-story from multiple-story housing) or to plan for an orderly retirement from the family business, large corporate executive position, or volunteer work at the hospital. This can be seen as another major change in how we view health and appropriate living. Supportive others can help older individuals maintain competence by proactive planning for normative changes that are likely to occur as they age. These might eventually be recognized as a revolutionary change in how we view old age, much as natural childbirth radically changed how we viewed the childbearing experience. Instead of assuming that aging is a phenomenon to be experienced passively, as child birth used to be experienced, we may need to educate ourselves that aging is a period of life for which we must take a proactive, planning role. Similar, but perhaps somewhat less broad in scope, are the changes that have been achieved in other areas, such as seat-belt fastening, cigarette smoking, and drinking when pregnant.

Links to the Socioemotional Selectivity Theory

As we move to the practical side of this, the research of Carstensen and Silverstein will be particularly useful. The socioemotional selectivity theory (Carstensen, 1992) suggests that people become more selective about the number of people with whom they maintain close relationships as they get older. Our speculations suggest that the number of supportive others is not critical as long as some supportive relationships do exist. Consequently, if older people become more selective about who they maintain a relationship with, this should not be problematic. Our data indicate that older people maintain close supportive relationships with significant others such as spouse, children, siblings, and close friends. Focusing on the more important close ties should, therefore, not threaten competence in any way. For general well-being, satisfaction or quality of relationship is important, not increased numbers of interactive relationships. The major threat to competence here is the lose of a significant relationship through death. The death of a spouse, for example, is not likely to be readily compensated for no matter how big one's network might be. Nevertheless, one can usually maintain other significant, if less close, relationships. Interventions may, therefore, best be directed at maintaining the quality of these relationships.

Links to the Needs Matching Theory

Silverstein's research, especially some of his work with Eugene Litwak but also more recent studies with Bengtson (Silverstein & Bengtson, 1991) and Waite (Silverstein & Waite, 1993), directly suggests that supportive interactions should match the needs of the individual. This is very useful for understanding and designing interventions that allow supportive others to directly target the threat. Thus the individual with health problems or reduced functional capacity would benefit more by specific interactions or instrumental support that targets the specific threat, for example, someone available to provide a ride to the hospital when experiencing chest pains, rather than high quality, globally positive support such as a warm and loving marital relationship. Once the individual's situation is understood, threats to competence can be ascertained and the specific supports needed identified. Then the appropriate support might be reinforced, encouraged, developed, or maintained. The maintenance of competence in old age is a practical problem that involves real people. What we are dealing with is a moving target. As this chapter has suggested, however, it will be possible to develop both prevention and intervention programs that will be effective in helping the individual maximize competency.

SUMMARY AND CONCLUSIONS

Although a great deal of research has been conducted in this area and a great deal is yet to be done, we believe we can offer, based on relatively sound empirical evidence, suggestions for how social relations may help the older person maintain competence in a variety of life situations across the health continuum. Three overall principals are relevant: (1) social relations involve both intra as well as interpersonal processes; (2) social relations are life span, longitudinal, and developmental in nature; and (3) social relations and health involve bidirectional influences. Since the maintenance of competence in old age is a practical problem that involves real people, it is not surprising that such events are not likely to occur in isolation. With individuals, old as well as young, multiple factors interact and effect outcomes. This, too, tends to be a moving target, but as this chapter has suggested, it will be possible to develop prevention and intervention programs that will be effective in helping the individual maximize competency.

REFERENCES

Acitelli, L., & Antonucci, T. C. (1994). Gender differences in the link between marital support and satisfaction in older couples. *Journal of Personality and Social Psychology, 67*(4), 688–698.

Akiyama, H., & Antonucci, T. C. (1994). *Gender and depressive symptomology: A developmental and cross-cultural study.* Paper presented at the 48th annual scientific meeting of the Gerontological Society of America in Atlanta, GA.

Antonucci, T. C. (1985). Personal characteristics, social support and social behavior. In R. H. Binstock & E. Shanas (Eds.), *Handbook of aging and social sciences* (pp. 94–129). New York: Van Nostrand Reinhold Company.

Antonucci, T. C. (1986). Social support networks: A hierarchial mapping technique. *Generations, 10*(4), 10–12.

Antonucci, T. C., & Akiyama, H. (1987). Social networks in adult life: A preliminary examination of the convoy model. *Journal of Gerontology, 42*, 519–527.

Antonucci, T. C., & Depner, C. E. (1982). Social support and informal helping relationships. In T. A. Wills (Ed.), *Basic process in helping relationships* (pp. 233–253). New York: Academic Press.

Antonucci, T. C., Fuhrer, R., & Dartigues, J. F. (1995). *Social relations and mental health in a sample of community dwelling French elderly.* Unpublished manuscript.

Antonucci, T. C., Fuhrer, R., & Jackson, J. S. (1990). Social support and reciprocity: A cross-ethnic and cross-national perspective. *Journal of Social and Personal Relationships, 7*(4), 519–530.

Antonucci, T. C., & Israel, B. (1986). Veridicality of social support: A comparison of principal and network members' responses. *Journal of Consulting and Clinical Psychology, 54*(4), 432–437.

Antonucci, T. C., & Jackson, J. S. (1987). Social support, interpersonal efficacy, and health: A life course perspective. In L. L. Carstensen & B. A. Edelstein (Eds.), *Handbook of clinical gerontology*. New York: Pergamon Press.

Antonucci, T. C., Kahn, R. L., & Akiyama, H. (1989). Psychological factors and the response to cancer symptoms. In R. Yancik & J. W. Yates (Eds.), *Cancer in the elderly: Approaches to early detection and treatment* (pp. 40–52). New York: Springer.

Baltes, P. B., & Baltes, M. M. (1990). *Successful aging: Perspectives from behavioral science*. New York: Cambridge University Press.

Bandura, A. (1986). *Social foundations of thought and action*. Englewood Cliffs, NJ: Prentice-Hall.

Berkman, L. F., & Breslow, L. (1983). *Health and ways of living*. New York: Oxford University Press.

Berkman, L. F., & Syme, S. L. (1977). Social networks, host resistance, and mortality: A nine-year follow-up study of Alameda County residents. *American Journal of Epidemiology, 109*, 186–204.

Blazer, D. G. (1982). Social support and mortality in an elderly population. *American Journal of Epidemiology, 115*, 684–694.

Brody, S. J., Poulshock, S. W., & Masciocchi, C. F. (1978). The family caring unit: A major consideration in the long-term support system. *The Gerontologist, 18*(6), 547–555.

Caplan, R. D., Robinson, E. A. R., French, J. R. P., Jr., Caldwell, J. R., & Shinn, M. (1976). *Adherence to medical regimens: Pilot experiments in patient education and social support*. Ann Arbor: University of Michigan Institute for Social Research, Research Center for Group Dynamics.

Carstensen, L. L. (1992). Social and emotional patterns in adulthood: Support for socioemotional selectivity theory. *Psychology and Aging, 7*(3), 331–338.

Cassel, J. (1976). The contribution of the social environment to host resistance. *American Journal of Epidemiology, 104*, 107–122.

Cobb, S. (1976). Social support as a moderator of life stress. *PsychoMedical, 38*, 300–314.

Coe, R. M., Wolinsky, F. D., Miller, D. K., & Prendergast, J. M. (1985). Elderly persons without family support networks and use of health services: A follow-up report on social network relationships. *Research on Aging, 7*(4), 617–622.

Cohen, C. I., Teresi, J., & Holmes, D. (1985). Social networks, stress, adaptation and health. *Research on Aging, 7*(3), 409–431.

Doherty, W. J., Schrott, H. G., Metcalf, L., & Iasiello-Vailas, L. (1983). Effect of spouse support on health beliefs on medications adherence. *Journal of Family Practice, 17*(5), 837–841.

Dorian, B., & Garfinkel, P. E. (1987). Stress, immunity and illness: A review. *Psychological Medicine, 17*, 393–407.

House, J. S., Robbins, C., & Metzner, H. L. (1982). The association of social relationships and activities with mortality: prospective evidence from the

Tecumseh Community Health Study. *American Journal of Epidemiology, 116,* 123–140.

Ingersoll-Dayton, B., & Antonucci, T. C. (1988). Reciprocal and non-reciprocal social support: Contrasting side of intimate relationships. *Journal of Gerontology: Social Sciences, 43*(3), S65–S73.

Jemmott, J. B., & Magliore. (1988). Academic stress, social support, and secretory immunoglobulin A. *Journal of Personality and Social Psychology, 55*(5), 803–810.

Kahn, R. L., & Antonucci, T. C. (1980). Convoys over the life course: Attachment, roles, and social support. In P. B. Baltes & O. Brim (Eds.), *Life span development and behavior, Vol. 3* (pp. 253–286). New York: Academic Press.

Kahn, R. L., & Antonucci, T. C. (1984). *Supports of the elderly: Family, friends, professionals (Final report to the National Institute on Aging)*. Washington, DC: U.S. Government Printing Office.

Kaplan, G. A., Salonen, J. T., Cohen, R. D., Brand, R. J., Syme, L. S., & Puska, P. (1988). Social connections and mortality from all causes and from cardiovascular disease: Prospective evidence from eastern Finland. *American Journal of Epidemiology, 128,* 370–380.

Kiegolt-Glaser, J. K., Glaser, R., Shuttleworth, E. C., Dyer, C. S., Ogrocki, P., & Speicher, C. E. (1987). Chronic stress and immunity in family caregivers of Alzheimer's disease victims. *Psychosomatic Medicine, 49,* 523–535.

Krause, N., Goldenhar, L., Liang, J., & Jay, G. M. (1993). Stress and exercise among the Japanese elderly. *Social Science and Medicine, 36*(11), 1429–1441.

Langlie, J. K. (1977). Social networks, health beliefs, and preventive health behavior. *Journal of Health and Social Behavior, 18*(3), 244–260.

Lindsey, A. M., & Hughes, E. M. (1981). Social support and alternatives to institutionalization for the at-risk elderly. *Journal of the American Geriatrics Society, 29*(7), 308–315.

Litwak, E., & Messeri, P. (1989). Organizational theory, social support and mortality rates: A theoretical convergence. *American Sociological Review, 54,* 49–66.

Medalie, J. H., & Goldbourt, U. (1976). Angina pectoris among psychosocial and other factors as evidenced by a multivariate analysis of a 5 year incidence study. *American Journal of Medicine, 60,* 910–921.

McKinlay, J. B. (1980). Social network influences on morbid episodes and the career of help seeking. In L. Eisenberg & A. Kleinman (Eds.), *The relevance of social science for medical practice* (pp. 77–110). Hingman, MA: D. Reidel.

Orth-Gothmer, K., & Johnson, J. B. (1987). Social network interaction and mortality. A six year follow-up of the Swedish population. *Journal of Chronic Diseases, 40,* 949–957.

Rakowski, W., Julius, M., Hickey, T., Verbrugge, L. M., & Halter, J. B. (1988). Daily symptoms and behavioral responses results of a health diary with older adults. *Medical Care, 26*(3), 278–297.

Ruberman, W., Weinblatt, E., Goldberg, J. D., & Chaudhary, B. S. (1984). Psychosocial influences on mortality after myocardial infarction. *New England Journal of Medicine, 311,* 552–559.

Rundall, T. G., & Evashwick, C. (1982). Social networks and help-seeking among the elderly. *Research on Aging, 4*(2), 205–226.

Schoenbach, V. J., Kaplan, B. G., Fredman, L., & Kleinbaum, D. G. (1986). Social ties and mortality in Evans County, Georgia. *American Journal of Epidemiology, 123,* 577–591.

Shanas, E. (1979). The family as social support system in old age. *The Gerontologist, 19,* 169–174.

Silverstein, M., & Bengtson, V. L. (1991). Do close parent-child relations reduce the mortality risk of older parents? *Journal of Health and Social Behavior, 32,* 382–395.

Silverstein, M., & Waite, L. J. (1993). Are blacks more likely than whites to receive and provide social support in middle and old age? Yes, no, and maybe so. *Journal of Gerontology: Social Sciences, 48*(4), S212–S222.

Umberson, D. (1987). Family status and health behaviors: Social control as a dimension of social integration. *Journal of Health and Social Behavior, 38,* 306–319.

Wan, T. T. H., & Weissert, W. G. (1981). Social support networks, patient status and institutionalization. *Research on Aging, 3,* 240–256.

Commentary: Social Relationships in Context and as Context: Social Support and the Maintenance of Competence in Old Age

Laura L. Carstensen and Frieder R. Lang

C ritics have argued over the years that psychology's primary focus on the individual tacitly denies the social context in which humans develop (Baltes & Graf, 1994; Bronfenbrenner, 1979). This criticism is particularly relevant to the area of social development, where bidirectional influence is omnipresent. In a relatively recent history, however, the tides have begun to change. Social and developmental psychologists have joined forces with sociologists and epidemiologists to address an intriguing and reliable finding that places individuals squarely in a social context: namely, social ties predict morbidity and even mortality (Cassel, 1976; Cobb, 1976; Berkman & Syme, 1979; Blazer, 1982; House, Robbins, & Metzner, 1982). Nevertheless, disciplinary approaches have persisted. Sociological and epidemiological approaches have attempted to quantify and describe entire social networks. Psychological approaches have focused more exclusively on dispositional styles of individuals or interchanges in dyadic relationships. Subsequently, functional and interactional aspects of social relationships often have been lost in sociological conceptions of social networks, and the context of the broader social fabric has been lost in psychological studies of particular relationships independent of the encompassing social network.

We mention this backdrop because it illuminates the exception that Antonucci and her colleagues have been crossing disciplinary boundaries and fusing diverse conceptualizations of social relationships. In this commentary, we discuss the role that the theoretical formulations of the Convoy Model of Social Relations (Kahn & Antonucci, 1980) and the Support-Efficacy Model of Social Relations (Antonucci & Jackson, 1987) have played in this evolving research arena and provide additional theoretical and empirical support for these models. We also address the links that social support may have to competence in old age. Throughout the chapter, we draw on theoretical and empirical work of our own and others that reliably lends support and sometimes expands on the central points offered by Antonucci and Akiyama in this volume.

THE CONVOY MODEL OF SOCIAL RELATIONS

Conceptual Contributions

The Convoy Model of Social Relations, introduced by Kahn and Antonucci in 1980 and elaborated extensively thereafter (Antonucci, 1985a, 1985b, 1986, 1990, 1991; Antonucci & Akiyama, 1987, 1994; Antonucci, Fuhrer, & Jackson, 1990), provides a life-span developmental framework for considering how individuals construct and maintain lifelong social relationships with significant others. Social convoys are presumed to serve the individual in a number of ways, ranging from physical protection and instrumental assistance to providing a sense of embeddedness in the social world and generally facilitating feelings of well-being and adjustment. The model does not presume that convoy members exert a uniformly positive influence, nor does it assume that all convoy members serve similar functions. On the contrary, it is a hierarchical model, which presumes that closer social partners exert greater influence—whether positive or negative—than more distant ones. Social networks are not characterized a priori by roles, such as spouse, child, friend. Rather, the most important feature of a social partner is the degree to which a target individual feels emotionally close to that person. This avoids presumptions that, for example, spouses are by default emotionally close to one another or that different friends hold equal importance for the target individual.

A central feature of the Convoy Model of Social Relations is its life-span perspective. According to the model, people become increasingly aware of the strengths and weaknesses of their convoys and its members over time. The ever-increasing knowledge base allows people to better select particular social network members for particular functions. In other words, people learn over time who best to turn to when emotional support is needed, which social partners are best able to help with activities of daily living, and who is best suited to help in times of crisis. In short, accumulated expertise about a social network accrues over a lifetime and increasingly guides and refines access to potential functions of the social world.

No doubt, these convoys are critical to psychological development throughout life. Through repeated interactions with others, for example, self-concept is developed and maintained. The value of convoys to psychological status may be particularly important in old age, when many social structural features of the environment (e.g., work) disappear and self-defining roles (e.g., parent) become less active instrumentally.

Methodological Contributions

The Convoy Model of Social Relations leads directly to a methodological approach that captures essential structural aspects of social networks and hierarchical organization as it pertains to emotional closeness. The social network questionnaire consisting of three concentric circles (Kahn & Antonucci, 1980) and described by Antonucci and Akiyama (see Chapter 5 of this volume), is an elegantly simple measure that has great appeal to investigators. Research participants readily understand the concepts of interest. Vocabulary required for administration is limited, thus reducing potential influences of education or intellect on subjects' responses. Moreover, the measure is easily transportable across cultures and languages. We know of no other social network measure that has generated more culturally comparative findings than the Kahn and Antonucci measure. It has been used with great success in the United States, France, Japan, and Germany.

Links between the Social Convoy Model of Social Relations and Socioemotional Selectivity Theory

The notion that social networks are cultivated over time is consistent with both the Convoy Model of Social Relations (Kahn & Antonucci, 1980) and socioemotional selectivity theory (Carstensen, 1991, 1993, 1995). The former is described in Chapter 5 of this volume. The latter is a life-span theory of motivated social behavior premised on the assumption that social behavior is activated by the salience of specific social goals. Like the Convoy Model, goals or functions of interaction are presumed to range from basic survival, such as protection from physical danger and the satisfaction of hunger or thirst, to psychologically relevant goals, such as the development and maintenance of self-concept and the regulation of emotion. The central premise of socioemotional selectivity theory is that, even though an essential social goal constellation operates throughout life, the salience of specific goals within this constellation fluctuates systematically as a function of past learning, psychological perceptions of the future and opportunity structures in the environment to satisfy goals. As elaborated below, the theory suggests that the regulation of emotion becomes increasingly salient over time, while the acquisition of information and the desire to affiliate with unfamiliar others becomes less so.

Changes in the salience of specific social goals are influenced to a considerable degree by the ability of social partners in the environment to satisfy identified goals, a utility that interacts importantly with individual maturation and experience. Very early in life, virtually all social partners are useful sources of information. Social interaction is the *primary* means of cultural transmission and is also an excellent resource for self-relevant information. Because interactions are information-rich, motivation for contact, even with unfamiliar social partners, is high. However, with age, as one's factual knowledge base grows and the self becomes better defined, interaction with novel social partners becomes less useful precisely because such contacts do not provide novel information to the individual. At the same time information seeking via social contact is becoming less useful, however, benefits of contact with a selective few are increasing, due largely to accumulated knowledge about familiar social partners. This social expertise about close social partners allows for better predictability and control of interactions. Moreover, interaction with emotionally close social partners offers increasingly more valuable rewards over time. Social partners who share history and knowledge about a target individual can provide unmatched empathic responses in times of need, verify self-concept, offer advice informed by personal history, and serve as good resources for affect regulation. Thus there are gains and losses associated with changes in social partner contact over life. Novel social partners, on average, come to offer less, but familiar social partners come to offer more. We stress that, according to the theory, the entire constellation of social motives continues to operate throughout life. There are conditions when the oldest old will prefer novel over emotionally close social partners and conditions when the youngest young will sacrifice information for affect regulation. We are focusing on what we believe is an *average* shift in preferences and behavior reflecting age-related changes in motivation.

In addition to a gradual shift in social preferences that is anchored in experience, social preferences are influenced importantly by the psychological construal of the future. Socioemotional selectivity theory contends that when the future is perceived as limited, attention shifts to the present, and more immediate needs, most notably, the regulation of emotion, assume highest priority. When emotion regulation is the most salient goal, people become highly selective in their choice of social partners, nearly always preferring social partners who are familiar to them because goal attainment is most likely with them. As a result of such changes, relative to younger people, older people are less motivated to engage in emotionally bereft but otherwise functional social contact and make social choices based on the potential for emotional rewards. Thus, according to the theory, social preferences are influenced both by internal goals and the probability that the external environment can fulfill such goals.

It appears that social networks do become increasingly focused on emotionally close social partners across adulthood. In a reanalysis of a longitudinal data set from the Intergenerational Growth Studies housed at the University of California-Berkeley, Carstensen (1992) found evidence of a gradual and *selective* reduction in social contact from late adolescence to middle age. Contact with acquaintances declined over time, with the most pronounced reduction occurring between the ages of 18 and 30 years; however, rates of interactions slightly increased in emotionally close relationships. Even more importantly, emotional closeness increased or remained stable in emotionally close relationships even when actual contact was reduced.

ACTIVE AND PASSIVE SELECTION IN SOCIAL NETWORKS IN OLD AGE

Empirical research on social networks in old age has been, for the most part, descriptive. One of the major contributions of the Convoy Model of Social Relations has been to point to the dynamic interplay between structural and functional aspects of network characteristics. Antonucci and her colleagues suggest that social networks of older individuals comprise multiple individual relationships each with their own history and set of functions, and that together these singular relationships comprise a greater social "gestalt" that surrounds individuals as they pass through life. The fact that the overall size of these social gestalts is substantially reduced in old age has been a topic of considerable interest and concern to gerontologists for many years (Maddox, 1963) and has stimulated hotly debated discussions about the reasons for such change (Carstensen, 1987; Osgood, 1989).

One reason that social networks shrink in late life is clearly "passive selection," that is, the process by which social partners are lost due to mortality and morbidity. Put simply, the longer one lives, the more people one outlives. Antonucci and Akiyama's example of an old woman who has survived virtually all those people who knew her when she was young appears to be a common experience for people who survive into the ninth decade of life. It has been described by some as the experience of "being left behind" (Bury & Holme, 1991).

Perhaps because passive selection indubitably occurs in late life, there has been relatively little attention to proactive processes that may also operate on social networks toward the end of life. In particular, we have been exploring the idea—grounded in socioemotional selectivity—that older people actively shape their social networks such that they comprise a disproportionate number of emotionally close social partners (Lang & Carstensen, 1994; Lang, Staudinger, & Carstensen, under review). We reasoned that if networks are reduced primarily through deaths of network members, this reduction should occur on a relatively random basis throughout the social network regardless of how close social partners are to target individuals. If, instead, reductions are *motivated*, reflecting a diminished desire for contact with social partners who do not offer emotional rewards, there should be a selective reduction in social networks that operates increasingly with the emotional distance of network members. Thus we hypothesized that the number of emotionally close social partners would be highly comparable for younger and older people, whereas the number of less close social partners should drop significantly with age.

To address these questions, we examined data from the Berlin Aging Study (BASE), a large multidisciplinary research project based on a representative sample of old and very old people aged 70 to 104 years (see

Baltes, Mayer, Helmchen, & Steinhagen-Thiessen, 1993). We completed a cross-sectional age comparison between younger and older subjects.

The social network measure used in the project was the German version of the circle diagram developed by Kahn and Antonucci (1980). The hierarchical concepts underlying the measure were ideal for our purposes. We considered social partners classified in different concentric circles to be qualitatively different from one another along the dimension of emotional closeness, that is, persons named in the first circle were considered extremely close and persons named in the outer circles (or not named in the circles at all) were considered increasingly less close emotionally. Indeed, we found that the social networks of this relatively old sample were structured hierarchically according to the degree of emotional closeness with social partners. Subjects easily classified social network members into the circles. Spouses and children were named predominantly in the inner circle, whereas friends and acquaintances were named in less close or not so close categories. This was not always the case, however, supporting Antonucci and her colleague's contention that the hierarchical organization of social networks is not entirely role-based. In some cases, nuclear family members were named in outer circles or outside of the circles entirely, and friends were named in the inner circle.

Overall, findings supported our hypotheses. First, the number of network members described as very close did not differ between the older and younger subsamples. In contrast, the number of less close social relationships was considerably fewer for older versus younger people in the sample. Thus, while there were differences in overall network size between younger and older subjects, differences were not distributed evenly across levels of emotional closeness as one would expect if morbidity and mortality alone accounted for differences in network size. Rather, reductions in more peripheral relationships accounted for age differences.[1]

Perhaps even more important, we found evidence for the adaptiveness of the reduction in network size (Lang & Carstensen, 1994; Lang et al.,

---

[1]To ensure that the apparent selective reduction was not due to the fact that the people in the inner circle were simply younger and subsequently had longer life expectancies, we examined more closely the age composition of network members in each circle. We found that network members named in the outer circles were, on average, slightly older than those named in the inner circles; however, the difference was small—outer circles compared to inner circles contained only 5% more network members over the age of 75. Thus, even if all the older network members had died, it would not explain the robust differences (roughly 50%) in network size between younger and older subsamples.

under review). Recall that the observed pattern of reduction in network size is consistent with the notion of ''distilling.'' When more distant social relationships are not maintained but close ones are maintained, the overall density of emotionally close relationships in a respective network increases. In our first study (Lang & Carstensen, 1994), we found that this density was related to feelings of social embeddedness. With increasing age, social networks consist of relationships that are emotionally close. In a second study, we showed that a subsequent increase in the mean level of closeness of a network was associated with stronger feelings of social embeddedness (Lang et al., under review).

In an extension and replication of these initial findings, Lang et al. (under review) confirmed these patterns of selection in social networks in late life and differentiated more closely between the quantitative (i.e., network size) and qualitative (i.e., emotional closeness) aspects of social relationships. In addition, we considered personality dimensions that may explain age-related differences in social networks such as extraversion, openness, and neuroticism. We found that qualitative aspects of social networks, such as the degree of emotional closeness with network partners, contributed above and beyond network size and personality differences to social embeddedness. Regardless of individual differences, older people appear to profit from a distilling of the social network such that the proportion of emotionally meaningful social partners is increased. If the reduction in networks was due to mortality alone, older people would not profit from feelings of social and emotional satisfaction with networks. We contend that networks are not just ''dying out,'' but are actively constructed by older people.

Interestingly, among older people without a nuclear family (i.e., defined as people who had neither a spouse nor a child), the association between emotional closeness of social network partners and feelings of social embeddedness was even higher than among people who had a nuclear family. This is noteworthy because it suggests that socioemotional selectivity operates as an adaptive mechanism within the constraints and provisions of specific relational contexts. We expect that two factors may contribute to the strength of the relationship among older people without a nuclear family: First, in the absence of a nuclear family, people appear to exert even more active efforts to construct emotionally satisfying social networks, and, second, they are not obliged—for reasons related perhaps to experimental demand characteristics or the symbolic meaning of family—to classify family members as emotionally close even when they may not really function as such. This is related to Wills' (1985) concept of "status support," which refers to support derived from the sheer presence of a role-based social partner. In other words, the social relationships of people without a nuclear family are typically less binding and more voluntary. Subsequently, examination of the social networks of these people may provide the best evidence for active construction of social networks.

One final note regarding the social networks of people without a nuclear family. Even though people who had a nuclear family reported higher levels of social embeddedness, when people without a nuclear family included three or more social partners in their inner circle, they matched the levels of social embeddedness of people with a nuclear family. Thus people can (and do) compensate for the absence of a nuclear family in old age and, in some ways, have the opportunity to construct these networks according to individual preferences even more so than people who have a nuclear family.

As Antonucci and Akiyama (this volume) point out, the effects of status support are not always positive. The presence of a spouse when a marriage is difficult, for example, may exert negative effects. In fact, research on marriage provides an excellent illustration of the need for the conjoint consideration of qualitative and quantitative aspects of social relationships when evaluating their influence on mental and physical health. Quantitative approaches to social network analysis typically consider marital status a categorical variable, that is, a person is either married or single. Studies based on this approach have yielded numerous reports that marriage disproportionately benefits husbands. Married men, on average, are mentally and physically healthier than their single counterparts. Married women, on average, are less mentally and physically healthy than their single counterparts. When marital quality is considered, however, the picture changes and presents a potentially more interesting and informative piece of the puzzle. Specifically, it appears that unhappily married wives account for the reported deleterious effects of marriage on women (Hess & Soldo, 1985; Levenson, Carstensen, & Gottman, 1993). Happily married wives are not affected negatively. It is conceivable in light of the literature on gender differences in emotional experience and expression that the absence of emotional closeness affects men less (or at least differently) than women (Gottman & Levenson, 1988).[2] These findings underscore Antonucci and Akiyama's (Chapter 5 of this volume) assertion that "being married does not necessarily mean your spouse provides you with support, nor does it mean that all the people who are married are fortunate enough to be involved in high quality relationships." Clearly, both quality and quantity are fundamentally important aspects of social networks.

SOCIAL RELATIONSHIPS AND COMPETENCE IN OLD AGE

Social connectedness indubitably enhances competence in old age. A tremendous amount of support for daily functioning comes by way of instrumental assistance provided by close friends and relatives. Family members—typically female kin—are, by far, the principal supporters of older adults, surpassing support provided by formal government programs established for such purposes (Carstensen & Pasupathi, 1993). Reliance on others for assistance holds many benefits for older people. The adaptive role of dependency, for example, has been well articulated by Baltes (1995; see Chapter 4 of this volume), who argues that the judicious relinquishing of certain responsibilities can enhance rather than diminish the overall functioning of older adults.

In the remainder of this chapter, we concentrate on the more nebulous role social relationships appear to play in enhancing psychological competence in older adults. In this arena, Antonucci's contributions have, once again, been seminal. The Support-efficacy Model of Social Relationships, proposed by Antonucci and Jackson (1987), provides a social context within which to consider self-efficacy. Rather than tacitly view social support as a unidirectional process, the support-efficacy model characterizes social support as a process that depends on the personal characteristics of a target individual and support-giver within a specific relational opportunity structure. The support-efficacy model is truly relational in that social

---

[2]Levenson et al. (1993) speculate that emotionally toxic interactions may have more adverse effects on women than men because women typically assume the problem-solving role in heterosexual relationships and push toward resolution of conflicts, whereas men more likely withdraw in the face of emotional conflicts. Although withdrawal may create problems in the relationship, it may also serve a protective function by reducing physiological arousal associated with negative emotions.

support is conceptualized as a social transaction of at least two interaction partners who share a specific relationship. In the support-efficacy model, the support-receiver is considered an active agent in the social support process who exerts influence on when and from whom social support is received. On the one hand, social support can compensate for deficits in competence and thus contribute to the older person's adjustment. For example, Hobfoll (1989, Hobfoll & Freedy, 1990) has shown that the more social and personal resources are available, the better older people compensate for age-related losses. On the other hand, relying on social support resources also places specific demands on the older individual such as the normative obligation to reciprocate received supports (Antonucci & Jackson, 1990; Gouldner, 1960; Rook, 1987; Wentowski, 1981).

Moreover, the support-efficacy model is—to the best of our knowledge—the only attempt to link directly the social support literature with social learning theory and the concept of self-efficacy (Bandura, 1982, 1986, 1992). In doing so, the support-efficacy model opens the door to conceiving of supportive relationships not only as occurring within contexts but also as influencing relational contexts.

Just as Bandura (1986) differentiates between outcome expectancies and efficacy expectancies, support-receivers' expectations about the outcomes of specific instances of received support must be differentiated from individuals' self-related efficacy expectations pertaining to need for support and support-management within specific relationships.

Three distinct perspectives about the contextual and relational effects of social self-efficacy can be distinguished.

1. Individuals' general self-efficacy can mediate the effects of relational outcomes, such as self-affirmation or positive affect, on health and well-being. It appears that people who have a strong sense of control profit more from receiving social support than those who lack a comparably strong sense of control (e.g., Krause, 1987; Lefcourt, Martin, & Saleh, 1984; Riley & Eckenrode, 1986; Schulz & Decker, 1985). Control beliefs may allow older people to receive support without experiencing it as threatening to their self-competence and, thus, feel less burdened by support.

2. Subjective beliefs about the capacity to influence social transactions and their outcomes with social partners optimizes the potential for social support within particular relationships (Antonucci & Jackson, 1987; Baltes & Reisenzein, 1986; Riggio, Throckmorton, & DePaola, 1990;

Solano, 1989; Spitzberg & Hurt, 1989). For example, Kessler, Price, and Wortman (1985) argue that control beliefs influence how and when people mobilize social support (see also Heller & Swindle, 1983). Bandura (1982) proposed the concept of "proxy control" for such processes, referring to the allocation of control within a particular domain to another person, thereby maintaining indirect control within that domain. The use of proxy control in interpersonal contexts can allow older people to compensate for the loss of primary control.

3. The support-efficacy model contends that older individuals' subjective expectations about supporters' competencies influence the level of comfort experienced when support is enlisted. Most close relationships go through times of conflict or periods of relational crises that must be mastered if social partners will continue to be satisfied with the relationship (Antonucci, 1985a; Duck, 1986). Successfully managing the stable and varying as well as the positive and negative aspects of family ties or friendships is likely fundamental for high levels of social adaptivity throughout adulthood and late life (Lang, Featherman, & Nesselroade, 1995; Morgan, 1990). This means, as Antonucci and Akiyama (Chapter 5 of this volume) point out, that the stability of supportive transactions in a relationship is important for adequate support. Receiving support from unreliable sources who fluctuate in their readiness to give support may well cause strains in support-receivers and reduce a sense of control (Lang et al., 1995). We emphasize that everyday competence is not only related to performance in circumscribed activities of daily life, but is also associated with competence to deal effectively with interpersonal matters.

In closing, the relationship between social support and competence, in our view, represents a complex system of exchanges between persons and environments. Achieving competence throughout life—but particularly in old age—requires social resources. Too much support or too little support can have deleterious effects (Lawton, 1989). Since social resources are not stable commodities, but rather require ongoing negotiation, support exchange is a continuous regulatory process. Particularly in old age, the social support one receives reflects not only current needs and abilities, but lifelong patterns of support. Although a great deal is known about descriptive aspects of such resources in old age, we are only beginning to understand the active psychological and behavioral processes that maintain them. The theoretical and empirical work contributed by Antonucci and her colleagues have made major contributions toward this end.

REFERENCES

Antonucci, T. C. (1985a). Personal characteristics, social support, and social behavior. In R. H. Binstock & E. Shanas (Eds.), *Handbook of aging and the social sciences* (2. Aufl., S. 94–128). New York: Van Nostrand Reinhold.
Antonucci, T. C. (1985b). Social support: Theoretical advances, recent findings and pressing issues. In I. G. Sarason & B. R. Sarason (Eds.), *Social support: Theory, research and application* (pp. 21–37). Dordrecht, Netherlands: Nijhoff.
Antonucci, T. C. (1986). Measuring social support networks: Hierarchical mapping technique. *Generations, 10,* 10–12.
Antonucci, T. C. (1990). Social supports and social relationships. In R. H. Binstock & L. K. George (Eds.), *Handbook of aging and the social sciences* (3. Aufl., S. 205–226). San Diego: Academic Press.
Antonucci, T. C. (1991). Attachment, social support, and coping with negative life events in mature adulthood. In E. M. Cummings, A. L. Greene, & K. H. Karraker (Eds.), *Life-span developmental psychology: Perspectives on stress and coping* (pp. 261–276). Hillsdale, NJ: Erlbaum.
Antonucci, T. C., & Akiyama, H. (1987). Social networks in adult life and a preliminary examination of the convoy model. *Journal of Gerontology, 42,* 519–527.
Antonucci, T. C., & Akiyama, H. (1994). Convoys of attachment and social relations in children, adolescents, and adults. In F. Nestmann & K. Hurrelmann (Eds.), *Social networks and social support in childhood and adolescence* (pp. 37–52). Berlin: de Gruyter.
Antonucci, T. C., Fuhrer, R., & Jackson, J. S. (1990). Social support and reciprocity: A cross-ethnic and cross-national perspective. *Journal of Social and Personal Relationships, 7*(4), 519–530.
Antonucci, T. C., & Jackson, J. S. (1987). Social support, interpersonal efficacy, and health: A life course perspective. In L. L. Carstensen & B. A. Edelstein (Eds.), *Handbook of clinical gerontology* (pp. 291–311). New York: Pergamon Press.
Antonucci, T. C., & Jackson, J. S. (1990). The role of reciprocity in social support. In B. R. Sarason, I. G. Sarason, & G. R. Pierce (Eds.), *Social support: An interactional view* (pp. 173–198). New York: John Wiley.
Baltes, M. M. (1995). Dependencies in old age: Gains and losses. *Current Directions in Psychological Science, 4,* 14–19.
Baltes, M. M., & Reisenzein, R. (1986). The social world in long-term care institutions: Psychosocial control toward dependency. In M. M. Baltes & P. B. Baltes (Eds.), *The psychology of control and aging* (pp. 315–343). Hillsdale, NJ: Erlbaum.
Baltes, P. B., & Baltes, M. M. (1990). Psychological perspectives on successful aging: The model of selective optimization with compensation. In P. B.

Baltes & M. M. Baltes (Eds.), *Successful aging: Perspectives from the behavioral sciences* (pp. 1–34). New York: Cambridge University Press.

Baltes, P. B., & Graf, P. (1994). *Psychological and social aspects of aging: Facts and frontiers.* Paper presented at the Nobelsymposium Life-span Development of Individuals: A Synthesis of Biological and Psychological Perspectives, Stockholm, Sweden.

Baltes, P. B., Mayer, K. U., Helmchen, H., & Steinhagen-Thiessen, E. (1993). The Berlin Aging Study (BASE): Overview and design. *Ageing and Society, 13*, 483–515.

Bandura, A. (1982). Self-efficacy mechanism in human agency. *American Psychologist, 37*, 122–147.

Bandura, A. (1986). *Social foundations of thought and action.* Englewood Cliffs, NJ: Prentice-Hall.

Bandura, A. (1992). Exercise of personal agency through the self-efficacy mechanism. In R. Schwarzer (Ed.), *Self-efficacy: Thought control of action* (pp. 3–38). Washington: Hemisphere Publishing.

Berkman, L. F., & Syme, S. L. (1979). Social networks, host resistance and mortality: A nine-year follow-up study of Alameda County residents. *American Journal of Epidemiology, 109*, 186–204.

Blazer, D. (1982). Social support and mortality in an elderly community population. *American Journal of Epidemiology, 115*, 684–694.

Bronfenbrenner, U. (1979). *The ecology of human development.* Cambridge, MA: Harvard University Press.

Bury, M., & Holme, A. (1991). *Life after ninety.* London: Routledge.

Carstensen, L. L. (1987). Age-related changes in social activity. In L. L. Carstensen & B. A. Edelstein (Eds.), *Handbook of clinical gerontology* (pp. 227–237). New York: Pergamon Press.

Carstensen, L. L. (1991). Selectivity theory: Social activity in life-span context (pp. 195–217). *Annual review of gerontology and geriatrics, 11.* New York: Springer.

Carstensen, L. L. (1992). Social and emotional patterns in adulthood: Support for socioemotional selectivity theory. *Psychology and Aging, 7*, 331–338.

Carstensen, L. L. (1993). Motivation for social contact across the life span: A theory of socioemotional selectivity. In J. Jacobs (Ed.), *Nebraska symposium on motivation: 1992, Developmental Perspectives on Motivation, Vol. 40* (pp. 209–254). Lincoln: University of Nebraska Press.

Carstensen, L. L. (1995). Evidence for a life–span theory of socioemotional selectivity. *Current Directions in Psychological Sciences, 4*, 151–156.

Carstensen, L. L., & Pasupathi, M. (1993). Women of a certain age. In S. Matteo (Ed.), *Critical issues facing women in the '90s* (pp. 66–78). Boston: Northeastern University Press.

Cassel, J. (1976). The contribution of the environment to host resistance. *American Journal of Epidemiology, 104*, 107–123.

Cobb, S. (1976). Social support as a moderator of life stress. *Psychosomatic Medicine, 38,* 300–314.

Duck, S. (1986). *Human relationships.* London: Sage.

Gottman, J. M., & Levenson, R. W. (1988). The social psychophysiology of marriage. In P. Noller & M. A. Fitzpatrick (Eds.), *Perspectives on marital interaction* (pp. 182–200). Clevedon, England: Multilingual Matters.

Gouldner, A. W. (1960). The norm of reciprocity: A preliminary statement. *American Sociological Review, 25,* 2, 161–178.

Heller, K., & Swindle, R. W. (1983). Social networks, perceived social support and coping with stress. In R. D. Felner, L. A. Jason, J. Moritsugu, & S. S. Farber (Eds.), *Preventive psychology: Theory, research, and practice in community intervention* (pp. 87–103). New York: Pergamon Press.

Hess, B., & Soldo, B. (1985). Husband and wife networks. In W. J. Sauer & R. T. Coward (Eds.), *Social support networks and the care of the elderly: Theory, research and practice* (pp. 67–92). New York: Springer.

Hobfoll, S. E. (1989). Conservation of resources. A new attempt at conceptualizing stress. *American Psychologist, 44,* 513–524.

Hobfoll, S. E., & Freedy, J. R. (1990). The availability and effective use of social support. *Journal of Social and Clinical Psychology, 9,* 91–103.

House, J. S., Robbins, C., & Metzner, H. M. (1982). The association of social relationships and activities with mortality: Prospective evidence from the Tecumseh Community Health Study. *American Journal of Epidemiology, 116,* 123–140.

Kahn, R. L., & Antonucci, T. C. (1980). Convoys over the life course. Attachment, roles and social support. In P. B. Baltes & O. G. Brim (Eds.), *Life-span development and behavior* (pp. 254–283). New York: Academic Press.

Kessler, R. C., Price, R. H., & Wortman, C. B. (1985). Social factors in psychopathology: Stress, social support, and coping processes. *Annual Review of Psychology, 36,* 531–572.

Krause, N. (1987). Understanding the stress process: Linking social support with locus of control beliefs. *Journal of Gerontology, 42,* 6, 589–593.

Lang, F. R., & Carstensen, L. L. (1994). Close emotional relationships in late life: Further support for proactive aging in the social domain. *Psychology and Aging, 9,* 315–324.

Lang, F. R., Featherman, D. L., & Nesselroade, J. R. (1995). *Managing short-term variability in personal relationships: Evidence from the MacArthur Successful Aging Studies.* Manuscript under review.

Lang, F. R., Staudinger, U. M., & Carstensen, L. L. *Socioemotional selectivity in late life: How personality does (and does not) make a difference.* Manuscript under review.

Lawton, M. P. (1989). Behavior-relevant ecological factors. In K. W. Schaie & C. Schooler (Eds.), *Social structure and aging: Psychological processes* (pp. 57–78). Hillsdale, NJ: Erlbaum.

Lefcourt, H. M., Martin, R. A., & Saleh, W. E. (1984). Locus of control for affiliations and behavior in social interactions. *Journal of Personality and Social Psychology, 48,* 755–759.

Levenson, R. W., Carstensen, L. L., & Gottman, J. M. (1993). Long-term marriage: Age, gender, and satisfaction. *Psychology and Aging, 8,* 301–313.

Maddox, G. L. (1963). Activity and morale: A longitudinal study of selected elderly subjects. *Social Forces, 42,* 195–204.

Morgan, D. L. (1990). Combining the strengths of social networks, social support, and personal relationships. In S. Duck & R. C. Silver (Eds.), *Personal relationships and social support* (pp. 190–215). Newbury Park, CA: Sage.

Osgood, N. J. (1989). Theory and research in social gerontology. In N. J. Osgood & A. H. Sontz (Eds.), *The science and practice of gerontology. A multidisciplinary guide* (pp. 55–87). New York: Greenwood Press.

Riggio, R. E., Throckmorton, B., & DePaola, S. (1990). Social skills and self-esteem. *Personality and Individual Differences, 11,* 799–804.

Riley, D., & Eckenrode, J. (1986). Social ties: Subgroup differences in costs and benefits. *Journal of Personality and Social Psychology, 51,* 770–778.

Rook, K. S. (1987). Reciprocity of social exchange and social satisfaction among older women. *Journal of Personality and Social Psychology, 52,* 145–154.

Schulz, R., & Decker, S. (1985). Long-term adjustment to physical disability: The role of social support, perceived control, and self-blame. *Journal of Personality and Social Psychology, 48,* 1162–1172.

Solano, C. H. (1989). Loneliness and perceptions of control: General traits versus specific attributions. In M. Hojat & R. Crandall (Eds.), *Loneliness, theory, research, and applications* (pp. 201–214). Newbury Park, CA: Sage.

Spitzberg, B. H., & Hurt, H. T. (1989). The relationships of interpersonal competence and skills to reported loneliness across time. In M. Hojat & R. Crandall (Eds.), *Loneliness: Theory, research, and applications* (pp. 157–172). Newbury Park, CA: Sage.

Wentowski, G. J. (1981). Reciprocity and the coping strategies of older people: Cultural dimensions of network building. *The Gerontologist, 21,* 600–609.

Wills, T. A. (1985). Supportive functions of interpersonal relationships. In S. Cohen & S. L. Syme (Eds.), *Social support and health* (pp. 61–82). New York: Academic Press.

Commentary: Emerging Theoretical and Empirical Issues in the Study of Social Support and Competence in Later Life

Merril Silverstein

For more than 15 years Antonucci and her colleagues have made important conceptual and empirical contributions to the scientific study of interpersonal relationships over the life span. With Kahn, she developed a method to examine how networks of social relationships, or convoys, change in size and character through adult life (Kahn & Antonucci, 1980). Their introduction of the "sociogram"—a method that asks subjects to rate social distance from network members within a system of concentric circles—has provided an elegant analytic tool for assessing a matrix of social relations and has become the dominant paradigm in the social sciences for mapping the terrain of social relationships over time.

In their chapter, Antonucci and Akiyama review the literature of two distinct bodies of research:

1. studies of age-related or developmental influences on the composition, intensity, functions, and degree of reciprocity within social support networks, and
2. studies of the relationship between social support and disease.

They summarize what we have learned from these many studies and suggest new ways of conceptualizing and measuring social support and well-being in old age within a developmental perspective.

Antonucci's research has been concerned with identifying the structure and function of social networks, examining patterns of exchange between network members, and studying the value of social support for health and well-being. It is therefore not surprising that in this volume she has turned her attention to the consequences of socially supportive relationships for the maintenance of competence in later life. The "Convoy Model" again serves as a useful perspective from which to view the role played by informal support providers in promoting competence and improving the quality of life of older people. This approach incorporates both developmental changes *and* continuities in social networks over time. Thus, conclusions can be drawn about how networks are different in later life than they are in young adulthood (smaller and more selective, as suggested by Carstensen in the commentary to Chapter 5 of this volume), and how the relational *histories* of older people have consequences for contemporary support opportunities.

The processes by which social relations are developed, lost, or never made earlier in life have consequences for the types of supportive relations that are available in old age. For example, the "support bank" hypothesis (Antonucci, 1985) views reciprocity from a life-span perspective: early in the family life cycle, parents build a repository of social equity by investing in their dependent children, then in later life withdraw this equity in the form of social support from their (purportedly grateful) children. As the dynamic nature of social support networks is made explicit by the Convoy Model of Social Relations, so is the dynamic nature of *disease* made explicit in the Support/Efficacy model developed by Antonucci and Jackson (1987). This model proposes that specific responses are required from the social network to help the older person adapt to specific challenges imposed by health problems; the efficacy of the response is, thus, contingent on where in the health/disease-course continuum the older person is located.

A major conceptual contribution of Chapter 5 is in the recognition that the two key constructs discussed—social support and competence—are multidimensional and have different meanings at different stages of the life span. That both social support and competence are "moving targets" presents empirical challenges to the researcher, who is seeking broad generalizations. As I will suggest in this commentary, such analytic complexity makes the role of theory crucial for understanding the *process* that links specific kinds of social support to specific outcomes in later life.

In the body of this commentary I will discuss four issues, largely taken from a sociological perspective in gerontology, that inform and, in some instances, expand the explanatory power of the models discussed in Chapter 5:

1. the need to formally test competing theories of social support;
2. the role played by norms and culture in shaping the meaning and impact of social support;
3. negativity or dysfunctions of social support; and
4. the life-course approach and macrosocietal issues as they affect social support exchanges and their outcomes.

THEORY TESTING AND DEVELOPMENT

In the study of social relations there are many empirical findings but relatively few theories to explain them. Ever since Durkheim (1897/1955) linked empirical regularities in suicide rates using the umbrella concept of "social integration," there have been few general theories with the reach and ambition to explain seemingly disparate social facts.

Testing theoretically derived causal hypotheses is hampered in the study of naturally occurring relationships, where it is difficult or unethical to experimentally manipulate the intervention—in this instance, the social relationships of older adults. In one of the few studies that randomly assigns treatments to groups, Heller and Thompson (1991) found that older persons randomly assigned to a telephone companion showed levels of depression no different than a control group. Typically, social scientists rely on survey methods to collect data that can be statistically manipulated to *infer* causality. However, more than one theory may adequately account for the observed data. This dilemma puts great weight on the rigor and explanatory range of the competing theories when deciding which of them to accept.

For example, studies that demonstrate statistically significant associations between social relations and health have explained their findings using a variety of different theories, including:

1. those that stress instrumental benefits of social relations (Litwak & Messeri, 1989);

2. those that stress the ability of social ties to regulate health behaviors (Umberson, 1987);
3. those that stress the capacity of social integration to increase host resistance to disease (Berkman & Syme, 1977); and
4. those that stress the role of personality, sense of control, and depression (Friedman & Booth, 1987; Rodin, 1986; Temoshok, 1985).

How do we make sense of the large number of empirical findings in the study of social relationships and well-being? Which theories explain more of the findings? Meta-analysis is a powerful but underused tool for generalizing findings across studies in a circumscribed body of research. Messeri, Silverstein, and Litwak (1993) use this technique to resolve a debate in social gerontology between two models that have been used to predict social support to the elderly. Do social relations of the elderly substitute for each other hierarchically, or are they specialized for particular tasks? Messeri et al.'s analysis of 12 studies of social support to dependent populations reveals that the latter theory accounts better for the pattern of findings. Meta-analysis, thus, represents a promising method for testing competing theoretical explanations for findings in an emerging empirical literature.

NORMS AND CULTURAL VALUES

The obligations that people have toward each other are defined by the cultural context within which their social networks are embedded. For example, minority elderly and their network members have unique normative expectations concerning which and when significant others should provide help (Silverstein & Waite, 1993). Social support network configurations have their bases in the values and prescriptions as exemplified in norms of individualism and collectivism that define the worldview of ethnic cultures.

An emerging focus in social network studies is the area of immigration and acculturation, particularly with respect to immigrants from Spanish-speaking and Asian countries—currently the most rapidly growing segments of the older population. In such immigrant families, the oldest generation typically emphasizes traditional values with respect to treatment of the elderly, but pressures for acculturation among members of younger generations result in weaker ethnic identification and weaker adherence to culturally prescribed family obligations (Markides, Boldt, & Ray, 1986). What might be the effect of such intergenerational discontinuity? Recent research shows that Mexican-American elderly persons whose expectations for social support from children are unfulfilled have elevated mortality rates (Silverstein, 1995). Thus, culturally prescribed norms that govern expectations for social support imbue supportive behavior with meaning and value.

NEGATIVITY IN SOCIAL SUPPORT

Virtually all research on social support and well-being relies on the assumption—implicit in the use of linear models—that more support is better. Research to date, indeed, is equivocal about whether older persons derive psychological benefits from exchanging social support with members of their networks. Excessive support received *from* network members may increase distress by inducing dependence and eroding autonomy in the older recipient (Lawton, 1982), and excessive support provided *to* network members may increase distress by being burdensome to the older provider. Nonlinear representations may capture better the consequences of social support received and provided in later life (Silverstein, Chen, & Helier, 1996).

A useful paradigm to guide research can be found in the Social Breakdown Theory (Kuypers & Bengtson, 1973). In this theory excessive social support to the vulnerable elderly serves to encourage dependence and loss of function, leading to a downward spiral in mastery and in well-being. Depending on both the needs of the recipient and the intensity of the services provided, social support may variably improve or erode one's sense of competence.

Further, competence itself is a culturally relative construct. For instance, in the United States, where a high value is placed on self-reliance and productivity, competence may be defined as maximizing *independence*, where in other nations or subcultures, competence may be defined as maximizing social *interdependence*. In this way, the cultural milieu contextualizes the link between social support and competence.

LIFE-COURSE AND MACRO APPROACHES

The Convoy Model of Social Relations explicitly treats social support along a temporal dimension. Drawing on a developmental life-span perspective in psychology, this model incorporates the dynamic nature of social networks by taking into account the events, decisions, and exchanges experienced earlier in life in setting the stage for opportunities to receive social support in later life. Antonucci's ''support bank'' hypothesis, with its emphasis on lagged reciprocity, exemplifies the great potential of the life-span approach for understanding contemporary social support relations of older people. Within the sociology of age, an emerging paradigm for interpreting change and continuity in human lives is the *life-course* perspective in which heterogeneity in human development is interpreted within the context of personal and sociohistorical time. This perspective examines developmental trajectories that result from the unique historical and social experiences of birth cohorts as they age (Riley, Foner, & Waring, 1988).

What cohort/historical influences might influence the nature of social relations as people mature into later life? The divorce revolution that began in the 1960s has created a cohort of young and middle-aged adults who are more likely than past cohorts to enter old age either unmarried or remarried (Goldscheider, 1990). Consequently, in the 21st century the older family will consist of more complex step-families where both inter and intragenerational obligations may be ambiguous.

Population fertility represents another cohort-specific force that affects the opportunity to receive support in old age. While the current cohort of older parents benefit from having had relatively large families, the number of children available to subsequent cohorts of older people will be smaller because of the tendency for baby boomers to have small families or to be childless (Himes, 1992). Another change in family structure is occurring on a vertical or lineage axis. Increases in longevity mean that generations are spending more time cosurviving each other (Watkins, Menken, & Bongaarts, 1987). Thus children of older people are increasingly likely to be elderly themselves and may not be capable of providing support. Will grandchildren be the primary support providers to the oldest-old in the 21st century?

Changes in social norms also may result in social support networks being differently configured among future cohorts of elderly. If responsibilities in the postmodern family have become more voluntary and less obligatory in nature, then nonfamily and fictive kin may increasingly become important features in the social networks of the elderly (Allan & Adams, 1989). Recent changes in gender norms and a more egalitarian gender ideology may accelerate the number of men who enter supportive roles with respect to the elderly, although no evidence exists for such a behavioral shift.

Life-course research also considers the role of large social institutions—including the state and the economy—in shaping microlevel events in later life. Since elder-care is a shared function between informal and formal sectors of society (see Litwak, 1985), retrenchment in the welfare state may shift responsibility for elder-care from public to private sources. If political attacks against income, health, and social programs for the elderly result in cuts in public expenditures, future cohorts of elderly may put greater demands on family and other informal relations for needed financial and instrumental support (Bengtson, 1993).

CONCLUSION

In this commentary I have outlined some of the landmark contributions made by Antonucci over her career to the study of social support and well-being. As she suggests, we know with a fair degree of certainty that there are associations between support and well-being; the next challenge is to understand the intervening mechanisms that explain *how* the two domains are linked. I have suggested the use of meta-analysis to summarize what we already know about support and well-being in discernible patterns. The "disease-course" paradigm, that Antonucci suggests to predict which type of support best satisfies which type of health need, is a promising meta-theory that can be used to integrate findings from studies that focus on a diverse set of health conditions and subpopulations.

Competence, as manifested in functional ability or sense of mastery, may represent a mechanism that intervenes between social support and well-being in later life. If social support encourages healthful practices, elevates self-esteem, or enhances feelings of self-efficacy, then statistical models should focus on the *indirect* effects of support on well-being as mediated by competence. However, at present, the relationships among support, competence, and well-being are not well specified and many questions remain unanswered. How much support is needed to optimize competence without overly reducing environmental challenges? How do ethnic and other cultural values moderate these relationships? Does *providing* support to others have as much to do with feelings of competence as does *receiving* support in later life? Even before we begin to empirically address these questions, the literature needs to make a clearer conceptual distinction between subjective dimensions of competence and self-assessmenat of well-being. Is competence a form of well-being?

In summary, I have discussed emerging conceptual and analytic issues in social support that expand our understanding of the social worlds of the elderly. To empirically test these ideas, it will be necessary to contrast social support networks across different cultural groups using the same survey instrument, take into account the contribution made by formal organizations in support of the elderly, and follow the networks of multiple cohorts over time as they mature into old age. The availability of longitudinal data on social support exchanges collected from several cohorts as they age is crucial if we are to disaggregate aging, cohort, and historical influences on the structure and function of social networks of the elderly. Considering macrosocietal changes that lie along a historical dimension of time, *in conjunction* with developmental changes that lie along a personal dimension of time, will enhance our understanding of social support networks and their contribution to competence and well-being in later life.

REFERENCES

Allan, G., & Adams, R. (1989). Aging and the structure of friendship. In R. Adams & R. Blieszner (Eds.), *Older adult friendships: Structure and process* (pp. 45–64). Newbury Park, CA: Sage.

Antonucci, T. C. (1985). Personal characteristics, social support and social behavior. In R. H. Binstock & E. Shanas (Eds.), *Handbook of aging and the social sciences* (pp. 94–129). New York: Van Nostrand Reinhold Company.

Antonucci, T. C., & Jackson, J. S. (1987). Social support, interpersonal efficacy, and health: A life course perspective. In L. L. Carstensen & B. A. Edelstein (Eds.), *Handbook of clinical gerontology*. New York: Pergamon Press.

Bengtson, V. L. (1993). Is the contract across generations changing? In V. L.Bengtson & W. A. Achenbaum (Eds.), *The changing contract across generations* (pp. 3–24). New York: Aldine de Gruyter.

Berkman, L. F., & Syme, S. L. (1977). Social networks, host resistance, and mortality: A nine year follow-up study of Alameda County residents. *American Journal of Epidemiology, 109*, 186–204.

Durkheim. (1897/1955). *Suicide: A study in sociology*. Glencoe, IL: Free Press.

Friedman, H. S., & Booth, S. K. (1987). Personality, Type A behavior, and coronary heart disease: The role of emotional expression. *Journal of Personality and Social Psychology, 53*, 783–792.

Goldscheider, F. (1990). The aging of the gender revolution. *Research on Aging, 12*, 531–545.

Heller, K., & Thompson, M. G. (1991). Support interventions for older adults: Confidante relationships, perceived family support and meaningful role activity. *American Journal of Community Psychology, 19*, 139–146.

Himes, C. L. (1992). Future caregivers: Projected family structures of older persons. *Journals of Gerontology: Social Sciences, 47*, S17–S26.

Kahn, R. L., & Antonucci, T. C. (1980). Convoys over the life course: Attachment, roles and social support. In P. B. Baltes & O. Brim (Eds.), *Life span development and behavior, Vol 3* (pp. 253–286). New York: Academic Press.

Kuypers, J. A., & Bengtson, V. L. (1973). Social breakdown and competence: A model of normal aging. *Human Development, 16*, 181–201.

Lawton, M. P. (1982). Competence, environmental press, and the adaptation of older people. In M. P. Lawton, P. G. Windley, & T. O. Byerts (Eds.), *Aging and the environment: Theoretical approaches.* New York: Springer.

Litwak, E. (1985). *Helping the elderly: The complementary roles of informal networks and formal systems.* New York: Guildford Press.

Litwak, E., & Messeri, P. (1989). Organizational theory, social supports, and mortality rates: A theoretical convergence. *American Sociological Review, 54*, 49–66.

Markides, K., Boldt, J. S., & Ray, L. A. (1986). Sources of helping and intergenerational solidarity: A three generations study of Mexican Americans. *Journal of Gerontology, 41*, 506–511.

Messeri, P., Silverstein, M., & Litwak, E. (1993). Choice of optimal social supports among the elderly: A meta-analysis of competing theoretical perspectives. *Journal of Health and Social Behavior, 34*, 122–137.

Riley, M. W., Foner, A., & Waring, J. (1988). Sociology of age. In N. Smelser (Ed.), *Handbook of Sociology* (pp. 243–281). Newbury Park, CA: Sage.

Rodin, J. (1986). Health, control and aging. In M. M. Baltes & P. B. Baltes (Eds.), *The psychology of control and aging* (pp. 139–163). Hillsdale, NJ: Erlbaum.

Silverstein, M. (1995). *Social relations and mortality in later life.* Paper presented at the Brookdale Foundation Annual Retreat, Garden City, NY.

Silverstein, M., Chen, X., & Helier, K. (1996). Too much of a good thing? Intergenerational social support and the psychological well-being of older parents. *Journal of Marriage and the Family, 58*, 976–982.

Silverstein, M., & Waite, L. (1993). Are blacks more likely than whites to receive and provide social support in middle and old age? Yes, no, and maybe so. *Journals of Gerontology: Social Sciences, 48*, S212–S222.

Temoshok, L. (1985). Biopsychosocial studies on cutaneous malignant melanoma: Psychosocial factors associated with prognostic indicators, progression, psychophysiology and tumor-host response. *Social Science and Medicine, 20*, 833–840.

Umberson, D. (1987). Family status and health behaviors: Social control as a dimension of social integration. *Journal of Health and Social Behavior, 28*, 306–319.

Watkins, S. C., Menken, J. A., & Bongaarts, J. (1987). Demographic foundations of family change. *American Sociological Review, 52*, 346–358.

CHAPTER 6

The Physical Environment and Maintenance of Competence

Victor Regnier

INTRODUCTION

When architects approach the design of housing for the elderly, the design challenge is often defined by larger considerations, such as the organization and sequence of building spaces and the relationship between the site context and the massing of the building. Fitting a building to a site involves

1. reconciling infrastructure linkages, such as roads and utilities;
2. dealing with legal and environmental constraints; and
3. respecting off-site influences, such as views from the site and access to surrounding land uses.

Interior design decisions such as those involving finishes, furniture, fixtures, equipment, and case work are almost always considered after initial spatial relationships are established. These decisions involve materials, such as carpets, furniture, wall surfaces, fixtures and equipment. Unlike the building's structure, the walls and the windows, these interior fixtures and features have a relatively short life span.

When clinicians, researchers, and geriatric practitioners discuss the "environment," they are almost always referring to this "microenvironment,'' which is made up of interior design elements. Replacing the furniture, wall and floor coverings, fixtures, and equipment are typical ''environmental modifications'' that can easily be changed to improve existing conditions. Architects often characterize these minor modifications as trivial to the building design process, which to some degree is true. Interior refurbishing rarely involves major remodeling adjustments to the building. For example, walls, parking lots, unit configurations, common social spaces, and landscape features are not changed when furniture is replaced, carpet is relayed, and walls are painted every 7 to 10 years.

To make housing for frail older people a social and therapeutic success, all of the aspects of a design problem should be considered as part of a potential solution. In new projects or major renovations, the focus of problem solving is on organizing the sequence and placement of spaces, designing the facade of the building, working out site design and parking considerations, and organizing a functional plan.

Competency in this chapter refers to the ability of older residents to carry out Activities of Daily Living (ADLs) and Instrumental Activities of Daily Living (IADLs), as well as to engage in social interaction with others. The focus of this chapter is on designing an environment that provides many possibilities for exercising these competencies and helps to maintain and builds these abilities. An architect who seeks to affect the competency of individual residents must start by raising questions about how the layout, configuration, and ''design'' of the building can best affect the behavior of residents in the building. We know from postoccupancy evaluations of elderly housing projects that the placement of social spaces and the position of resident circulation patterns can create a situation that promotes or discourages social interaction (Howell, 1980).

THERAPEUTIC ARCHITECTURAL DESIGN

Building Design and Client Needs: An Interaction

Architects are trained as generalists and, thus, they are interested in the total environment. Their generalist training can leave them poorly informed about how the nuances of management philosophy, therapeutic regimens, informal family interventions, and changing functional considerations affect requirements for use. Buildings are rarely designed to change in response to the changing needs of residents, emerging new technologies, or reorganized staff patterns and policies. Brand (1994), in a book entitled *How Buildings Learn* attributes many of today's lawsuits and unhappy client-architect relationships to the fact that designers allow the building to fend for itself after the first day of occupancy and rarely pay attention to how clients have used and adapted the spaces designed for them as the building matures and requires change.

The evaluation literature often focuses on the microenvironmental scale of interior design features previously described. When function and use are compromised by features, such as a lack of light, poor grasp control, or an awkward transition caused by a joint between two floor materials, postoccupancy evaluations are very effective. However, architectural or clinical gerontology research evaluations rarely pinpoint how the building fails to support the "therapeutic" nature of the environment. The literature is moot on those issues that most designers consider "major" decisions. Issues like the placement of important therapeutic activities near heavily traveled corridors, the specification of special rooms that encourage competency-building activities, and the development of outdoor spaces that support a range of activities are rarely evaluated. Effectiveness is difficult to measure when alternative design options were not pursued and thus cannot be assessed.

When architectural design configurations facilitate caregiving and encourage therapeutic benefits, the environment can be a powerful tool. The design of the physical environment can make a major contribution toward increasing resident well-being and the beneficial impacts of staff interventions. The best architectural research and writing attempts to raise these questions and to define how the building's architecture can intervene in a way that adds to the quality of life by increasing opportunities for continued independence.

This chapter will focus on two issues: (1) the contribution the design of a building makes to the stabilization, maintenance, and enhancement of mental and physical competency of the older person; and (2) the combination of housing and services in residential models to reduce dependence on institutional solutions.

Shared Spaces and Residential Units

Much of the therapeutic benefit associated with housing for older people relies on how units are connected with shared spaces and the types of spaces set aside for resident activities. Residential units are designed and then replicated in patterns that cluster them along corridors to common meeting areas. These common meeting spaces create the context for a shared social life. The placement of common spaces, their sequence, their approachability, and their functional fit require accurate and insightful design decisions. A thoughtful analysis of common space is needed if they are to create a better therapeutic or social environment and increase resident independence.

The design of the dwelling or residential unit also plays an important role in supporting independence. In particular, kitchens and bathrooms can have deleterious impacts if they are not designed properly. This is an area where human factors knowledge has been very instrumental in guiding and informing alternative design solutions. Human factors knowledge plays a very important role in the specification of cabinets, access tolerances, floor surfaces, and fixtures. The researchers working in this area have contributed a great deal to understanding the relationship between functional manipulation and body dynamics (Charness & Bosman, 1992; Faletti, 1984; Fozard, 1981).

ASSISTED LIVING: AN IMPORTANT HOUSING TYPE

Assisted living is one housing type that has the potential to play an important role in building the competency of mentally and physically frail older adults (Kane & Wilson, 1993; Regnier, Hamilton, & Yatabe, 1995). This housing type is a reinvention of the "home for the aged," which in its modern reincarnation seeks to emphasize independence, autonomy, service choices, self-care, and family integration, in contrast to a fixed, highly regulated, institutional formula for long-term care.

The concept of "assisted living" embraces the potential for increasing resident competency by using programs and policies that intervene to stabilize, build, and maintain higher levels of mental and physical function. Although rehabilitation activities in nursing homes have long reflected this philosophy, they have been considered relatively ineffectual because they are often "too little—too late." Nursing home residents that are assigned physical therapy have often lost their ability to benefit from this activity.

Use of the architecture of the building in a strategic way to increase its therapeutic potential is an underexplored topic in both the design and the clinical aging literature. Much of the research on programs deal with institutional settings such as rehabilitation hospitals or nursing homes (Brody & Ruff, 1986; Kemp, Brummel-Smith, & Ramsdell, 1990; Smyer & Frysinger, 1985). In these settings therapy is defined in a formal manner and carried out in rooms with equipment and procedures that maximize functional outcome and minimize staff time. These short bursts of therapeutic activity are not as effective as a building designed to support a lifestyle that values social interaction, peer support, activity generation, and family interaction.

To take steps forward in the design of therapeutic housing for the frail, we must examine how the setting can be configured to support greater independence and autonomy while providing a safety net of service supports and programs that build both mental and physical competency. Although mental impairments and physical disabilities are common characteristics in the frail population, the approach to dealing with them therapeutically calls upon very different resources, facilities, and therapeutic interventions. The issue of physical competency seems well represented in the exercise physiology literature with numerous recent articles touting the benefits of exercise, movement therapy, and even weight lifting (Emery, Burker, & Blumenthal, 1991; Schmidt, 1993; Spirduso & Gilliam-MacRae, 1991). Articles dealing with how to arrest mental decline through behavioral interventions are more rare. Most of the literature deals with assessment and hints at useful strategies for improving function, recall, and counteracting depression. A few articles begin to suggest how the environment can play a role in therapy (Reifler & Teri, 1986; Wilson, 1989; Zarit, Zarit, & Reever, 1982).

In the United States, years of institutional building types, reinforced by codes, state laws, and archaic professional behaviors have led to a narrow vision of how long-term care environments should be designed. For some architects, creating a therapeutic environment that appears residential in character is antithetical to their understanding of basic building types. Policies regulating group housing environments are based on the level and intensity of services provided. This is accomplished by creating special categories of housing within narrow and prescribed guidelines for performance and quality. Thus homes for the aged, nursing homes, intermediate care settings, group homes, and continuing care retirement communities operate under separate and often very different standards that focus on the competency level of residents. Codes for these building types are often specified in laborious detail outlining everything from the square footage of space to the surface friction of wall coverings.

In contrast to the excessive codes established for institutional settings, relatively little attention has been given to residential environments. When residential environments are mentioned in the rehabilitation literature, they often refer to activities that take place in private residential dwellings (Boling, 1993; Pynoos, 1992). These discussions often begin with the assumption that one "makes do" and intervenes with only modest adjustments. Modifying the bathroom and kitchen to increase safety for the older person and using gadgets that facilitate the manipulation of the environment are commonly referred to as "home modifications."

ARCHITECTURAL LITERATURE AS A GUIDE FOR DESIGN DECISIONS

Most of the literature of interest to designers focuses on functional considerations. Plans and simple descriptions of intentions and building concepts are used to communicate a range of solutions (American Institute of Architects' Committee on Architecture for Health, 1992). These are often devoid of any evidence of performance assessment or evaluation, which limits their usefulness in prescribing effective design solutions. Other texts identify generic design solutions that can aide resident independence (American Institute of Architects Foundation, 1985; Bush-Brown & Davis, 1992; Carstens, 1985; Greene, Fedewa, Johnston, Jackson, & Deardorff, 1975; Zeisel, Epp, & Demos, 1977; Zeisel, Welch, Epp, & Demos, 1983).

The literature often specifies solutions that have proven to be successful in past applications. However, in many cases there is very little empirical data to verify under what conditions these design solutions were effective. Design standards often reflect sensitive issues where incorrect design judgments can impair everyday use.

A common technique is to sensitize designers to the effects of aging through direct experience. Pastalan (1977) has devised a set of empathic eyeglasses and other devices that simulate movement and perception in old age. Hiatt (1987) has focused much of her research on how changing sensory acuity affects the older person's ability to perceive and navigate the environment.

In schools of architecture there has been an attempt to establish theoretical frameworks that conceptualize how older users are affected by the environment. Frequently, there is an attempt to link social and behavioral theories to design situations. This has provided a rich source of theoretical exploration that has led to the development of environmental psychology programs and to an emphasis in some schools on the relationship between social science inquiry and design research activities. The work of Zeisel (1981) and Sommer and Sommer (1983) has helped designers to pursue data collection and refinement techniques that can aide design decision making.

In the aging literature, several edited volumes were produced as a result of the Aging and Environment curriculum project, cosponsored by the Gerontological Society of America in the 1970s (Lawton, Windley, & Byerts, 1982). Surprisingly little of the theoretical work, however, has found its way into the practice of architecture. Twenty years later one might expect that there would be a generation of socially sensitive architects who had been exposed to this perspective and employed behaviorally based information in design decision making. However, the weak link between theory and practice has made it difficult for this to become a reality.

The AIA/ACSA Research Council is currently involved in new curriculum development based on the earlier Aging and Environment curriculum. The focus is on studio-design problem-solving so that students and faculty "translate" problems into solutions in the studio. This approach is in contrast to the focus on the derivation of practical solutions based solely on theoretical formulations.

CASE STUDY EVALUATION RESEARCH

Case studies have been employed to identify and describe important issues in the design of housing for the aged (Cohen & Day, 1993; Hoglund, 1985; Howell, 1980; Regnier, 1994; Salmon, 1993; Valins, 1988; Weal & Weal, 1988). Some studies have focused on specific problems such as the design of housing for dementia residents (Calkins, 1988; Cohen & Weisman, 1991); small congregate houses (Welch, Parker, & Zeisel, 1984) and product design considerations (Koncelik, 1976, 1982; Pirkl, 1994; Raschko, 1982). A few sources have used marketing data in conjunction with design and management concepts to reflect on the experiences of private pay facilities marketed to middle- and upper-middle-class residents (Goodman & Smith, 1992; National Association of Home Builders, 1987).

Others have attempted to link research findings to design and policy decisions (Regnier & Pynoos, 1987).

Much of the research in the 1970s coincided with federal programs for the design and construction of age-segregated independent housing for moderate income people. The focus of much of this research was to understand how the design of these settings could increase social exchange. Howell's (1980) classic research monograph, *Design for Aging: Patterns of Use*, used case study data to hypothesize how patterns of circulation and the location of common spaces in elderly housing projects could lead to socially integrated ''friendly'' buildings. Conversely, it also documented how socially ineffectual buildings can be when planned improperly. Since a major goal of early housing programs was to create a socially conducive ''friendly'' environment, this research was important in securing more predictable social outcomes.

There is growing recognition that management and services play an important role in the design of housing for the frail. Of particular concern is the way that dwelling units should be organized to relate to one another. Lawton (1975) was a pioneer of this approach with his landmark study *Planning and Managing Housing for the Aged*. This book, which benefited greatly from the findings of the 1971 National Survey of Housing for the Elderly, raised questions regarding the manner in which services and management philosophy could support the independence of residents in planned housing. Zeisel's work continued this line of analysis through his consultation with the Captain Eldridge congregate house (Zeisel, 1981) and through his collaboration with Welch in *Independence through Interdependence* (Welch et al., 1984).

Gelwicks and Newcomer (1974) and Hiatt (1991) used planning and program facility management experience to inform facility administrators regarding the planning and design process. A range of issues associated with new facility design and remodeling were addressed in their work.

The most recent work of Cohen and Day (1993), Regnier (1994), and Regnier, Hamilton, and Yatabe (1995) conceptualizes the design of facilities for mentally and physically frail individuals as one that depends in large measure on how well the design of the facility supports an independent residential lifestyle while also facilitating staff support and nurturing the relationship between residents, their families, and the surrounding neighborhood. These research monographs employ case studies and a series of ''therapeutic goals'' to suggest how the environment can be deinstitutionalized while still providing the professional service support necessary for satisfying quality of life considerations.

The concept of a "therapeutic environment" is concerned with how a setting extends quality of life by allowing the individual to stay as independent and autonomous as possible while still leading a safe, socially engaging, and challenging lifestyle. The two major impediments to this goal are diseases and chronic conditions that impair memory and physical ability.

The physical and mental problems of the aged require differing strategies to optimize the therapeutic benefit of the environment. One set of interventions should focus on stimulating physical exercise, and the second should focus on emotional, social, cognitive, and spiritual development.

PROMOTING INDEPENDENCE

Five Environmental Design Issues

As a framework to guide interventions that increase independence, five types of environmental design decisions are considered.

Building Design

These include issues associated with the concept of the building, its placement on the site, the relationship of indoor-outdoor spaces, and the internal organization of common spaces. Arranging units in patterns that allow mentally frail residents to orient themselves better and avoid the frustration of being lost can lead to a higher level of self-control. For physically frail residents, the distance from their dwelling unit to meal service can greatly affect independence.

Environmental Modifications and Details

These involve modifications of equipment and furniture or the specification of special colors, textures, and treatments. Changes in furnishings that make the environment easier to remember ease way-finding for those with mental confusion. Modifications to equipment, devices, and fixtures that allow residents with severe arthritis or lowered grip strength to manipulate the environment are also included here.

Therapeutic Activities

Although activities are often programmed separately from the design of the environment, their placement, visibility, and the way they are configured can increase their utilization and effectiveness. Mental stimulation can be greatly supported by library spaces and music rooms that are designed to carry out therapies that stimulate mental function in a natural way. Design of space for physical therapy, occupational therapy, and exercise activities should attract attention, making residents aware of their presence and encouraging their use.

Socialization

Countering depression through informal social exchange and friendship formation is one of the most important activities a facility can nurture. Clustering unit entry doors to encourage informal helping behaviors between neighbors can increase patterns of interdependence. Programming spaces to support activities and linking common activity spaces and circulation patterns stimulates social activities.

Management and Service

Older residents sometimes require help from aides or family members. The environment should be configured to create the greatest level of independence and privacy while facilitating formal and informal help when necessary. Families can provide enormous effective and emotional support. It should be easy to involve family members in the life of a facility. Caregiving activities like moving, bathing, lifting, and monitoring should supplement a resident's own abilities and should be delivered in a way that encourages the older person to take as much responsibility as possible for his or her own self-care.

Therapeutic Interventions: Capitalizing on Element of Building Design

A housing environment that is designed to stimulate resident competency should make accessible a range of therapeutic activities. The four categories described in the next section include 20 different activities that stimulate mental and physical functioning. Each can produce options for residents seeking a healthy, independent lifestyle. To optimize their effectiveness, these therapeutic activities should be located, sequenced, and related to one another.

Physical Therapies

Walking Therapy

Walking within and around the facility is one of the most popular forms of exercise for both physically impaired and physically fit individuals. Walking can occur inside, by using corridors, or outside around the site or within the neighborhood. Many memory impaired "wanderers" can take advantage of looped pathways. Garden areas and sidewalks that loop the site and the neighborhood can be used for "laps."

Stretching Therapies

Physically impaired residents should have a place to stretch and tone muscles. A large room is needed for this type of group activity. Access to chairs as exercise props and a relatively resilient floor for calisthenics and running is useful. This type of exercise therapy can be experienced by a wide range of individuals.

Upper and Lower Body Exercise Therapies

Equipment such as exercise bicycles, treadmills, and arm exercisers if placed in a location that encourages their use can be physically stimulating and socially engaging activities. Special equipment fitted to the capacities of older users is required, but it doesn't have to be placed in a room dedicated solely to that purpose. Many applications flourish in public spaces where spur of the moment use is possible. These can be social as well as therapeutic activities. Having friends involved in the activity builds esprit de corps and increases motivation.

Outdoor Exercise Therapy

In Sunbelt states, outdoor exercise can take place all year round. Courtyards can be used for walking, stretching exercises, and the location of equipment. When exercises are in a fixed location they should be sheltered from the wind and the sun. Although these are most feasible in places with a moderate climate, spaces that are screened, covered, and protected but still open to the fresh air can work well in other locations.

Swimming Therapy

Swimming is a powerful and effective form of physical exercise. While an inside pool permits year round use, in the summer, inside pools are less appealing because of their poor acoustics, chlorine smell, and the excess humidity generated. Unfortunately, swimming pools are expensive to install and to maintain.

Weight Therapies

Building upper and lower body strength through the use of special weight equipment is becoming more popular. A room dedicated to this purpose is required with equipment calibrated for the capacities of the older person. In recent research this type of therapy has shown to be very effective, but professional guidance is necessary.

Occupational and Activity Therapies

Occupational or Ergo-Therapy

These activities exercise small muscles and stress motor- and eye-hand coordination. Since they result in the production of products such as rugs and fabrics, they are often popular with a range of residents. Occupational therapy should focus on activities that stimulate mental function, encourage creative expression, develop better hand to eye coordination, and encourage manipulating small objects. A special room with higher light levels and special equipment may be required.

IADL and ADL Therapy

Normal activities of daily living are employed to provide structure, meaning, stimulation, and a feeling of participation to memory impaired residents. In smaller scale facilities for memory impaired residents, normal daily activities associated with food preparation (setting the table, busing dishes, preparing food) and with laundry (folding laundry, putting laundry in the machine, sorting it into colors) are used to engage residents in meaningful activities.

Training Kitchen Therapy

Providing a place where residents and friends and family can engage in the basics of food preparation can build or maintain competency. Such activities can be useful to residents who are regaining their ability to manage tasks independently in their own apartment. Individuals making the transition from hospital to their home after a stroke or acute medical episode may need training to regain lost abilities.

Adult Day Care Therapy

Intellectually, socially, and physically stimulating activities can be provided to both facility residents and people living in the surrounding neighborhood. Day care activities are targeted toward the mentally frail. A high staff ratio allows activities to be customized to the interests of participants.

Mixed Land Use Settings

Nearby neighborhood resources provide attractive destinations for residents to visit while also making them less dependent on the facility for all of their needs. Zoning laws that encourage mixed housing, commercial and office land usage allow the frail older person easily to reach convenience stores and make weekly or monthly health visits. In European neighborhoods where mixed land uses are common, housing for the independent elderly is supported by nearby services.

Social and Mentally Stimulating Therapies

Social Exchange and Friendship Formation

Locating spaces that overlook activities and provide opportunities for previewing give residents a sense of control over their interactions with others. One of the advantages of a group living arrangement is the possibility it provides for residents to make new friends and create meaningful social relationships. This is an outcome that should be pursued in the design and placement of common areas. It can be best accomplished by clustering spaces to stimulate informal friendship formation; placing common activity spaces near heavy trafficked corridors; and creating informal opportunities for meeting one another.

Activity spaces can be classified into three types: destination spaces, spur of the moment activity spaces, and spaces for simple, short-lived informal exchanges. Each building has a ''100% corner'' where the activity and the potential for social exchange is the greatest. Placing activity magnets near the primary circulation pathways add to the potential for social exchanges in various areas of the building.

Reading and Intellectually Stimulating Therapies

Providing places for reading the morning paper or listening to music encourages these types of intellectually stimulating activities. Puzzles, games, newspaper and magazine racks stimulate novel mental activity and enhance recall.

Art and Sheltered Workshop Therapy

Allowing residents to explore two- and three-dimensional artwork often stimulates creativity and augments other forms of therapy that involve music and reading. Residents explore art and craft activities to satisfy self-expression, to gain new skills, and to socialize with others. These activities can be stimulating and fun, especially for memory impaired residents who may still be able to partake in these activities.

Spiritual and Emotional Therapies

Sensory Stimulation Therapy

Smell, touch, sound, taste, and sight can enhance interest in the environment and encourage its use. Sensory stimulation is particularly applicable in gardens with smells, colors, sounds, and textures. It can also encompass an attitude about stimulation in the environment that might include color selection, a variety of textures and surfaces, differing light levels, cooking smells, and music. Nursing homes are often criticized for having too much noise and too few experiences that stimulate the senses.

Pet Therapies

Providing opportunities for residents to give and receive affection from warm-blooded mammals has therapeutic benefit. These therapies seem particularly effective with memory impaired residents. The unconditional affection that animals show and the opportunity to pursue nurturing behaviors are generally positive. Spaces adjacent to sunlight that facilitate ventilation are effective. Three-season porches have been popular settings for this activity.

Plant Therapies

Plants are important to many residents and provide continuity for those who have lifelong interests in gardening and nurturing plants. Gardening gives older residents the satisfaction of watching things grow while providing an outlet for nurturing behaviors. Outdoor areas for plants, raised planting beds, greenhouse spaces, and plant shelves in each dwelling unit are some of the ways the environment can support interest in this activity.

Intergenerational Therapy

Activities that involve young children can be a source of emotional pleasure. These can include playgrounds next to the building that make it possible to watch children play, as well as direct participation in programs. Some facilities invite children to interact with residents within the facility. Involvement in teaching as well as various activities can be both stimulating and nurturing.

Religious Services

Providing an outlet for fellowship and spiritual expression is important to many residents. Religious services can take place in a room that has been transformed to support these activities. It should accommodate guests, be flexible in design, and have an appropriate location for the display of religious objects used in the service.

Residential Appearance

Giving the building the look and feel of a residential setting encourages noninstitutional behaviors and attitudes from visitors, family members, staff, and residents themselves. Utilizing a compact plan and making the building appear smaller in scale from the street can make it more approachable. Porches, low eaves heights, and residential detailing reinforce a homelike character.

CONCLUSIONS

The architectural design of the building can support a range of physical, occupational, emotional, mental, spiritual, and social therapies providing the older resident stimulating choices. Developing a design plan that facilitates a range of therapeutic activities is a powerful way to foster independence and well-being. Most facilities utilize a less effective approach. Either activities are not planned around a therapeutic agenda or trivial home modifications are relied upon to stimulate effective therapeutic responses. We need to design programs, management systems, informal resident helping networks, and family support systems in a way that challenges the architecture of the building to perform at a higher level of social and therapeutic accountability. Design that is planned and executed in this way becomes a powerful mechanism for supporting the ultimate desire of increasing quality of life.

Architects designing special purpose facilities should focus much more of their creative energy on establishing the basic therapeutic framework for facility design. Using this as an organizational framework, traditional issues such as site placement, common space organization, and unit design can take on a far more significant therapeutic role in affecting the daily lives of residents.

REFERENCES

American Institute of Architects' Committee on Architecture for Health. (1992). *Design for aging: 1992 review*. Washington, DC: AIA.

American Institute of Architects Foundation. (1985). *Design for aging: An architect's guide*. Washington, DC: AIA Press.

Boling, P. (1993). Safety in the home. In T. Yoshikawa, E. Cobbs, & K. Brummel-Smith (Eds.), *Ambulatory geriatric care* (pp. 159–165). St. Louis, MO: Mosby.

Brand, S. (1994). *How buildings learn: What happens after they are built*. New York: Viking.

Brody, S., & Ruff, G. (1986). *Aging and rehabilitation: Advances in the state of the art*. New York: Springer.

Bush-Brown, A., & Davis, D. (1992). *Hospitable design for healthcare and senior communities.* New York: Van Nostrand Reinhold.

Calkins, M. (1988). *Design for dementia.* Owings Mills, MD: National Health Publishing.

Carstens, D. (1985). *Site planning and design for the elderly: Issues, guidelines and alternatives.* New York: Van Nostrand Reinhold.

Charness, N., & Bosman, E. (1992). Human factors and age. In F. Craik & T. Salthouse (Eds.), *Handbook of aging and cognition* (pp. 495–551). Hillsdale, NJ: Erlbaum.

Cohen, U., & Day, K. (1993). *Contemporary environments for people with dementia.* Baltimore, MD: The Johns Hopkins University Press.

Cohen, U., & Weisman, J. (1991). *Holding on to home: Designing environments for people with dementia.* Baltimore, MD: The Johns Hopkins University Press.

Emery, C., Burker, E., & Blumenthal, J. (1991). Psychological and physiological effects of exercise among older adults. In K. W. Schaie (Ed.), *Annual review of gerontology and geriatrics* (Vol. 11, pp. 218–238). New York: Springer.

Faletti, M. (1984). Human factors research and functional environments for the aged. In I. Altman, M. P. Lawton, & J. Wohwill (Eds.), *Human behavior and environment: Advances in theory and research: Vol. 7. Elderly people and the environment* (pp. 191–237). New York: Plenum.

Fozard, J. (1981). Changing person-environment relations in adulthood. *Human Factors, 23*(1), 7–27.

Gelwicks, L., & Newcomer, R. (1974). *Planning housing environments for the elderly.* Washington, DC: National Council on the Aging.

Goodman, R., & Smith, D. (1992). *Retirement facilities: Planning. design and marketing.* New York: Watson-Guptill Publications.

Greene, I., Fedewa, B., Johnston, C., Jackson, W., & Deardorff, H. (1975). *Housing for the elderly: The development and design process.* New York: Van Nostrand Reinhold.

Hiatt, L. (1987). Designing for the vision and hearing impairments of the elderly. In V. Regnier & J. Pynoos (Eds.), *Housing the aged: Design directives and policy considerations* (pp. 341–371). New York: Elsevier.

Hiatt, L. (1991). *Nursing home renovation designed for reform.* Stoneham, MA: Butterworth Architecture.

Hoglund, D. (1985). *Housing for the elderly: Privacy and independence in environments for the aging.* New York: Van Nostrand Reinhold.

Howell, S. (1980). *Designing for aging: Patterns of use.* Cambridge: MIT Press.

Kane, R., & Wilson, K. (1993). *Assisted living in the United States.* Washington, DC: American Association of Retired Persons.

Kemp, B., Brummel-Smith, K., & Ramsdell, J. (1990). *Geriatric rehabilitation.* Boston: Little, Brown.

Koncelik, J. (1976). *Designing the open nursing home.* Stroudsburg, PA: Dowden, Hutchinson and Ross.

Koncelik, J. (1982). *Aging and the product environment.* Stroudsburg, PA: Hutchinson and Ross.

Lawton, M. P. (1975). *Planning and managing housing for the elderly.* New York: John Wiley.

Lawton, M. P. (1980). *Environment and aging.* Monterey, CA: Brooks-Cole.

Lawton, M. P., Windley, P., & Byerts, T. (1982). *Aging and environment: Theoretical approaches.* New York: Springer.

National Association of Home Builders. (1987). *Seniors housing: A development and management handbook.* Washington, DC: NAHB.

Pastalan, L. (1977). The empathic model: A methodological bridge between research and design. *Journal of Architectural Education, 31*(1), 14–15.

Pynoos, J. (1992). Strategies for home modification and repair. *Generations, 16*(2), 21–25.

Raschko, B. (1982). *Housing interiors for the disabled and elderly.* New York: Van Nostrand Reinhold.

Regnier, V. (1994). *Assisted living housing for the elderly: Design innovations from the United States and Europe.* New York: Van Nostrand Reinhold.

Regnier, V., Hamilton, J., & Yatabe, S. (1995). *Assisted living for the frail and aged: Innovations in design. management and financing.* New York: Columbia University Press.

Regnier, V., & Pynoos, J. (1987). *Housing the aged: Design directives and policy considerations.* New York: Elsevier.

Reifler, B., & Teri, L. (1986). Rehabilitation and Alzheimer's disease. In S. Brody & G. Ruff (Eds.), *Aging and rehabilitation: Advances in the state of the art* (pp. 107–121). New York: Springer.

Salmon, G. (1993). *Caring environments for frail elderly people.* New York: John Wiley.

Schmidt, R. (1993). Physical activity and exercise. In T. Yoshikawa, E. Cobbs, & K. Brummel-Smith (Eds.), *Ambulatory geriatric care* (pp. 187–195). St. Louis, MO: Mosby.

Sommer, R., & Sommer, B. (1983). *A practical guide to behavioral research.* New York: Oxford University Press.

Spirduso, W., & Gilliam-MacRae, P. (1991). Physical activity and quality of life in the frail elderly. In J. Birren, J. Lubben, J. Rowe, & D. Deutchman (Eds.), *The concept and measurement of quality of life in the frail elderly* (pp. 226–255). San Diego, CA: Academic Press.

Smyer, M., & Frysinger, M. (1985). Mental health interventions in the nursing home community. In C. Eisdorfer (Ed.), *Annual review of gerontology and geriatrics* (Vol. 5, pp. 283–320). New York: Springer.

Valins, M. (1988). *Housing for elderly people: A guide for architects and clients.* New York: Van Nostrand Reinhold.

Weal, F., & Weal, F. (1988). *Housing for elderly people: Options and design.* New York: Nichols Publishing.

Welch, P., Parker, V., & Zeisel, J. (1984). *Independence through interdependence.* Boston, MA: Department of Elder Affairs, Commonwealth of Massachusetts.

Wilson, B. A. (1989). Designing memory-therapy programs. In L. Poon, D. Rubin, & B. Wilson (Eds.), *Everyday cognition in adulthood and late life* (pp. 615–638). Cambridge: Cambridge University Press.

Zarit, S., Zarit, J., & Reever, K. (1982). Memory training for severe memory loss. *Gerontologist, 22,* 373–377.

Zeisel, J. (1981). *Inquiry by design: Tools for environment-behavior research.* Monterey, CA: Brooks/Cole.

Zeisel, J., Epp, G., & Demos, S. (1977). *Low-rise housing for elderly people: Behavioral criteria for design.* Washington, DC: U.S. Government Printing Office.

Zeisel, J., Welch, P., Epp, G., & Demos, S. (1983). *Mid-rise elevator housing for older people.* Boston, MA: Building Diagnostics.

Commentary: The FSU Approach to Design: Feedback from Senior Users

Neil Charness*

Regnier's chapter chronicles the planner's dilemma, which is rather like that of a politician trying to be elected: "how to be all things to all people." As he points out, architectural training focuses primarily on the organization and sequence of building spaces and the relationship between a building's form and its site. It is concerned with the constraints of building codes and services, and with the ever-present budget bottom line. In these lean times, the architect cannot, as legend portrays Ludwig Mies van der Rohe (e.g., see Simon, 1981, p. 175), sit down with a client, pour him a fine drink, light up cigars, and convince him to accept a design that is a better fit to the architect's vision than the client's. Today's financing client for seniors' housing is often the public, and they are not in the mood for expenditures, let alone overexpenditures.

---

*One way to escape from the top-down nature of architectural design is to involve the user in the process. The author calls this the "Feedback from Senior Users" (FSU) approach. He outlines several ways to improve user input into the design process, particularly by probing his or her beliefs about what would make the dwelling more strongly resemble a home. Resident goals could help to constrain the design process, improve the functionality of the building, and, ultimately, improve the competence of the resident.

Regnier also makes some important points about the problems that architects face when trying to design buildings, particularly when crossing over from their discipline's central focus to come closer to that of the clinician and gerontologist interested in providing a "therapeutic environment." It may be helpful to look first at the discipline's history to appreciate Regnier's dilemma.

The New Grolier Multi-Media Encyclopedia (1993, release 6, s.v. 6.03) gives a definition of the discipline of architecture by Vitruvius, the famous Roman architect:

> Vitruvius said that architecture was a building that incorporated utilitas, firmitas, and venustas, which Wotton translated as "commodotie, firmness, and delighte." This definition recognizes that architecture embraces functional, technological, and aesthetic requirements: it must have commodotie (utilitarian qualities), firmness (structural stability and sound construction), and delighte (attractive appearance).

This chapter is concerned primarily with the first feature: functionality. The encyclopedia notes that Western architecture initially stressed *art* as the primary function. Architecture was a means to honor the gods. The goal of the architect was to design in such a way that the gods would be pleased. That is indeed a prime example of "top-down" design. In contrast, one of the first principles of the historically recent field of human factors is "Honor thy user," a saying meant to stress the "bottom-up" nature of design. We will be concerned with the tension between creating a work of art and creating a functional work. A potential solution path for this design dilemma is the FSU approach: "Feedback from Senior Users." We need to involve seniors in the design process.

Design is a fallible process. Since human information processors have a limited information processing capacity, a truism of cognitive psychology, they cannot possibly foresee all the implications of a given design. So, as Regnier comments, architects rely on the accepted wisdom and findings of their fellow designers and attempt to design in accord with those principles.

The tension that Regnier's chapter makes apparent is that architectural design has not generally focused on the microenvironments that are the small-scale results of building design writ large. Unfortunately, it is precisely at the microenvironmental level that the senior users of the building have to function. Thus there is the potential for a *mismatch* in the hierarchy of design specifications that a large-scale building entails, as seen in Figure 6.1. Top-down design typically puts the concerns of the specific resident last, although it undoubtedly seeks to accommodate residents generally. As Regnier outlines, such a result is due in no small part to rather rigid guidelines and to building codes for assisted-living dwellings. One way to address this potential imbalance is to recast the architect's problem from that of designing a dwelling to that of making a dwelling a home. I want to suggest that we look more at the possibility of designing from the bottom up, starting with what makes a dwelling a home to the senior.

Such an emphasis has its roots in 20-century architect Le Corbusier, whose later work considered design from the perspective of the people who will inhabit the structured environment (urban planning). To turn

Hierarchical Top-Down Design

Site

Codes

Financing

Aesthetic Concerns

Client Wishes

Resident Goals

FIGURE 6.1 Architectural design as a hierarchical top-down process.

the legendary architect Ludwig Mies van der Rohe on his head, at least figuratively, I might be so bold as to argue not for "Less is More," but "More is More." The more the consultation with the senior population, the more functional will be the resulting building at the microenvironmental level. Given the difficulty of the design task, design should also be an iterative process. It will take some living in a structure to point out the interactions that create difficulties for the residents that were unforeseeable in the original design plan. Further, resident populations may change over time. Money needs to be set aside from the original proposal to modify the building over time (with appropriate budgeting for the discounted value of money).

I don't for a moment believe that changing the process to be more bottom-up will prove to be a panacea for design. One of the truisms in aging research is that older people are a very diverse group, as work by Schaie and his colleagues on longitudinal study of intellectual functioning has made abundantly clear (e.g., Schaie, 1983). This probably holds true for functioning in the assisted-living dwelling as well, since people there run the gamut from being relatively intact to being completely bedridden. Thus there are many (probably too many) residents from whom to scale up design plans. Different cohorts and men and women may also have markedly different preferences (e.g., for baths versus showers: Cranz, 1987).

I chose the term "mismatch" to point to a potential solution-path for complex design: goals. Though proposing goals as solution paths seems "oxymoronic" to the cognitive psychologist, it may have some redeeming grace. For design to work, it should ask the questions who, how, and what. Who are you designing for? How do you know that the design works? What is the cost-effectiveness of the design? These issues form the core of the classical problem-solving process (Newell & Simon, 1972). The who question translates to, "What is the problem to be solved?" The how question transforms to, "How do you test a proposed solution?" The what question addresses the issue of "Optimized versus satisficed solutions."

WHO DO YOU DESIGN FOR?

"Who do you design for" is a difficult question. Clearly, as in Regnier's case of a nursing home, you typically design in a top-down hierarchical fashion: first for your building site, then the building codes, then for your client, often a privately run institution or a governmental body. Specifications at these levels may not fit too well with those of the ultimate resident population, the caregivers and the patients.

How can we ensure that designers meet up with the functional needs of the user population? ''Feedback'' is the magic word. As psychology learned long ago, there is no learning without knowledge of results— ''reinforcement'' or ''feedback.'' When you consider architecture, feedback is hard to come by, excepting the rather crude case of going out of business for lack of clients. Feedback on aesthetics probably occurs often enough (there are many prizes for notable building shapes). But feedback for function is not as likely to occur. In all your years of inhabiting buildings, how many times have you ever been queried by an architect (or builder) about how well the building works? In my case the answer is once, for the new house I moved into recently, and I suspect that the modal answer for most of the readers is never. In all your years of going to restaurants, how often have you been asked by your waiter if the meal was satisfactory? Regnier and Pynoos (1987) have already alluded to this problem and Regnier points to a recent book (Brand, 1994) that highlights the issue.

But are the users the right group to ask? Would a resident in a nursing home have a reasoned opinion about what works for her? I'm not certain that architects can count on the users for appropriate feedback, though I think that this is an open question and one that is definitely worth asking. Regnier (1987) has already pioneered studies of user preferences, using checklists of potential features with upper-income seniors. Still, what people say they want to do and what they actually do frequently don't match up, to the never-ending sorrow of those in the business of running marketing surveys.

I also don't want to minimize the problem of dealing with conflicting claims. Some residents will prefer a setting with prominent spaces to socialize. Others (perhaps many after a while: e.g., Carp, 1987) will complain about open spaces leading to people sitting around and gossiping about them. They will prefer privacy over inviting areas in which to socialize. Geddis (1993) argues that privacy concerns are sufficiently fundamental that they ought to override extant building regulations. Some data we collected in Waterloo underline this observation.

Perhaps the right level of feedback is whether the building works in a way that facilitates the users' goals. What would users like to be able to do when in the dwelling, as opposed to what we as designers think they ought to be doing? I'm not too certain that I would willingly opt for a "therapeutic environment," no matter how elegantly it is designed, when disabilities force me leave my home.

One of my former students, Claudine Carlson (1991), took seriously the word "home" in terms such as "nursing home" and "home for the aged." Thus she set her goal to try to understand something about the meaning of home to older adults, comparing a community-dwelling group with two other groups living in institutional settings for short (2–4 years) and longer (5+ years) periods of time (all groups $N = 25$, all aged 70 +). Carlson measured important aspects of home with a checklist of 25 items, rated in importance from extremely important to unimportant on a 5-point Likert scale. Residents also checked off whether the feature was, or was not, available where they resided. She also asked people about how happy they were, using a 6-point single item scale.

Not too unexpectedly, the concept of home was similar across groups (e.g., Rutman & Freedman, 1988), and not surprisingly, those living in the community experienced greater levels of happiness than those in institutions. Critical, however, was the finding that the perceived availability of aspects of home was a primary correlate of happiness across the groups. Happiness correlated highly (r (73) = .63) with a summed score of perceived availability of the 25 features of home.

What were the most important aspects of a home? Items such as "having friends or relatives visit me," "feeling safe and secure," "having my own private place," "feeling comfortable", and "having a quiet place to think and pray" were rated between "quite" and "extremely" important aspects of a home. Less important were things such as "regular contact with place of worship," "having a pet," "being part of clubs or organizations," and "cooking my own food." These items sound pretty much like goals to me, rather than bricks and mortar attributes.

How do these attributes fit with the lengthy list of features that Regnier outlines in his chapter? He focuses on trying to create a "therapeutic environment" that allows the individual to stay "as independent and autonomous as possible" while leading a "safe, socially engaging, and challenging lifestyle." To achieve this he proposes designing to stimulate physical exercise as well as to focus on emotional, social, cognitive, and spiritual development. In the latter stages of the chapter he lists an ambitious set of architectural features that may address these design concerns, ranging from outdoor exercise spaces to indoor chapel arrangements. I'm not confident, though, that there is a close fit between these features and those functions that the residents believed to be important in creating a homelike residence.

My concern is that there may be a gap between what architects believe to be optimal and what the typical resident desires. There may also be a gulf between what the resident believes she desires and what would truly improve her sense of well-being. People do not always know (or act in accord with) what is best for them, but we are probably safer to err in favor of their wishes, than our preconceptions.

Although Carlson's limited study did not probe a very extensive list of amenities or goal structures that go into making up a home atmosphere, her work does provide the beginnings of a methodology for doing bottom-up research into the crafting of homelike buildings. Having private places for residents seems pretty critical to satisfying some of the most important aspects of a homelike atmosphere, as Geddes (1993) argued.

There are important caveats. One puzzling finding was that those resident in an institution for a longer period of time, 5.5 or more years, perceived lower availability of these attributes than their more newly arrived peers, those institutionalized for 2–4 years. The explanation for this finding was not clear (perhaps the health of longer term residents was poorer, meaning they could less easily access these features). Nonetheless, perceptions, not necessarily realities, dictated happiness. Perhaps this finding underlines the very important difference between *availability* and *accessibility*. It is one thing to have a swimming pool available and another for it to be easily accessible. Bridging this gap may require the strategy of setting aside funds for later remodeling. Observational studies of usage patterns seem like a good first step in identifying mismatches.

Aside from the usual objective-item questionnaires, Carlson also engaged in some open-ended interviews with the residents. One older woman's complaint was telling: she was unable to make a cup of tea for Carlson when she came for the interview. The staff could provide tea for visitors (in a styrofoam cup), but did not allow the residents to partake in the ceremony, something that certainly would have made this older woman feel more at home. Now I suspect that there were good safety reasons not to allow frail older residents to come in contact with stoves and boiling water. Styrofoam cups are also probably far more economical than china. Missing in the equation, however, was a functional analysis of user goals.

To be able to entertain a guest, whether an anonymous interviewer or a family member, meant to be able to act as a host with all the small gestures of civility that go along with that role. I also recall the case of an older resident in a wheelchair I once met in a nursing home, who mentioned to me that he always carried candies in his robe. It was his way of preserving an essential goal: to be a host to visitors, particularly small children. I needn't remind you all of the way in which reciprocal exchange is an essential component for successful social interchanges. The point I want to make is that there is no way to help Victor Regnier and other architects design for older users unless the goals of the user can bubble to the top of the specifications list. We need feedback from senior users, before and after construction.

"Who to design for" also means the caregivers working in the dwelling, to enable them to assist those residing there, as Regnier points out. If residents are too frail to make tea, they could be provided with a teapot filled with water, and given the choice of adding the tea to the top of the pot. (Langer & Rodin, 1976, showed the benefits of improving such simple choice patterns for older nursing home residents.) Having a tap that provides boiling water could make the caregiver's task fairly easy. The manufacture of teapots in a pottery workshop could solve the problem of breakage.

I don't want to minimize the interactive nature of top-down and bottom-up design. For one, you can't design just for the incoming residents. The average length of stay in chronic care institutions is sometimes only a few years, because the incoming population is becoming older and sicker. With rapid staff turnover in many facilities, the caregiving population also boasts a regrettably short longevity. The critical issue is whether the patient and caregiver mix (and their associated goals) is changing drastically over time or not. Mrs. Smith's goals may or may not be predictive of Mrs. Smith II's goals. Perhaps it is the very volatile nature of the user population that dictates a top-down design process. Finances will always be tight, and building materials are less likely to change drastically over a 5–10-year span than the population being served. Stronger constraints shape the problem space more than weaker ones.

In short, surveys of goals of the inhabitants may well be a useful place to begin the design process. If people don't typically desire to bowl, building a bowling alley or bowling green makes little sense. (It must be admitted, though, that design is sometimes a push-pull situation. You may find that you attract retired bowling enthusiasts to your setting if you do put in a bowling alley.)

HOW DO YOU KNOW THAT THE DESIGN WORKS?

Maintaining competence is the theme of Regnier's chapter. Such a theme does a good job of restricting the problem space for evaluating the success of the design process. By definition, a good design will maintain competence better than a poor one. Competence, however, is not that easy to define. It brings us up against such issues as skill (e.g., Bosman & Charness, 1996) and compensation (Bäckman & Dixon, 1992). Competence, to a cognitive psychologist interested in expertise, implies the means to pursue your goals in an effective, if not efficient, way.

First, we might note that both physical and mental competence cannot be judged without knowledge of a person's goals. Although ability to perform activities of daily living (ADLs) such as toileting, feeding, bathing, grooming, and dressing would seem to be relatively easy to determine, more important instrumental activities of daily living (IADL) such as daily finances may be more difficult to judge.

Silberfeld (1992) discusses the notion of risk in decision making about competence, pointing out that competence is not a binary situation, and that even in the case when someone is judged incompetent for financial management in terms of his or her estate, he or she still might be permitted to engage in small-scale daily financial transactions. The consensus developing seems to favor the notion of *situational competence* rather than general competence. For instance, someone might be deemed mentally competent to make decisions about informed consent for health care, but not financial matters.

Attempting to judge competence in the absence of knowledge of goals leads to some peculiar conclusions. For instance, this writer is remarkably incompetent at hundreds if not thousands of things: nuclear physics research, tightrope walking, molecular biology research, surgery, printed circuit board assembly, auto repair, and backgammon. Fortunately, most are not particularly important activities for me. It seems reasonable to probe a person's goals for institutional living and to try to design in a way that such goals are reachable, and that people do not need to change too many of their goals, since feelings of self-efficacy and well-being may well be tied to success at achieving personal goals (e.g., Brandstätder & Rothermund, 1994).

A useful heuristic is to consider that the sphere of goals that people strive for may become narrower as they age. They may set less lofty ambitions as their physical and mental abilities lessen. As a result, they may become supremely dependent on the flexibility of their microenvironments to support even modest goals. (There is an apocryphal story of the gradual diminution in the sphere of goals as we age. It concerned a man who, when young, managed a broad expanse of farmland, taking joy from the activity of growing crops. When less physically firm, he shifted back to a large vegetable garden, then to a smaller garden, and finally, when severely mobility-restricted, to an indoor windowsill of plants.)

When it comes to frail older adults, the issue of competence often does come down to ADLs or IADLs. Still, there is more to life than dressing, feeding, bathing, toileting, and even shopping and banking. I suspect that few of us who are currently able-bodied would consider our lives satisfactory if we had perfect competence at IADLs, let alone ADLs, *but that is all that we were able to do*. To be fair, I suspect that building design that could render ADLs and IADLs manageable for the frail older adult will be a remarkable achievement. It is an excellent first step.

Ensuring mental competence, particularly in the face of disease processes such as dementia, is a particularly difficult goal for building design. Regnier makes a number of valuable suggestions for supporting dementia victims through the design of therapeutic environments. Still, it is probably necessary to engineer at a microenvironmental level and with specific people in mind. An older man I met recently mentioned that Alzheimer's Disease caused his wife to have difficulty finding her room in the institution she had moved into. It, of course, disturbed other residents to have her and others wandering into their rooms. Putting names on the door did not work. The husband mentioned that before her disease, she was an accomplished musician. Perhaps using soft music as the cue to her room might work. Perhaps color-coding of doors might help. A combination of environmental design and behavior modification training using spaced practice and fading techniques may be useful (Camp et al., 1993).

The main point is that it is likely to be necessary to design the microenvironments after the specific residents have arrived, hence the need for budgeting funds for redesign. Given the difficulty of becoming an expert at all facets of design, it also may rest to other professionals to collaborate with architects on this level of design. We have interior decorators. Why not entertain the possibility of therapeutic designers?

In answer to the question ''How do you know when a design works?'' we can tentatively answer that it works when residents function well at ADLs and IADLs and show high levels of satisfaction with their built environment and its microenvironmental niches. We need to ask the users to determine their satisfaction levels. There is a large well-being literature that can be tapped for measurement instruments (e.g., Ryff & Essex, 1991). In the case of the demented elderly resident, we need to ask proxies, such as family and staff, and perhaps we will have to settle for more modest outcomes, such as continence, freedom from bedsores, and absence of gross behavioral disturbance.

An alternative technique for getting at the atmosphere of an existing institution, presumably for the purpose of redesign, is to use standardized instruments such as the Multiphasic Environmental Assessment Procedure (MEAP: Lemke & Moos, 1986). A good adjunct to determining the microenvironmental side would be to observe patterns of use of facilities, either directly or perhaps by doing time-budget surveys with residents (e.g., Moss & Lawton, 1982).

WHAT IS THE COST-EFFECTIVENESS OF THE DESIGN?

Surely the slogan ''Less is More'' is highly appropriate when it comes to financing building projects today, or perhaps ''Less, More Often.'' Although Regnier provides a virtual cornucopia of examples of therapeutic design based on showcase assisted-living facilities around the world, the reality we face is that all-encompassing facilities will be the exception rather than the rule for new buildings. We probably cannot command adequate resources (cognitive or financial) to provide optimal designs. Rather, the designer's task is to ''satisfice'' (Simon, 1981), find ''good-enough'' solutions within the existing (financial, site, code, client) constraints. Perhaps we need to focus on minimalist design. What, at a minimum, ought to exist in every facility? (We ask the question from a functional perspective, not a building-code perspective that dictates back the square footage for rooms.) Further, we need some cost-effective analyses to assess what works and what doesn't work. We might want to use increments in self-reported well-being of both residents and staff (with residents' ratings weighted more highly) as the evaluation currency.

A serious problem with doing cost-effective evaluation of designs is that we cannot do experimental studies wherein we erect several different building variants, randomly assign people to those variants, and measure their satisfaction levels. We undoubtedly have to accept less satisfactory field studies using case-control methodologies.

ALTERNATE APPROACHES
TO ENVIRONMENTAL DESIGN

Although Regnier restricts his overview to multiple-dwelling structures, we should not forget that the majority of older adults live in private, single-family residences, and many, if not most, would prefer to stay there (e.g., Harootyan, 1993). Given the debtor status of most governments, the chances are slim that they will soon sponsor large-scale congregate housing and assisted-living building projects, so retrofitting the existing housing stock is likely to be where the major design and redesign efforts are concentrated over the next decade or so. When there is but one client, the owner, chances are the retro-fits will reflect the client's goals. (Then again, the architect might have a fighting chance with wine, though perhaps not with cigars.)

As well, we probably can become more proactive in designing single-family dwellings, working toward creation of that mythical home that permits "aging in place" using so-called "universal design." My suspicion is that universal design, design that fits all types of residents, from infant to old adult, is a quixotic quest, given the variability in inter and intraindividual abilities across the life span. Still, it is clear now that some designs are far more successful than others (e.g., single lever faucets in sinks, lever door handles) and economies of scale should bring their costs into line with less expensive alternative designs.

Finally, counter to notions of "aging in place" are notions of moving to appropriate housing as needs change. Designers may not be able to provide a multifunctional building structure that meets everyone's needs in a cost-effective way. We may have to consider options such as relocating residents to new quarters as residents' competence diminishes and they slip outside the "comfort zone" (as defined in a person-environment fit model: e.g., Lawton, 1977). Still, we cannot envision having residents move every few months as their competence declines, so the bandwidth of design flexibility needs to be fairly wide across levels of care.

In conclusion, although therapeutic environmental design is a noteworthy goal, it should be tested against the goals of the residents by getting feedback from senior users. Competence is situation-specific and dependent upon a resident's goals. We only can hope to increase competence with environmental modifications when we are careful to take those goals into consideration.

ACKNOWLEDGMENTS

This work was supported by grants from the Natural Sciences and Engineering Research Council of Canada, NSERC A0790, and by the Canadian Aging Research Network (CARNET), one of 15 Networks of Centres of Excellence supported by the Government of Canada.

REFERENCES

Bäckman, L., & Dixon, R. A. (1992). Psychological compensation: A theoretical framework. *Psychological Bulletin, 112*, 259–283.

Bosman, E. A., & Charness, N. (1996). Age differences in skilled performance and skill acquisition. In F. Blanchard-Fields & T. Hess (Ed.), *Perspectives on cognition in adulthood and aging* (pp. 428–453). New York: McGraw-Hill.

Brand, S. (1994). *How buildings learn: What happens after they are built.* New York: Viking.

Brandstädter, J., & Rothermund, K. (1994). Self-percepts of control in middle and later adulthood: Buffering losses by rescaling goals. *Psychology and Aging, 9*, 265–273.

Camp, C. J., Fos, J. W., Stevens, A. B., Reichard, C. C., McKitrick, L. A., & O'Hanlon, A. M. (1993). Memory training in normal and demented elderly populations: The E-I-E-I-O Model. *Experimental Aging Research, 19*, 277–290.

Carlson, C. V. (1991). *The concept of ''home'' in elderly populations.* Unpublished master's thesis, Research Project, Department of Psychology, University of Waterloo, Waterloo, Ontario, Canada N2L 3G1.

Carp, F. (1987). The impact of planned housing. A longitudinal study. In V. Regnier & J. Pynoos (Eds.), *Housing the aged* (pp. 43–79). New York: Elsevier.

Cranz, G. (1987). Evaluating the physical environment. In V. Regnier & J. Pynoos (Eds.), *Housing the aged* (pp. 81–104). New York: Elsevier.

Geddis, B. L. (1993). The quest for privacy in the design of living environments for the aging. In *Life-span design of residential environments for an aging population* (pp. 29–31). Proceedings of an invitational conference convened by Forecasting and Environmental Scanning Department, American Association of Retired Persons, Washington, DC, and Stein Gerontological Institute, Miami Jewish Home and Hospital for the Aged, Miami, FL. Available from the American Association of Retired Persons.

Harootyan, R. A. (1993). Aging, functional abilities, and life-span design. In *Life-span design of residential environments for an aging population* (pp. 29–31). Proceedings of an invitational conference convened by Forecasting and Environmental Scanning Department, American Association of Retired Persons, Washington, DC, and Stein Gerontological Institute, Miami Jewish Home and Hospital for the Aged, Miami, FL. Available from the American Association of Retired Persons.

Langer, E. J., & Rodin, J. (1976). The effects of choice and enhanced personal responsibility for the aged: A field experiment in an institutional setting. *Journal of Personality and Social Psychology, 34,* 191–198.

Lawton, M. P. (1977). The impact of the environment on aging and behavior. In J. E. Birren & K. W. Schaie (Eds.), *Handbook of the psychology of aging* (pp. 276–301). New York: Van Nostrand Reinhold.

Lemke, S., & Moos, R. H. (1986). Quality of residential settings for elderly adults. *Journal of Gerontology, 41,* 268–276.

Moss, M., & Lawton, M. P. (1982). The time budgets of older people: A window on four lifestyles. *Journal of Gerontology, 37,* 115–123.

The New Grolier Multimedia Encyclopedia. (1993). (Dos version 6.0). Danbury, CN: Grolier Electronic Publication.

Newell, A., & Simon, H. A. (1972). *Human problem solving.* Englewood Cliffs, NJ: Prentice-Hall.

Regnier, V. (1987). Programming congregate housing. Preferences of upper income elderly. In V. Regnier & J. Pynoos (Eds.), *Housing the aged* (pp. 207–226). New York: Elsevier.

Regnier, V., & Pynoos, J. (1987). *Housing the aged.* New York: Elsevier.

Rutman, D. L., & Freedman, J. L. (1988). Anticipating relocation: Coping strategies and the meaning of home for older people. *Canadian Journal on Aging, 7,* 17–31.

Ryff, C. D., & Essex, M. J. (1991). Psychological well-being in adulthood and old age: Descriptive markers and explanatory processes. In K. W. Schaie (Ed.), *Annual review of gerontology and geriatrics* (Vol. 11, pp. 144–171). New York: Springer.

Schaie, K. W. (1983). The Seattle longitudinal study: A 21-year exploration of psychometric intelligence in adulthood. In K. W. Schaie (Ed.), *Longitudinal studies of adult psychological development* (pp. 64–135). New York: Guilford Press.

Silberfeld, M. (1992). The use of ''risk'' in decision-making. *Canadian Journal on Aging, 11*, 124–136.

Simon, H. A. (1981). *The sciences of the artificial* (2nd ed.). Cambridge: MIT Press.

Commentary: The Maintenance of ADL and IADL Functioning Through Design

Paul G. Windley

egnier's chapter, "The Physical Environment and Maintenance of
Competence," describes how the designed environment enhances
the competence of older people. His focus on therapeutic settings
for "assisted living" targets the segment of the older population most
likely to benefit from a therapeutic environment. His description of 5
environmental interventions, coupled with his 19 therapies provide the
elements of his therapeutic environment concept. One aim of a therapeutic
environment is to enhance quality of life by promoting autonomy and
independence among older people. Autonomy results from the ability to
function independently (Grimely-Evans, 1984; World Health Organization, 1984). Loss of autonomy has far-reaching effects in any society, but
is particularly significant among older populations in more developed
countries, as noted by Davies (1985):

> While the majority of the elderly are capable of maintaining their autonomy,
> a proportion, increasing at each age, becomes frail and in need of support,
> care or institutional life for the rest of its days. As absolute numbers of
> those requiring care increase, so does the drain on the communal and public
> purse, and the miracle of increased longevity becomes the "problem" and
> the "burden" of old age. (p. 12)

Regnier argues that autonomy and independence among older persons
enhance competence. For our purposes, autonomy will include "the ability

to cope with daily life in spite of chronic morbidity—and decreased levels of activity, and the aggravating factors which change disease to impairments and impairments to handicaps'' (Davies, 1985). A more complete review of how autonomy affects the quality of life can be found in Andrews and Withey (1976); Campbell, Converse, and Rogers (1976); Birren, Lubben, Rowe, and Deutchman (1991); and, more recently, Abeles, Gift, and Ory (1994).

The core of Regnier's therapeutic model is the 19 therapies and the environmental attributes that support them. Because each therapy is based on a unique body of research with its own design implications, the descriptive and predictive usefulness of the model as a whole will require an understanding of the conceptual premises and environmental requirements of each therapy. To illustrate, this chapter discusses underlying premises for Regnier's ADL/IADL Therapy, and then notes its design implications.

Many investigators assess autonomy and independence by measuring functional performance in the activities of daily living (ADLs) and the instrumental activities of daily living (IADLs) (Katz, Ford, Moskowitz, Jackson, & Jaffe, 1963; Spector, Katz, Murphy, & Fulton, 1987; Lawton & Brody, 1969). Although there is no definitive list of ADLs and IADLs, those most studied are Katz et al. (1963) original list: bathing, dressing, toileting, transferring, continence, and feeding. The basic IADL's include shopping, housekeeping, using public transportation, laundry, and cooking. Other investigators have measured additional activities such as walking, money management, using the telephone, and taking medications (Lawton & Brody, 1969). Functional performance in these activities is usually assessed by asking two questions: How difficult is it for you to perform this activity? and Can you perform this activity without help?

Activity difficulty, while less precisely defined than dependence, describes operational problems encountered in performing daily activities. Researchers and designers ask: What is difficult about performing specific activities? Are some activities more difficult than others? What products and space configurations lead to reduced difficulty in the home? When does difficulty prevent one from doing an activity? When does activity difficulty lead to activity dependence; that is, what is the difficulty threshold a person will tolerate before aid is sought from mechanical means or from another person?

Activity dependence addresses somewhat different questions: What are the different degrees of dependence? When do individuals perceive themselves to be dependent? Does dependence lead to loss of self-esteem?

What are the social and personal costs for those who are caregivers? Can dependence be predicted?

The distinction between activity difficulty and activity dependence is important for designers because the design requirements for each are often different. For example, design interventions aimed at reducing difficulty in bathing are different from interventions that aid a caregiver in helping a person bathe. This chapter argues that a consideration of both activity difficulty and dependence provides a more integrated view of personal autonomy in daily functioning. The narrative that follows elaborates further on these concepts and discusses their design implications.

ACTIVITY DIFFICULTY AND DEPENDENCE

Dependence

Lawton and Brody's (1969) early work established the notion of a combined ADL/IADL hierarchy. Researchers have subsequently shown that older people appear to become dependent in IADLs and ADLs in the following predictable sequence: shopping, housekeeping, using public transportation, laundry, cooking, bathing, dressing, toileting, transferring, continence, and feeding (Katz et al., 1963; Spector et al., 1987). Katz and Akpom (1976), and Asberg-Hulter and Son (1988) later demonstrate that these activities can be indexed hierarchically, thus enabling individuals to be ranked, compared, and their changes in performance predicted over time. They also present considerable evidence that these activities are sociobiologically based, with functional decline among the elderly occurring in the opposite order as functional development occurs in small children. Analyses of large data sets that included functional performance among older populations (compare Jette & Branch, 1981; and the National Center for Health Statistics, 1987) also suggest a similar dependence hierarchy. More recent evidence supporting an ADL/IADL hierarchy is reported by Lazaridis, Rudberg, Furner, and Cassel (1994).

This hierarchy provides designers with tools to predict over time the environmental needs of older people and their caregivers. For example, if designers know where an individual lies in the hierarchy, design interventions can be tailored to address the individual's current as well as anticipated future needs. The hierarchy also helps designers establish priorities by assuring that the most prevalent needs are addressed first by design interventions. For example, interventions for community-based older people should address shopping and transportation problems before housekeeping and laundry. The hierarchy also identifies design criteria for evaluation. Once current and future design needs are identified, an individual's performance can be monitored over time and the effectiveness of the design intervention assessed.

Difficulty

No similar hierarchy exists for activity difficulty. In fact, only a few researchers have examined the role activity difficulty plays in the performance of ADLs and IADLs. For example, the 1984 National Health Interview Survey: Supplement on Aging (National Center for Health Statistics-Department of Health and Human Services, 1987) assessed the degree of difficulty older people had performing specific ADLs and IADLs. Nagi (1976) reported on the degree of difficulty older people had performing 10 activities ranging from hand manipulations to whole body movements. These studies show no evidence of a difficulty hierarchy. Although activity difficulty as a concept lacks the validity of activity dependence, the relationship of difficulty to dependence may provide designers and planners with an additional tool to more effectively target environmental interventions for older people. This relationship will be explored next with potential environmental design implications recommended.

THE RELATIONSHIP BETWEEN
ACTIVITY DEPENDENCE AND DIFFICULTY

Few investigators have gathered or analyzed activity dependence and difficulty data from the same subjects or discussed their relationship (Windley, 1990). However, Figure 6.2 shows such data gathered by staff at the Herman Miller Research Corporation under the direction of the author.[1] Percentage distributions of difficulty and dependence data for selected ADLs and IADLs are shown for a small unrepresentative sample

---

[1]These data were collected under the direction of the author while working with the Herman Miller Research Corporation. Special recognition goes to Dr. Sidney Katz, who developed the ''Living Arts Studio'' project in which the data were collected.

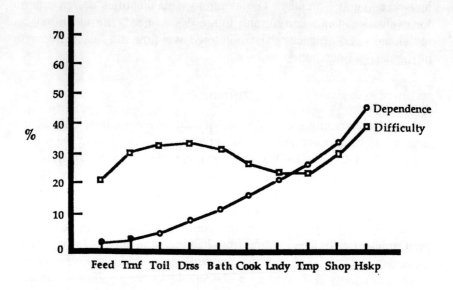

FIGURE 6.2   Percent distribution on ADL and IADL for dependence and difficulty. (The curves in Figure 6.2 are based on a polynomial regression of the original data and should be considered as lines of best fit.)

of 66 community-based older people. The analyses suggest a number of interesting speculations about the possible relationship between activity dependence and difficulty. The percentage distribution for dependence was expected given the dependency hierarchy. But the distribution for difficulty is intriguing. Two general speculations based on these distributions will be discussed here.

1.   The percentages of individuals who experienced difficulty and dependence for IADLs are similar in magnitude, although the higher percentage for dependence than for difficulty is curious. We concluded that because many of the 66 individuals were living with a spouse (40%) and came from a high socioeconomic bracket, assistance in performing these activities was readily available regardless of need. However, for

ADLs, the percentage of people who experienced difficulty relative to dependence increased dramatically. Here we speculate that it is easier to accept assistance with less personal IADLs than with more private ADLs. That is, individuals may endure higher thresholds of difficulty before requesting assistance when the activity is personal hygiene rather than self-maintenance.

2.   The percentage gap between difficulty and dependence for ADLs narrowed as the most personal activities in the hierarchy were approached. We suspect this phenomenon occurred because the threshold of difficulty tolerance peaked for many, and out of necessity individuals became increasingly willing to accept assistance in the most basic ADLs.

Although speculative at this time, these data suggest that while activity difficulty usually precedes dependence, the tolerance threshold for difficulty is activity-specific and not hierarchical. The relationship between difficulty and dependence for IADLs is also likely to be affected by the availability of a caregiver and financial resources. While hypothetical, it may be possible to return activity-dependent individuals to a state of independence be reducing activity difficulty first, rather than increase the caregiver role. Even though this relationship is conceptual and based on a small unrepresentative sample, it improves our understanding of how difficulty and dependence may interact in a residential context and suggests some hypotheses for further consideration. The design implications of this relationship will now be discussed.

DESIGN IMPLICATIONS

What significance do activity difficulty and dependence have for environmental designers? Two factors seem important here.

1.   Design interventions should address activity difficulty before dependence. Individuals who are now activity dependent, for example, in grocery shopping, may become independent if the difficulty could be reduced. This might be accomplished by making food commodities more reachable by lowering shelves and providing better means for carrying commodities to the automobile. If the attempt to reduce difficulty is not successful, interventions may then be directed toward assisting the caregiver. This might be accomplished by designing a grocery cart with

a seat to transport an older person, or installing a bench where an older person can rest and watch store activity while the caregiver shops.

2.   Interventions that attempt to reduce difficulty or dependence in a specific activity in the hierarchy such as for dressing, must anticipate that recipients will likely be dependent in the preceding activity of bathing. Individuals who experience difficulty toileting will soon have difficulty transferring, and so on through the hierarchy. Therefore, to avoid a series of singular, rapidly obsolete, and often expensive corrective measures, designs should be a coordinated system, easily adaptable over longer periods of time, and targeted to a broad range of disability. These efforts should recognize functions in individuals that have already been lost. For example, a design strategy to assist older shoppers should simultaneously aid in the storing of grocery items in cupboards. The strategy must include assistance in transportation to other locales as their older clients become less able to use public transportation. Similarly, designers who try to reduce toileting problems with new bathroom layouts should also add amenities that aid in dressing. These amenities must in time also accommodate individuals who have problems transferring.

CONCLUSIONS

Current design strategies to support ADL and IADL functioning are seldom based on the preceding principles. After initial design solutions are implemented, subsequent design modifications to accommodate changing needs are added haphazardly, and often defeat the purpose of the original design and create unexpected problems. For example, many older persons have replaced chairs difficult to transfer to and from with lounge chairs more accommodating, but less comfortable for long-term seating. Food trays and writing surfaces may then be added to the chair hindering egress. A further addition may include a portable reading lamp creating an unbalanced and unevenly lighted surface. This unplanned and incremental approach to design seldom leads to increased accommodation. Of course, ADL therapy is not enhanced under these conditions. If such objects are to facilitate ADL therapy, they must be approached comprehensively, taking into account the dynamics of both activity dependence and difficulty.

Regnier's ADL Therapy will also be enhanced by a more careful study of specific body movements involved in performing ADLs and IADLs.

These include upper and lower body movements, fine motor movements, range of motion, and dexterity. Human factors data will be helpful here.

The purpose of this chapter was to demonstrate how one of the 19 therapies can be operationalized in conceptual and environmental design terms. Regnier's therapeutic environment concept is timely and a significant addition to the maintenance of competence in old age, and to the aging and environment literature. Further research should elaborate upon other therapies in a similar fashion and identify common themes running through the therapies.

REFERENCES

Abeles, R. P., Gift, H. C., & Ory, M. G. (1994). *Aging and quality of life*. New York: Springer.

Andrews, F. M., & Withey, S. B. (1976). *Perceptions of life quality*. New York: Plenum Press.

Asberg-Hulter, K., & Son, U. (1988). The cumulative structure of personal and instrumental ADL. *Scandinavian Journal of Rehabilitative Medicine*.

Birren, J., Lubben, J., Rowe, J., & Deutchman, D. (Eds.), (1991). *The concept and measurement of quality of life in the frail elderly* (pp. 50–89). New York: Academic Press.

Campbell, A., Converse, P. E., & Rogers, W. L. (1976). *The quality of American life*. New York: Russell Sage.

Davies, A. M. (1985). Epidemiology and the challenge of ageing. *International Journal of Epidemiology, 14*, 1, 9–21.

Grimley-Evans, J. (1984). Prevention of age-associated loss of autonomy: Epidemiological approaches. *Journal of Chronic Disease, 37*, 353–363.

Jette, A. K., & Branch, L. G. (1981). The Framingham Disability Study: Physical disability among the aged. *American Journal of Public Health, 71*, 1211–1216.

Katz, S., & Akpom, C. A. (1976). A measure of primary sociobiological functions. *International Journal of Health Services, 6*(3), 493–507.

Katz, S., Ford, A. B., Moskowitz, R. W., Jackson, B. A., & Jaffe, M. W. (1963). Studies of illness in the aged. The index of ADL: A standardized measure of biological and psychosocial function. *Journal of the American Medical Association, 186*, 914–919.

Lawton, M. P., & Brody, E. (1969). Assessment of older people: Self-maintaining and instrumental activities of daily living. *The Gerontologist, 30*, 497–502.

Lazaridis, E. N., Rudberg, M. A., Furner, S. E., & Cassel, C. K. (1994). Do activities of daily living have a hierarchical structure? An analysis using the longitudinal study of aging. *Journal of Gerontology, 49*, 2, M47–M51.

Nagi, S. Z. (1976). An epidemiology of disability among adults in the United States. *Milbank Memorial Fund Quarterly, 54,* 439–468.

National Center for Health Statistics: Department of Health and Human Services. (1987). Health statistics on older persons, analytic and epidemiological studies, Series 3, No. 25, DHHS Publication No. (PHS) 87-1409.

Spector, W. D., Katz, S., Murphy, J. B., & Fulton, J. P. (1987). The hierarchical relationship between activities of daily living and instrumental activities of daily living. *Journal of Chronic Disease, 40*(6), 481–489.

World Health Organization. (1984). Uses of epidemiology in aging: Report of a scientific group, 1983, Geneva, Switzerland. *Technical Report Series, 6.*

Windley, P. G. (1990). *Autonomy in the residential setting: The role of ADL dependence and difficulty.* Paper presented at the 43rd annual scientific meeting of the Gerontological Society of America, Boston, MA.

Author Index

Aaronson, W., 178, 181
Abbey, J., 167, 172, 181
Abeles, R. P., 132, 135, 267, 273
Abramson, L. Y., 143, 162
Acitelli, L., 196, 203
Adams, O., 4, 22
Adams, R., 228, 230
Akiyama, H., 134, 184, 192, 195, 198–199, 203, 208, 209, 216, 218–219, 223
Akpom, C. A., 268, 273
Al-Assaf, A. F., 177, 180
Albrecht, 125, 128
Allan, G., 228, 230
Allison, P. D., 110, 127
Alverno, L., 174, 180
American Heritage Dictionary of the English Language, 51, 64
American Institute of Architects' Committee on Architecture For Health, 237, 247
American Institute of Architects Foundation, 237, 247
Amigo, E., 60, 65
Anda, R., 134–135
Andersen, R. M., 98, 127
Andres, R., 96, 110, 116, 123, 128
Andrews, F. M., 267, 273
Aneshensel, C. S., 95–96, 112, 127, 137, 141

Antonucci, T. C., 134, 183–185, 187, 189, 192, 194–196, 198, 199, 203–205, 208–209, 213, 216–219, 221, 223–224, 230–231
Arnold, R. M., 126–127, 129
Asberg-Hulter, K., 268, 273

Babcock, R. L., 69, 82
Bäckman, L., 259, 263
Baddeley, A., 68, 80
Baer, D. J., 144, 162
Baltes, M. M., 87, 92, 143, 145, 147–148, 152, 154, 157, 159–160, 162–165, 170, 172, 197, 204, 216–217, 219
Baltes, P. B., 154, 159–160, 163, 170, 172, 197, 204, 207, 213, 219, 220
Bandura, A., 191, 204, 217–218, 220
Barefoot, J. C., 134–135
Barrett, V., 170, 172
Baume, R. W., 46, 48
Bebbington, A. C., 4, 20
Belanger, A., 13, 14, 21
Bengston, V., 125, 129
Bengston, V. L., 191, 202, 206, 227, 229–231
Bennett, R. G., 178, 181
Berkman, L. F., 183–184, 204, 207, 220, 226, 230
Berkowitz, N., 60, 65
Bierman, E. L., 96, 110, 116, 123, 128

Birren, J., 267, 273
Black, B., 60, 65
Blass, J. P., 96, 110, 116, 123, 128
Blazer, D. G., 8, 13, 14, 21, 183, 204, 207, 220
Blow, F. C.. 40, 48
Blumenthal, J., 236, 248
Blumenthal, S., 177, 181
Boldt, J. S., 227, 231
Boling, P., 237, 247
Bongaarts, J., 228, 231
Booth, S. K., 226, 230
Borchelt, M., 152, 154, 162–163
Bosman, E. A., 235, 248, 259, 263
Branch, L. G., 2, 13, 14, 20, 21, 137, 141, 268, 273
Brand, R. J., 183, 205
Brand, S., 234, 247, 255, 263
Brandstätder, J., 260, 263
Brannon, D., 168, 172, 179–180
Braudel, F., 150, 163
Braun, J. V., 120, 123–124, 127
Brayne, C., 5, 21
Breslow, L., 184, 204
Brody, E. M., 57, 65–66, 81, 267–268, 273
Brody, J. A., 167, 172
Brody, S. J., 184, 204, 236, 247
Bronfenbrenner, U., 207, 220
Brouard, N., 10, 12, 21
Brummel-Smith, K., 236, 248
Bucquet, D., 7, 10, 21, 25, 33
Burgio, K. L., 167–168, 172
Burgio, L. D., 167–168, 172, 178, 180
Burker, E., 236, 248
Burnett, J., 177–178, 181
Burns, B. J., 132, 135
Bury, M., 212, 220
Bush-Brown, A., 237, 248
Byerts, T., 238, 249
Byrd, M., 68, 71

Caldwell, J. R., 184, 204
Califf, R. M., 134–135
Calkins, M., 238, 248
Callahan, D., 126–127

Callahan, C. M., 94–97, 99–100, 112–114, 120–121, 129–131, 136–141
Camp, C. J., 260, 263
Campbell, A., 267, 273
Caplan, R. D., 184, 204
Carlson, C. V., 256, 263
Carnes, B. A., 167, 172
Carp, F., 255, 263
Carstens, D., 237, 248
Carstensen, L. L., 134, 194, 201, 204, 210–216, 220–222
Cassel, C. K., 132, 133, 135, 167, 172, 268, 273
Cassel, J., 183, 204, 207, 220
Castle, N., 179–180
Cavanaugh, J. C., 75, 81
Charness, N., 69, 80, 235, 248, 259, 263
Chaudhary, B. S., 184, 206
Chen, X., 227, 231
Cherry, K. E., 71, 81
Chesney, M. A., 134, 135
Chyba, M. M., 100, 104, 128
Clark, D. O., 100, 127
Cobb, J., 43, 45, 48–49
Cobb, S., 183, 204, 207, 221
Coe, R. M., 41, 49, 184, 204
Coffey, R. J., 176, 180
Cohen, C. I., 184, 204
Cohen, R. D., 183, 205
Cohen, U., 238–239, 248
Cohn, M., 168, 172
Coleman, B., 179, 180
Collopy, B. J., 150, 163
Colton, T., 46, 48
Colvez, A., 7, 21
Concato, J., 113, 127
Converse, P. E., 267, 273
Cooley, C. H., 85–86, 92
Corder, L., 17, 21, 29, 33
Costa, P. T., 38–40, 48–49
Counte, M. A., 177, 180
Coupland, N., 88, 92
Cowan, C. A., 94, 129
Cowling, W. R., 120, 123–124, 127
Craik, F. I, M., 68, 71–72, 80
Cranz, G., 254, 263

Crimmins, E. M., 2, 4, 7–8, 13, 15–18, 21, 23, 29, 31–33, 35–36, 38–39, 42, 46–47, 49
Cronqvist, A., 177–178, 181
Croog, S. H., 46, 48
Culler, S. D., 100, 129
Cumming, E., 134–135
Cupples, A., 42, 46
Czaja, S. J., 79, 80

D'Agostino, R., 42–43, 45, 48–49
Dartigues, J. F., 198, 203
Davies, A. M., 266–267, 273
Davis, D., 237, 248
Day, K., 238–239, 248
Dean, J. W., 179–180
Deardorff, H., 237, 248
Decker, S., 217, 222
Deming, W. E., 176, 180
Demos, S., 237, 250
DePaola, S., 217, 222
Department of Health and Human Services, 269, 274
Depner, C. E., 185, 203
Deutchman, D., 267, 273
Diehl, M., 59–60, 63–65
Dimant, J., 176, 178, 180
Dixon, R. A., 259, 263
Doherty, W. J., 184, 204
Dorian, B., 191, 204
Duara, R., 60, 65
Duck, S., 218, 221
Dudley, W. N., 71, 82
Durkheim, 225, 230
Dyer, C. S., 191, 205

Earles, J., 68, 82
Eckenrode, J., 217, 222
Educational Testing Service, 59, 63–64
Edgecome, J. L., 40, 48
Eisdorfer, C., 60, 65
Elias, J. W., 38, 41, 48
Elias, M. F., 38, 40, 42–46, 48–49, 79–80
Elias, P. K., 38, 43, 48, 79–80
Emery, C., 236, 248

Engel, B. T., 178, 180–181
Epp, G., 237, 250
Erickson, P., 25, 33
Essex, M. J., 261, 264
Evans, J. R., 179–180
Evashwick, C., 184, 206
Everett, D. F., 30, 33

Faletti, M., 235, 248
Farmer, M. E., 42, 49
Featherman, D. L., 218, 221
Fedewa, B., 237, 248
Feinleib, M., 42, 49
Feinstein, A. A., 113, 127
Feldman, J. J., 94, 99, 128, 129
Fillenbaum, G. G., 56, 64
Firth, M., 78, 81
Fischer, D. H., 126–127
Fischer, L., 126, 127, 129
Fitti, J. E., 99–100, 104, 127–128
Fitzgerald, J. F., 95–97, 99–100, 110, 112–114, 120–121, 128–130, 136–137, 141, 152, 163
Fogerty, T. E., 167, 172, 177, 181
Foley, D. J.,13–14, 20
Folstein, M. F., 57, 64
Folstein, S. E., 57, 64
Foner, A., 228, 231
Ford, A. B., 100, 128, 267–268, 273
Foss, J. W., 260–263
Fozard, J., 235, 248
Frasure-Smith, N., 134–135
Fredman, J. N., 100, 127
Fredman, L., 183, 206
Freedman, J. A., 152, 163
Freedman, J. L., 256, 264
Fredman, J. N., 100, 127
Freedy, J. R., 217, 221
French, J. R. P., 184, 204
Friedman, H. S., 226, 230
Friedman, S., 17–18, 21, 42, 46, 49
Frieske, D., 68, 78, 81, 82
Frysinger, M., 236, 249
Fuhrer, R., 196, 198, 203, 208, 219
Fulton, J. P., 267–268, 274
Furner, S. E., 268, 273

Gage, P., 79, 80
Gaines, C., 68–82
Garfinkel, P. E., 191, 204
Gatz, M., 132, 135
Gaucher, E. J., 176, 180
Geddis, B. L., 255, 257, 264
Gelwicks, L., 239, 248
Gensini, G. G., 40–41, 49
Gift, H. C., 132, 135, 267, 273
Giles, H., 88, 92
Gilliam-MacRae, P., 236, 249
Gittelman, B., 60, 65
Glandon, G. L., 177, 180
Glaser, R., 141, 205
Glasgow, R. E., 91–92
Glass, A. P., 178, 180
Goffman, E. L., 127–128
Goldberg, J. D., 184, 206
Goldbourt, U., 184, 205
Goldenhar, L., 191, 205
Goldscheider, F., 228, 230
Goodman, R., 238, 248
Gottman, J. M., 215–216, 221–222
Gouldner, A. W., 217, 221
Graf, P., 207, 220
Greene, I., 237, 248
Greene, V. L., 94, 99, 113, 128
Greenberg, D. F., 118, 128
Grimely-Evans, J., 38, 49, 266, 273
Gruber-Baldini, A., 2, 22
Guralnik, J. M., 8, 13–14, 20–21, 30, 33
Gustafson, D. H., 176–177, 180
Guterman, A., 60, 65

Hall, W. D., 46, 48
Halter, J. B., 191, 206
Hamburg, D. A., 166, 172
Hamilton, J., 235, 239, 249
Haney, T. L., 134–135
Hanley, J. A., 108, 128
Harootyan, R. A., 262, 264
Harris, T., 99, 128
Hatton, F., 7, 21
Havighurst, R., 125, 128
Hawkins, A., 178, 180
Hay, J. F., 70, 80

Hayward, M. E., 2, 8, 15–18, 21, 23, 29, 32, 35–36, 38–39, 42, 46–47, 49
Hazzard, W. R., 96, 110, 116, 123, 128
Heller, K., 218, 221, 225, 227, 231
Helmchen, H., 154, 163, 213, 220
Henry, E. W., 134–135
Hess, B., 215, 221
Hiatt, L., 237, 239, 248
Hickey, T., 191, 206
Hill, J. P., 177, 180
Himes, C. L., 228, 231
Hlatky, M. A., 134–135
Hobfoll, S. E., 217, 221
Hoglund, D., 238, 248
Holford, T. R., 113, 127
Holme, A., 212, 220
Holmes, D., 170, 172, 184, 204
Horgas, A. L., 147, 163, 165
Hosmer, D. W., 108–109, 111, 113–115, 128
House, J. S., 183, 204, 207, 221
Howell, S., 233, 238–239, 248
Hughes, E. M., 184, 205
Hurt, H. T., 218, 222
Hurwitz, D., 60, 65

Iasiello-Vailas, L., 184, 204
Idler, E. L., 114, 128
Ingegneri, D., 4, 7, 16, 21
Ingersoll-Dayton, B., 195, 205
Institute of Medicine, 124, 128, 179–180
Israel, B., 195, 203

Jackson, M. M., 177, 181
Jackson, B. A., 100, 128, 267–268, 273
Jackson, J. S., 183, 189, 196, 203–204, 208, 216–217, 219, 224, 230
Jackson, W., 237, 248
Jacoby, L. L., 70–80
Jaffe, M. W., 100, 128, 267–268, 273
Jagger, C., 5, 21
Jay, G. M., 59, 65, 85, 92, 191, 205
Jemmott, J. B., 191, 205
Jenkins, C. D., 46–48
Jennings, J. M., 68, 70, 72, 80

Jette, A., 5, 6, 22, 26–27, 34, 137, 141, 268, 273
Johnston, C., 237, 248
Johnson, J. B., 183, 205
Johnson, R. J., 95–97, 99–100, 111–115, 120–121, 128–130, 136–137, 141
Joint Commission on Accreditation of Healthcare Organizations, 176, 180
Jones, D., 134–135
Jones, L. T., 178–180
Julius, M. J., 191, 206

Kahn, R. L., 167, 172, 182, 184, 187, 194, 199, 204, 205, 208–209, 213, 221, 223, 231
Kane, R., 235, 248
Kane, R. A., 95, 109, 123, 128
Kane, R. L., 95, 109, 123, 128
Kane, R. M., 124, 128, 140–141
Kaplan, B. G., 183, 206
Kaplan, E., 42, 49
Kaplan, G. A., 132, 134–135, 183, 205
Kasl, S., 114, 128
Katz, S., 20, 100, 128, 267–268, 273–274
Kaufmann, P. G., 132, 135
Kemp, B., 236, 248
Kessler, R. C., 118, 128, 218, 221
Keuthen, N. K., 38, 49
Kidder, D. P., 77, 81
Kiegolt-Glaser, J. K., 191, 205.
Kiel, J. E., 134–135
Kincaid, D., 78, 81
Kirscht, J., 87, 92
Kittner, S. J., 42, 49
Kleinbaum, D, G., 183, 206
Kleinman, J. C., 99, 128
Kliegl, R. A., 68, 81
Kohout, F. J., 13–14, 20
Koncelik, J., 238, 249
Kovar, M. G., 30, 33, 99–100, 104, 127–128
Kramer, A., 175, 181
Krater-Wood, R. E., 177, 181
Krause, N., 85, 92, 191, 205, 217, 221
Kritchevsky, S. B., 176–177, 181

Ku, L., 2, 20
Kuypers, J. A., 227, 231

LaCroix, A. X., 30, 33
Lafronza, V. N., 71, 81
Land, K., 8, 13, 14, 21
Lang, F. R., 157, 163, 212–214, 218, 221
Langer, E., 166, 172, 258, 264
Langlie, J. K., 184, 205
Lautenschlager, G., 68, 78, 81–82
Lawton, M. P., 57, 65, 66, 81, 150–152, 163–164, 169, 172, 218, 221, 227, 231, 238–239, 249, 261, 262, 264, 267–268, 273
Lazaridis, E. N., 268, 273
Lazenby, H. C., 94, 129
Leahy, E., 178, 180
Lefcourt, H. M., 217, 222
Lehr, U. M., 150, 163
Leibum, S. R., 46, 48
Lelaidier, S., 7, 21
Lemeshow, S. W., 108–109, 111, 113–115, 128.
Lemke, S., 261, 264
Lenfant, C., 132, 135
Lennon, B., 125, 129
Lespearance, F., 134, 135
Letenneur, L., 5, 21
Letsch, S. W., 94, 129
Levenson, R. W., 215–216, 221–222
Levit, K. R., 94, 129
Lewis, M. A., 87, 93
Lezak, M. D., 42–43, 46, 49
Liang, J., 191, 205
Lidz, C. W., 126–127, 129
Lindenberger, U., 68, 81
Lindsey, A. M., 184, 205
Litwak, E., 191, 205, 225–226, 229, 231
Liu, K., 25, 31, 33
Loewenstein, D. A., 60, 65
Lubben, J., 267, 273
Lynch, P., 177, 181

Maas, I., 152, 164, 162–163
Maddox, G. L., 212, 222

Magliore, 191, 204

Maier, S. F., 37, 49

Malmberg, B., 170–172

Manton, K. G., 17, 21, 25, 29, 31, 33

Mark, D. B., 134–135

Markides, K., 227, 231

Marks, J., 178, 181

Mars, E., 42, 49

Marsiske, M., 59, 63, 65, 157, 163

Martin, D. K., 100, 127, 152, 163

Martin, R. A., 217, 222

Masciocchi, C. F., 184, 204

Mathers, C., 10, 12, 21, 25, 33

Mattis, S., 57, 65

Mattson, D. E., 174, 180

Mayer, K. U., 154, 163, 213, 220

Mayhorn, C. B., 77, 81

Mayr, U., 68, 81, 152, 163

McCormick, K., 178, 180, 181

McCrae, R. R., 39–40, 48

McHugh, P. R., 57, 64

McIntyre, N. J., 57, 65

McKinlay, J. B., 184, 205

McKitrick, L. A., 260, 263

McManara, P., 42, 49

McNeil, B. J., 108, 128

Mead, G. H., 125, 129

Medalie, J. H., 184, 205

Menken, J. A., 228, 231

Merton, R. K., 123, 129

Messeri, P., 191, 205, 225–226, 231

Metcalf, L., 184, 204

Metzner, H. L., 183, 204

Metzner, H. M., 207, 221

Miller, D. K., 41, 49, 184, 204

Mitchell, D. R., 69, 82

Monaco, C., 170–172

Moos, R. H., 261, 264

Morel, B., 7, 21

Morgan, D. L., 218, 222

Morley, J., 124, 129

Morrell, R. W., 71, 77–78, 81, 82

Moskowitz, R. W., 100, 128, 267–268, 273

Moss, M., 151, 164, 169, 172, 261, 264

Murphy, J. B., 267–268, 274

Nagi, S. Z., 103, 129, 269, 274

National Association of Home Builders, 238, 249

National Center for Health Statistics, 99, 268, 269, 274

Nesselroade, J. R., 218, 221

Neumann, E. M., 148, 163

Newcomer, R., 239, 248

Newell, A., 254, 264

Newman, D. R., 167, 172, 177–178, 181

Nuland, S. B., 134–135

Ochberg, F. M., 166, 172

Ogrocki, P., 191, 205

O'Hanlon, A. M., 260, 263

Oleske, D. M., 177, 180

Olshansky, S. J., 132–133, 135, 167, 172

Ondrich, J. I., 95, 99, 113, 128

Orth-Gothmer, K., 183, 205

Ory, M. G., 132, 135, 167, 170, 172, 177, 181, 267, 273

Osgood, N. J., 212, 222

Osterweil, D., 124, 129, 177, 181

Ostfeld, A.,13–14, 20

Ouslander, J. G., 124, 129, 177, 181.

O'Keefee, J. E., 132, 135

Palmer, M. H., 178,181

Palmon, R., 69, 82

Park, D. C., 68–69, 71, 75–78, 81–82

Parker, S. B., 132, 135

Parker, V., 238–239, 250

Parmalee, P. A., 150, 164

Parsons, T. P., 123, 129

Pastalan, L., 237, 249

Pasupathi, M., 216, 220

Patrick, D. L., 25, 33

Pearlin, L. I., 95–96, 112, 127, 137, 141

Perry, H. M., 46, 48

Peterson, J., 125, 129

Pierce, T. W., 42, 48

Poon, L. W., 77, 81

Pope, A. M., 26, 33

Poulshock, S. W., 184, 204

Prendergast, J. M., 41, 49, 184, 204

Price, R. H., 218, 221

Pryer, D. B., 134–135
Puglisi, J. T., 71, 81, 82
Puska, P., 183–206
Pynoos, J., 237, 239, 249, 255, 264

Rakowski, W., 191, 205
Ramirez, M., 170, 172
Ramsdell, J., 236, 248
Raschko, B., 238, 249
Ray, L. A., 227, 231
Reever, K., 236, 250
Regnier, V., 235, 238–239, 249, 255, 264
Reichard, C. C., 260, 263
Reichert, M., 147, 164
Reifler, B., 236, 249
Reisenzein, R., 145, 162, 217, 219
Reoma, J., 2, 22
Reynolds, S. L., 31, 33
Rhodes, S. R., 69, 82
Rice, A. P., 40, 48
Rice, D. P., 94, 128
Riggio, R. E., 217, 222
Riley, D., 217, 222
Riley, M. W., 228, 231
Ritchie, K. C., 5, 10, 11, 21
Robbins, C., 183, 204, 207, 221
Robbins, M. A., 40, 42, 48, 79, 80
Robine, J. M., 7, 10–12, 21, 25
Robinson, E. A. R., 184, 204
Rodin, J., 166, 172, 226, 231, 258, 264
Rogers, A., 2, 13–14, 21, 33
Rogers, R., 2, 13–14, 21
Rogers, W. L., 267, 273
Rook, K. S., 87, 93, 217, 222
Rosko, M., 178, 181
Rothermund, K., 260, 263
Rowe, J., 267, 273
Ruberman, W., 184, 206
Rudberg, M. A., 132, 133, 135, 167, 172, 268, 273
Rudman, D., 174, 180
Ruff, G., 236, 247
Rundall, T. G., 184, 206
Rutman, D. L., 256, 264
Ryff, C. D., 261, 264

Saito, Y., 2, 4, 8–7, 15–16, 21, 31, 33
Saleh, W. E., 217, 222
Salmon, G., 238, 249
Salonen, J. T., 183, 205
Salthouse, T. A., 66, 68, 69, 82, 83, 84
Sanders, B., 3, 22
Saunders, W. B., 134–135
Schaie, K. W., 59–60, 63–65, 254, 264
Scheve, A., 178, 180
Schick, F. L., 58, 65
Schick, R., 58, 65
Schmele, J. A., 177, 180
Schmidt, R., 236, 249
Schnelle, J. F., 167, 172, 177–178, 181
Schoenbach, V.J., 183, 206
Schrott, H. G., 184, 204
Schular, R. H., 95–96, 112, 127, 137, 141
Schultz, N. R., 42, 48
Schulz, R., 217, 222
Seligman, M. E. P., 143, 162, 164
Selvin, S., 112, 123, 129
Shanas, E., 192, 206
Sharit, J., 79–80
Shaughnessy, P., 175, 181
Shinn, M., 184, 204
Shuttleworth, E. C., 191, 205
Siegler, I. C., 38, 49, 132, 134–135
Silberfeld, M., 259, 265
Silverstein, M., 190, 202, 206, 226–227, 231
Simon, H., 175, 181, 251, 254, 261, 264–265
Simmons, B. P., 176–177, 181
Skinner, E. A., 143, 163
Skovronek, E., 69, 82
Smith, A. D., 71, 75, 81–82
Smith, D. B., 100, 108, 127, 129, 238, 248
Smith, D. M., 152, 163
Smyer, M. A., 132, 135, 168, 172, 236, 249
Solano, C. H., 218, 222
Soldo, B., 215, 221
Sommer, B., 238, 249
Sommer, R., 238, 249

Son, U., 268, 273
Sovacool, M., 71, 81
Spector, W. D., 267–268, 274
Speicher, C. E., 191, 205
Spirduso, W., 236, 249
Spitzberg, B. H., 218, 222
Splaine, M., 170, 172
Spuck, J., 178, 181
Stallard, E., 17, 21, 25, 29, 31, 33
Staudinger, U. M., 212, 214, 221
Steinhagen-Thiessen, E., 154, 163, 213, 220
Stevens, A. B., 260, 263
Strickland, B. R., 39, 49
Stump, T. E., 99–100, 111, 114–115, 127, 129–131, 136, 138–140
Sullivan, D. F., 3, 22
Suzman, R., 99, 128
Swindle, R. W., 218, 221
Syme, S. L., 183, 204, 205, 207, 220, 226, 230

Talajic, M., 134–135
Tarlov, A. R., 26, 33
Taube, C. A., 132, 135
Teasdale, J. Y., 143, 162
Temoshok, L., 226, 231
Teresi, J., 170, 172, 184, 204
Teri, L., 236, 249
The New Grolier Multimedia Encyclopedia, 252, 264
Thomae, H., 150, 163
Thomas, W. I., 85, 86, 93
Thompson, M. G., 225, 231
Throckmorton, B., 217, 222
Thuras, P. D., 87, 93
Tombaugh, T. N., 57, 65

Umberson, D., 191, 206, 226, 231

Valins, M., 238, 249
Verbrugge, L., 2, 3, 5–6, 22, 26–27, 30, 33–34, 191, 206
Vladeck, B., 124, 129
Volner, T. R., 177–178, 181

Wahl, H. W., 87, 92, 145, 147, 163–164
Waite, L., 202, 206, 226, 231
Walston, K. A., 167, 172, 177, 181
Wan, T. T. H., 98, 129, 184, 206
Waring, J., 228, 231
Watkins, S. C., 228, 231
Weal, F., 238, 250
Webster's Seventh New Collegiate Dictionary, 51, 65
Wechsler, D., 68, 82
Weinberg, G., 60, 65
Weinblatt, E., 184, 206
Weisman, J., 238, 248
Weissert, W. G., 184, 206
Welch, P., 237–239, 250
Wentowski, G. J., 217, 222
Wetle, T. T., 13–14, 20
White, L. R., 42–43, 45, 48–49
White, M., 167, 172, 177–178, 181
Wiemann, J. M., 88, 92
Wilkie, F., 60, 65
Wilkins, R., 4, 22
Williams, R. B., 134–135
Williamson, D., 134–135
Willis, S. L., 51, 59–60, 62–65
Wills, T. A., 215, 222
Wilms, H. U., 152, 154, 162, 163
Wilson, B. A., 236, 250
Wilson, K., 235, 248
Windley, P., 238, 249
Windley, P. G., 269, 274
Wisoki, P. A., 38, 49
Withey, S. B., 267, 273
Wolf, P. A., 42, 43, 48–49
Wolinsky, F. D., 41, 49, 94–97, 99–100, 110–115, 120–121, 127–131, 134, 136–141, 152, 157, 163, 184, 204
Wolz, M., 42, 49
World Health Organization, 34, 266, 274
Wortman, C. B., 218, 221
Wright, L. K., 124, 130
Wykle, M. H., 120, 123–124, 127

Yatabe, S., 235, 239, 249
Yonelinas, A. P., 70, 80

Zank, S., 148, 163
Zarcone, V., 166, 172
Zarit, J., 236, 250
Zarit, S. H., 170–172, 236, 239, 250

Zeisel, J., 237–239, 250
Zinn, J., 178–181
Zwahr, M., 68, 82

Subject Index

Active life, 1, 3–8, 10, 14–16, 36–38
Active Life Expectancy (ALE), 1–8, 10,
    12, 14–15, 19, 23–33, 35–36, 39, 47
    model, 2, 10, 12, 15–17, 42
    tables, 3, 39
    sex differences, 12, 14–15, 19, 30
Active theory, 125, 132, 134, 140
Activities of Daily Living (ADL), 4, 14,
    24–25, 27, 56–59, 85–88, 90–91, 95,
    100–104, 106, 108–111, 115, 117,
    119–120, 139, 152, 157, 169, 209,
    218, 233, 243, 259–261, 266–273
Adaptive mechanisms, 214
Adjusted Odds Ratio (AOR), 95, 105–
    106, 108–116, 133, 137
Advanced Activities of Daily Living, 152
Age differences, 14, 67, 113, 193, 195,
    213
Age
    -cohort differences, 42, 45, 228, 254
    -related differences, 68, 211, 214
    -specific risks, 17, 42
Alzheimer's disease, 60, 95–96, 100, 102,
    106, 108–109, 133, 260
Architectural , 234, 251
    design , 233–235, 247, 252, 260
    feedback, 255, 258, 263
Assessment(s), 50, 52–53, 55–57, 60, 64,
    118, 151, 178–179, 236, 237
    competence, 51, 53, 56–61, 151

Assistive devices, 6, 151
Assisted living, 171, 235, 261–262, 266
    dwellings, 171, 253–254, 261
Attitudes toward aging, 168
Autonomy, 127, 142, 148, 170–172, 174,
    227, 235–236, 240, 266–267
Average length of competent life, 1, 37

Basic Competencies (BaCo), 152, 154–
    155, 157, 159, 169–170
Behavioral
    dependency, 87, 142–143, 159–160,
    173
    model, 88, 98–99, 119, 121, 139
    modification, 50, 53–56, 61–64, 260
    observations, 54, 60–61, 88
Berlin Aging Study (BASE), 154, 157,
    212

Cancer, 100, 102, 106, 108, 111, 184,
    198–199
Capability, 32, 57, 60, 86
Caregiver, 95, 147–148, 159, 162, 174,
    255, 258, 268, 271–272
Caregiving, 148, 157, 159, 162, 174, 176,
    234, 241
Caretaker, 87
Cerebrovascular Accident (CVA), 100,
    102

Cognitive
    activities, 30, 67–68, 72
    aging, 66–69, 71
     competence, 5, 36, 42
    demands, 66–67, 69, 71–78
    deficits, 46, 143
    functioning, 17, 42–44, 46, 57, 61, 63,
        70, 83–86, 123, 151
    impairment, 5, 17–18, 42, 47, 123
    impairment–free, 17–18, 42
    incompetence, 5, 38
    resources, 67–69, 71, 77–78
Competence (competency), 1–7, 14–15,
        19–20, 35–39, 42, 47, 50–57, 60–64,
        66–67, 69, 71–72, 74, 76–78, 83–87,
        91, 129, 131, 142, 150–151, 154–
        155, 157–159, 161–162, 165, 169–
        171, 174, 182–184, 189–190, 192,
        197, 201–203, 207–208, 216–218,
        223–224, 227, 229–230, 251, 259,
        262–263, 266
    change(s), 2, 5–6, 197
    difference(s), 2, 5
    everyday, 142, 150–154, 157, 159,
        161, 218
    loss of, 5–6, 47, 62–63, 83
    maintenance of, 78, 131, 190, 194,
        196–202, 207, 224, 232, 244, 259,
        266, 273
    measures, 62–64
Competent life, 1–2, 6, 10, 15, 35, 37
Community-dwelling, 17–18, 42, 116,
        123, 147, 154–155, 161, 256, 269
Conditions
    fatal, 30
    nonfatal, 30
Congregate housing, 238–239, 262
Convoys of social relations, 182, 186–
        189, 208–211, 224, 227–228
Cornell Medical Index (CMI), 40–41
Cultural
    context, 209, 226–227
    differences, 91, 109, 152, 196, 199,
        209, 230

Death, 2, 8, 30, 37, 61, 79, 95–96, 98,
        104–105, 112–113, 116, 122–125,
        138–139, 188, 201, 212

Death rates, 2, 5, 8, 16
Deliberate recollection, 70–71
Demands
    perceptual, 72, 74–76, 78
    physical, 66–67, 72–76
    sensory, 67, 72–75
    tasks, 66, 71–72, 74, 77
Dementia, 17, 42, 47, 57, 95, 122, 124,
        167, 170–171, 178, 238, 260
    free life expectancy, 17, 46
    free living, 17, 46
Dementia Rating Scale (DRS), 57
Dependence/Dependency, 142–144, 150,
        159–161, 165–167, 170, 173–174,
        216, 227, 268–272
    behavior, 144–145, 147–148, 150, 159,
        173, 177
    support script, 87, 145–148, 157, 159,
        165, 167–171
Dependent life, 14
Depression, 40, 123, 132–134, 143, 159,
        225–226, 236
Design
    bottom-up, 252–254, 257–258
    top-down, 252–254, 258
Diabetes, 45, 100, 102, 106, 108, 111,
        115, 132
Digit–Symbol Substitution Test, 46
Direct Assessment of Functional Status
        (DAFS), 60
Disability(ies), 2–7, 10, 12, 14–17, 19–
        20, 23–31, 36, 38–39, 46, 172, 236,
        256
    age–related changes, 30
    incidence, 28–29, 32
    multiple (or codisability), 30
    prevalence, 16, 28–29, 32
    sociology, 28, 31
    trends, 6, 29, 32
Disability-Adjusted Life Years (DALY),
        25
Disability free life (expectancy), 10, 12,
        36
Disabled life (see also Inactive Life), 4,
        23–24, 31
Disablement process, 5–6, 36

Disengagement theory, 134, 140
Dynamic model(s), 8, 20, 38–39, 47, 97–98, 121–122
Dysfunction, 6, 20, 24, 71, 147, 160, 225

ETS Basic Skills Test, 59, 63
Efficacy support model, 216–218, 224
Eldercom, 79
Emotional closeness, 183, 187, 195, 200–201, 208–215
Emotional Therapy (see Therapeutic Interventions)
Environmental
 changes, 6, 167
 design, 166–167, 233, 240, 260, 269, 271, 273
 support, 6, 66–67, 71–72, 74–76, 246
Environmental assessment procedure, (see Multiphasic Environmental Assessment Procedure)
Environments (see physical and social environments)
Epidemiology, 31–32, 43, 142, 183, 196–197, 207
Ethnicity (race), 91, 100, 104, 109, 123, 226–227
Everyday Problems Test (EPT), 59
Expanded Competencies (ExCo), 152, 154–155, 157, 159, 169–170

Failure-to-thrive, 120, 123–125, 132, 134, 139–140
Feedback from Senior Users (FSU), 251–252, 255, 263
Financial management, 71, 76, 78–79
Frail elderly (older), 68, 75, 79, 87, 131, 159, 166, 233, 235–236, 239, 244, 257, 260–261, 266
Framingham Heart Study, 42, 45–46
Functional
 assessment, 60
 disability, 41, 47, 167, 227
 independence, 235–236, 266–267
 limitations, 5, 36, 47, 140, 155, 157, 199, 202

status, 100, 104, 117–119, 121, 123, 125, 139, 157, 173–174, 211
Functioning, 2–3, 12, 15, 34, 53–54, 56–57, 62–64, 160–161, 166, 171, 254
 ability, 2–4, 6, 24, 54, 159, 161, 166, 171, 216, 229, 236

Gender differences, 12, 28, 30, 39, 105, 111, 113, 145, 155, 215, 228
Gensini Index, 40
Group homes, 170–171, 236, 244

Health, 3–5, 8, 12, 15–16, 19, 28, 30–31, 35, 42, 47, 94, 100, 113–114, 126, 131, 133–134, 154, 183–187, 189–190, 192, 201–202, 217, 224–225, 229
Health–Adjusted Life Expectancy (HALE), 25
 care, 94, 124–125, 176–177
 behaviors, 87, 104, 184, 190–191, 198–200, 226, 236
 services (utilization), 72, 98–101, 104, 115, 118, 121
 status, 39–40, 61, 84–85, 90, 95–98, 100, 103, 110, 115–116, 119, 121–123, 136–138, 145, 197
Health/disease continuum, 190–192, 198, 200, 202, 204, 224
Healthy Life Expectancy (HLE), 27, 29, 30
Heart disease, 5, 38, 40, 100, 102, 106, 109, 111, 132–133, 184, 200
Hosmer-Lemeshow Statistics, 108–109, 111, 113–115
Housing environments, 6
Hypertension, 42–44, 102, 106, 111, 115, 132–133

Impairment(s), 4–5, 17–19, 31, 36, 39, 42, 70, 144, 155, 167, 174, 201, 236, 267
Inactive life, 3–4, 7–8, 14–16, 38
Incompetent, 1, 3, 15, 37, 51, 54–55
Incompetence/Incompetent, 1, 3–5, 15, 35, 37, 42, 51–52, 54–55, 143–144, 150, 159, 162, 166, 173, 259

Incontinence, 167–168, 177–178
Independence-ignore script, 145, 148
Independence/Independent , 142, 159,
    165, 168, 174, 227, 235–237, 239–
    240, 266–267, 271
  behaviors, 145, 147–148, 150, 168
  living, 4, 50, 52, 56–64, 74, 83–88,
    91–92, 110, 127, 152, 235, 239, 242,
    244
International classification of impair-
    ments, disabilities and handicaps, 4,
    26
International Network on Active Life Ex-
    pectancy (REVES), 4
Intervention(s), 50, 54–56, 61–62, 64, 77,
    83, 131, 142, 144, 147–148, 167–
    168, 170, 178, 183, 196, 202–203,
    225, 234, 236, 240, 272
  design, 92, 196, 268–269
Institutional(ization), 17, 24–25, 96, 109–
    110, 114, 116, 123, 126, 133–134,
    137–139, 142, 145, 147, 154–155,
    157, 159, 165–168, 170–171, 173–
    174, 179, 184, 257, 266
  discrimination, 109
  noninstitutionalized, 133–134, 155, 159
Instrumental Activities of Daily Living
    (IADL), 4, 24–25, 27, 56–57, 66–73,
    75–76, 78–79, 84–88, 90–91, 95,
    103, 109–110, 152, 157, 233, 243,
    259–261, 266–273

Kaplan-Albert Neuropsychological Test
    battery, 42–46

Learned
  dependency, 143, 148
  helplessness, 37, 143, 148
Life
  cycle, 1–3, 12, 14, 19–20, 224
  expectancy, 2, 5, 12, 14–17, 24–25, 27,
    29, 35, 40, 42, 47, 113
  satisfaction, 195
  span, 10, 38, 182, 187–189, 194, 197,
    202, 208–210, 223–224, 227–228,
    232, 262

Life table, 2–3, 8, 14, 42
  population, 7
Life table model, 2–3, 5
  incidence-based, 8, 28–29
  (Markov-based) multistate (increment–
    decrement), 8, 10
  prevalence-based, 7–8, 10, 28–29
Long-term
  care, 137–138, 140, 142, 144, 159,
    161, 166, 169–171, 173–175, 178–
    179, 235
  disability, 4
  environments, 161, 236
Longitudinal Study of Aging (LSOA), 29,
    97, 99–100, 104–105, 109–113,
    115–118, 121–122, 132–133, 136,
    138, 140, 254

Measurement, 52–56, 59, 63–64, 100,
    151, 261
Medication, 59, 76, 178
  adherence, 62, 78–79, 184
  information, 77
  taking, 71, 77–79, 267
Memory, 68–69
  research, 68
  tasks, 68
Mental therapy (see Therapeutic In-
    terventions)
Mentally competent, 17, 234, 236,
    259–260
Mini-Mental Questionnaire, 42
Mini-Mental Status Exam (MMSE), 57
Minimum Data Set/Resident Assessment
    Protocol (MDS/RAP), 174, 178
Morbidity, 16, 26–29, 31–32, 95–97, 99,
    104, 116, 119–122, 126, 136–140,
    183–184, 207, 211–213
  chronic, 16, 27, 267
Mortality, 1–2, 12, 15–16, 18–19, 24, 27–
    31, 95–99, 104–106, 111–114, 116,
    120–122, 126, 132, 134, 136–138,
    140, 159, 183, 207, 211–214
  decline, 3, 139
  old age, 16, 30
  rates, 3, 7, 16–17, 114, 159, 177, 227

sex differences, 15, 31
Multigenerational households, 114
Multiinfarct disease, 38
Multiphasic Environmental Assessment
    Procedure (MEAP), 261
Multistage life table, 42, 47
Multistate life table, 14–17, 24–25
Multistate model, 14–15
Myocardial infraction, 45, 100, 102, 108,
    132, 191

Nagi/Institute of Medicine Scheme, 26
National Death Index (NDI), 97, 99, 104,
    121, 136
National Health Interview Survey(NHIS),
    29, 99, 133, 269
National Long-Term Care Survey
    (NLTCS), 17, 29
Neuropsychological test, 42–43, 45
Nondementia, 42
Nondisabled, 3, 23–25, 27, 29
Nondisabled life (see also Active Life), 4,
    7
Noninstitutionalized, 95, 133–134, 155,
    159
Nonkin social support(s), 100, 106, 109,
    111, 115, 228
Nuclear family, 213–215
Nursing home, 71, 94, 96–98, 104, 108–
    110, 114, 125–127, 131–134, 136–
    137, 139, 145, 154, 159–162,
    165–168, 170–171, 174–175, 177–
    179, 235–236, 245, 255–256, 258
    placement, 95–99, 103–124, 126, 131,
        136–140
    probability of dying, 95–96, 112, 114,
        121–123, 137
    risk of dying, 95, 98, 111–113, 115,
        122, 137–138

Observational Task of Daily Living
    (OTDL), 60, 63
Older adults, 56, 58, 66–71, 75–79, 83,
    86, 89–92, 94–96, 99, 109, 111,
    113–115, 120, 123–126, 139, 145,
    155, 157, 160–162, 194, 211, 213–

    214, 216–217, 224–225, 228, 234,
    243, 254, 262, 268, 272
    work performance, 66–68

Passive selection, 201, 211–212
Personnes Agees Quid (PAQUID),
    197–198
Physical
    ability, 12
    dependency, 234, 239, 244, 267, 269
    disability, 144, 189, 236
    environment, 6, 20, 61–62, 67, 150,
        155, 159, 189, 201, 210, 232, 234,
        266
    support, 6, 189
    therapy (see Therapeutic Interventions)
Population, 1–5, 7–8, 14, 17, 24, 27–29,
    31–32, 35–36, 39, 42, 46, 61, 101,
    106, 131–132, 226, 228, 254–255
    community dwelling, 17, 256, 270
    disability, 5, 16, 19, 23, 28
    health, 5, 15–16, 23, 30–31, 39
    older, 4, 8, 10, 13–14, 31, 228, 258,
        266, 268
    subgroups, 1–4, 19, 29
    trends, 28, 258

Quality of life, 3, 25, 33, 125, 131, 152,
    161, 165, 167, 169–170, 224, 234,
    240, 247, 266–267
Quality-Adjusted Life Expectancy
    (QALE), 3–4, 25

Receiver Operating Characteristic (ROC),
    107–109, 111, 113–115
Reliability, 52, 55, 58–60, 145

Self-care, 4, 53, 56, 144–146, 151, 155,
    157, 159, 161, 235, 241, 271
Self-efficacy, 152, 216–217, 229, 259
Self-fulfilling prophecy, 123, 132, 134,
    139
Self-report(s), 38–41, 84, 104, 112, 186,
    261
Short Portable Mental Status Question-
    naire, 17, 42

Significant (supportive) other(s), 84, 86–
    92, 188–189, 192, 195, 199–202,
    208, 226
Social activities, 1, 38, 151, 241–242
Social Breakdown Theory, 211, 227
Social convoy model, 207, 209, 223–224
Social
    context, 38, 47, 91, 154–155, 157–159,
        161, 173, 207
    differences, 6, 10
    environments, 6, 19–20, 39, 61–62,
        142–144, 147, 159, 173, 210, 235
    goals, 162, 210–211
    groups, 19, 148
    isolation, 126, 211–212
    networks, 86–87, 89, 110, 157, 169,
        185, 187, 192, 194, 198, 207–209,
        211–216, 223–224, 226–230, 244
    partners, 144–145, 147–148, 151, 155,
        157, 208, 210–215, 217–218
    roles, 3, 19, 32, 39, 125–126, 150, 152
    support, 6, 79, 95, 109–110, 125, 134,
        154, 157, 183–187, 189, 192, 194–
        198, 202, 207–208, 216–218,
        223–230
    therapy (see Therapeutic Interventions)
Sociodemographic, 19, 28, 31
Socioeconomic status, 14–15, 109, 154,
    194, 201, 210–211, 214, 270

Socioemotional selectivity theory, 194,
    209–212, 214
Spiritual Therapy (see Therapeutic In-
    terventions)
Status support, 215
Stroke, 38, 42–43, 45, 100, 102, 106,
    111, 114–115, 122, 244
Support/efficacy model of social rela-
    tions, 183, 189, 200, 208, 216–218
Supports of the Elderly Study, 194, 196,
    198, 226

Therapeutic
    environment, 233–236, 240, 252, 256,
        260, 263, 266, 273
    interventions (types of), 236, 241–246,
        266–267
Total life expectancy, 12, 14, 15, 17
Total Quality Management (TQM),
    175–179

Validity, 52, 54–55, 60–61

Well-being, 161, 187, 189, 192, 196–197,
    199, 201, 208, 217, 224, 226–227,
    229–230, 234, 247, 257, 259, 261
Wechsler Adult Intelligence Scale
    (WAIS), 42, 68
Yesterday Interview, 151, 155, 161, 169

The Aging Individual
Physical and Psychological Perspectives
Susan Krauss Whitbourne, PhD

In this text, Dr. Whitbourne forges a new understanding of the psychological aspects of physiological change in aging persons. This volume integrates theoretical perspectives that are needed for teaching courses in the psychology of aging. Complex biological concepts are illustrated in a clear and accessible style throughout.

The book describes physical and cognitive changes as a result of the aging process and the various ways that individuals age and think about their own aging. The benefits of this unique perspective will allow the reader to gain a new understanding of how biology and psychology interact in the aging individual.

Contents:
- Models of Identity and the Aging Process
- How Aging is Studied
- Aging of Appearance and Mobility
- Cardiovascular and Respiratory System
- Physiological Control System
- The Nervous System
- Sensation and Perception
- Cognitive Processes
- Intelligence
- Identity and Personality

1996   328pp   0-8261-9360-9   hardcover

536 Broadway, New York, NY 10012-3955 • (212) 431-4370 • Fax (212) 941-7842

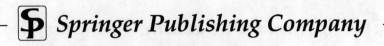
Springer Publishing Company

Life Beyond 85 Years
The Aura of Survivorship

Colleen L. Johnson, PhD
Barbara M. Barer, MSW

Those 85 years and older — the Oldest Old — are now the fastest growing group in the U.S. Using their original research, the authors examine how the oldest old adapt to daily challenges and what competencies are needed to survive and continue living in the community. The authors address the topics of health and physical status, family and social relationships, quality of life, as well as the implications that increases in life expectancy have for families and society. The book features illuminating vignettes that illustrate how the oldest old perceive and interpret their world, and thereby convey the aura of their survivorship.

Contents:

- Introduction
- Studying the Oldest Old: The Context of Survivorship
- Are Very Old People Different?
- Stability and Change in Physical Status: A Naturalistic Account
- Late Life Family Relationships
- Social Networks: A Continuum from Sociability to Isolation: The Processes of Adaptation
- Managing Daily Routines
- Discourses on Self and Time
- Sustaining Emotional Well-Being: The Content of Emotional Life
- Profiles in Survivorship
- Preparing for Death
- Summary and Conclusions
- Afterword by *Lillian Troll*

Springer Series on Life Styles & Issues in Aging
1996 280pp 0-8261-9540-7 *hardcover*

536 Broadway, New York, NY 10012-3955 • (212) 431-4370 • Fax (212) 941-7842